Mission Matters

Essays on the Theory, Practice and Contexts of Mission

Kieran Beville

EP BOOKS

Faverdale North

Darlington

DL3 0PH, England

web: http://www.epbooks.org

e-mail: sales@epbooks.org

EP Books are distributed in the USA by:

JPL Distribution

3741 Linden Avenue Southeast

Grand Rapids, MI 49548

E-mail: orders@jpldistribution.com

Tel: 877.683.6935

First published 2014

British Library Cataloguing in Publication Data available

ISBN: 978–0–85234–940–3

To Jackie and her late husband Chris
whose sacrificial love for the Lord
is an inspiration and a challenge.

Contents

'Kieran Beville offers a well-informed and up to the minute reflection on some of the major challenges that face contemporary Christians who are serious about their mission. His own position is well rooted in conservative evangelical theology and will be of particular interest to those who share the same roots. This book is broad in the span of topics it tackles, clear in expression and designed to enable an effective articulation of the Christian message. It is a valuable book arguing well thought out responses to contemporary needs.'

Dr Nigel G. Wright, former principal, Spurgeon's College, London.

'These diverse essays by Kieran Beville probe critical issues related to missionary theory and practice and they provide keen insights along the way. From serious discussions of 'isms' and 'issues' related to gospel ministry and missionary endeavours to reports on God's work in various countries, Kieran challenges the reader to think about mission and missions and to assess their own personal commitment to the Great Commission and the Christ of the Commission. The reader will be both informed and challenged through this thoughtful and interesting collection of essays, which together present in no uncertain terms that mission matters.'

David Olford Ph.D., President of Olford Ministries International, Inc., Professor of Expository Preaching, Union University, Jackson, Tennessee, USA.

Foreword

What is desperately needed in the realm of missiology today are missionary theologians or practitioners who are reflective on the whole activity and world of mission. It is great to have men and women on the field sharing Christ, planting churches, and engaging in the joyful, though at times arduous, task of mission. It is also helpful to have thinkers about the task of mission, who devote themselves to the study of the history and theology of mission. But oh, to have the two combined!

Such a figure was the Apostle Paul. Clearly, a man devoted to church planting—see Romans 15:14–21 and the account of Paul's ministry in Acts. But he was also a theologian *par excellence*, who grounded his mission in a robust theology of divine sovereignty, Christological new-covenant fulfillment, and human responsibility.

Such a man was also Irenaeus of Lugdunum/Lyons, who, in the late second century, after twenty years or more of ministry in the now-extinct Celtic language of Gaulish to the inhabitants of south-eastern Gaul, wrote a fabulous theological tome popularly known as *Against heresies*. In this book, he yokes mission and theology to the mission of the Son and the Spirit who have come from the Father to bring us back to God.

Such a person was also Patrick of Ireland, who, in the mid to late fifth century, defends his mission with rich theological reflection. Despite his protestation that he was a man 'most unlearned' (*rusticissimus*), his *Confession*, written not long before his death, provided theological direction and inspiration for the missionary activity of the Celtic Church over the next two hundred and fifty years.

And I am happy to find in this book also a writer who is both a missional practitioner and theologian, missions-minded and theologically reflective. Kieran's analyses of the various trends of culture world-wide and how this impacts mission are extremely helpful, as are his reports from the field that reveal a man who is not simply content to think about mission from the cosy warmth of his southern Irish home. And what gives this book added value is knowing the author to be a genuine man of God, passionate for the glory of God in the salvation of those lost in the dark maze of this world. I am honored that he has asked me—a historian who does spend most of his time simply reading, thinking and writing—to write a foreword commending this book that combines both missionary act and theology.

Michael A. G. Haykin
Professor of Church History & Biblical Spirituality
The Southern Baptist Theological Seminary

Acknowledgements

Some of the chapters in this work have been published as articles in various magazines and journals over a period of several years, others were conference papers. As such they are independent essays relevant to the theory and practice of mission as well as the contexts in which mission takes place. They explore the biblical mandate, historical development and cultural contexts of mission and propose a strategic approach going forward. The fact that these chapters were written over a period of time and for different audiences is reflected in their diverse and distinctive voices. They are brought together here in one place as part of what I hope will be a helpful discussion about mission. As the title '*Mission Matters*' suggests these are essays pertaining to the theme of mission but they also emphasize the importance of mission by stating that it matters.

'Understanding Postmodernism' was a paper first read to the Society of Oxford Scholars at a banquet in Rewley House, Kellogg College, Oxford University in January 2009. It was later incorporated into my book, *Preaching Christ in a Postmodern Culture*, 2010 and is used here with permission from Cambridge Scholars Publishing. 'Militant Secularism' was published in two parts in *Evangelical Times* in May and June, 2012. 'China: Changing Contours' appeared in *Evangelical Times*, September, 2012. 'Aggressive Atheism' was included in *Foundations*: *International Journal of Evangelical Theology*, spring, 2012. 'The Church Community in Contemporary Culture: Evangelism and Engagement' was published in *Puritan Reformed Theological Journal*, July, 2011. 'The Rhythm of God's Heartbeat: Biblical Perspective on Mission Theology' featured in *Churchman,* autumn, 2012. 'Identifying the way Forward: Keeping Mission Central to Church Life' was presented at the ISPCK tercentenary conference in Delhi in October, 2010. 'Religious Freedom in Serbia' was published in *Evangelical Times*, April, 2005. 'Religious Revolution in Romania' was published in *Evangelical Times*, June, 2005. 'A Taste of India first appeared in abridged form under the title 'India Training Trip' in *Evangelicals Now*, October, 2009.

In the chapter 'What About Those Who Have Never Heard the Gospel' I have used a short extract from my book *Jonah: Pride and Prejudice* (2010) with permission from ISPCK and I have also drawn on my article 'Unconditional Election' published in *Grace* (the magazine of the Grace Baptist churches [Reformed] in the U.K.), January, 2005. Although there is some overlap with these works the chapter is, nevertheless almost entirely new material.

I wish to thank Roger Fay (*Evangelical Times*), Peter Milsom and Matthew Evans (*Foundations),* Joel Beeke (*Puritan Reformed Theological Journal*), Gerald Bray (*Churchman*) and John Benton (*Evangelicals Now*). These men do a tremendous job in providing helpful, contemporary, relevant and inspiring articles for the

Christian reader and I am honoured that they have considered my humble contributions worthy of inclusion in their publications.

I thank Ezzat S. and Jackie L. for allowing me to tell their story in 'A Student's Story'. Their courage and commitment to the Christ is exemplary. I have been intentionally vague about some details.

I also acknowledge the assistance of Dane Vidović a Christian publisher in Belgrade for helping me understand the issues pertaining to religious freedom in Serbia, and Jasmine from the Bread of Life ministry who acted as my interpreter when I was teaching and preaching in Belgrade.

Doru Hnatiuc and I first met in 1997 in Memphis, Tennessee as students of expository and evangelistic preaching at the Stephen Olford Center for Biblical Preaching. We met again (2004) in Romania and he subsequently came to Ireland (2005). We travelled throughout the country where he spoke about what God had done in Romania, especially in and through Emanuel Baptist Church in Oradea. I am grateful to him for all I learned during those weeks and for the relevant photographs.

I am sincerely thankful to Dr Michael Haykin (Professor of Church History and Biblical Spirituality and Director of The Andrew Fuller Center for Baptist Studies, at The Southern Baptist Theological Seminary, Louisville, Kentucky, USA) for writing the 'Foreword' to this work. Although he is a man of renown with 'name recognition' Michael has retained an endearing humility. It is an honour to have his contribution published here.

I am indebted to Dr Nigel Wright (former Principal of Spurgeon's College, London) for writing a commendation for this work and also to Dr David Olford (President of Olford Ministries International, Inc. and Professor of Expository

Preaching, Union University, Jackson, Tennessee, U.S.A.) who endorsed it and made very helpful suggestions for revision of some of the material.

I would also like to express my sincere thanks to Graham Hind and the board of Evangelical Press and its chairman, Roger Fay, for their insightful comments and gracious manner in offering some advice which helped me to refine one of the chapters. The readers they appointed were astute and diligent and I am grateful for their comments.

Daniel and Clodagh McAllen read this manuscript, at short notice and found punctuation and typo issues that needed to be addressed, for this I am very grateful.

I would like to express my sincere thanks to Trudy Kinloch, who edited this manuscript, for her professionalism and patience. I am also thankful to Quinta Press for the typesetting.

Last, but by no means least, I am very grateful to my wife Ber for taking an interest in my work and her willingness to proof-read the manuscript. She had the difficult job of offering advice and comments at the risk of incurring my displeasure. Invariably she has been right and I am blessed that she has the integrity to challenge me because the process of engaging with her has helped to refine the work.

I take full responsibility for the theological perspectives expressed in this work. I am not so naïve as to assume that everybody mentioned here agrees with everything I have written. So they are absolved from responsibility for any residual mistakes which might remain or opinions expressed which might differ to their own. If I have failed to mention anybody who feels he/she ought to have been acknowledged I beg their indulgence, *mea maxima culpa*.

Soli Deo gloria.

Part 1

1

Aggressive Atheism

Recently I read again the story of the encounter between David and Goliath in the Valley of Elah and how the champion of the Philistines taunted the people of God. Goliath was arrayed in impressive armour of bronze and heavily armed. But David, who declined to wear the armour of King Saul, approached this awesome opponent in the name of the Lord. What impressed me most about the account is how David was grieved in his spirit that the Lord's name should be profaned in such a way. He had an unshakeable confidence that God would grant him victory in this amazing confrontation. Goliath taunted the army of Israel and this had the effect of discouraging God's people. The most unlikely person (a shepherd boy) had the most astonishing victory over the most powerful adversary in an unpredictable manner—with a sling-shot. The words of that youth are a trumpet-call for the valiant who have more confidence in their

God than fear in the face of awesome odds: 'You come to me with a sword and with a spear and with a javelin, but I come to you in the name of the LORD of hosts … whom you have defied. This day the LORD will deliver you into my hand …' (1 Samuel 17:45–46).

David emerged from obscurity and the shadow of the contempt his brothers had for him. An unlikely person worked an improbable victory that day in the Valley of Elah. David selected five smooth stones from the brook and put them in his shepherd's pouch. However, he also possessed five notable qualities. He entered that valley with confidence in God, experience in defending the flock, a spirit that was grieved to hear the Lord's name being profaned, a courageous heart and a desire 'that all the earth may know that there is a God …' (1 Samuel 17:46). Thus armed, David stepped into the valley to face a formidable foe and God granted him success. Those who possess such qualities are needed today to act as valiant champions in the cause of the Lord. It is my hope that God will grant success today to those courageous shepherds of the flock who step forward to defend the honour of the Lord against the giants who mock God and deride faith as an intellectual cop-out—the New Atheists. If we are to conduct mission effectively in contemporary culture we must understand the challenges that atheism presents.

What is atheism?

Atheism is sometimes defined as the rejection (or absence) of belief in the existence of God. But it is more accurate to define it as belief that there is no God.[1] Whereas a theist is someone who believes in God, an atheist is someone whose disbelief in God is central to his worldview. Atheism, therefore, is not merely uncertainty or doubt about the existence of God such as agnosticism or scepticism. Although atheism is a minority view in Western culture, it is nevertheless growing in popularity. Historically, atheism would have been scandalous, but today it is far less objectionable and, in some circles, well-respected.

Historical overview

The Greek word *atheoi*, as it appears in the Epistle to the Ephesians, 'remember that you were at that time separated from Christ, alienated from the commonwealth of Israel and strangers to the covenants of promise, having no hope and without God in the world' (2:12) is usually translated into English as 'without God'. In ancient Greek the adjective *atheos* meant 'godless'. It was first used as a term of censure roughly meaning 'ungodly' or 'impious'. In the fifth century BC the word began to indicate more deliberate and active godlessness in the sense of 'severing relations with the gods' or 'denying the gods'. Atheists were those who impiously denied or disrespected the local gods, even if they believed in other gods. Thus the word 'atheist' was originally used pejoratively and as such was an insult. Nobody would willingly have assumed such a title.

The Greek philosopher Epicurus (c. 341–270 BC) disputed many religious doctrines, including the existence of an afterlife or a personal deity. He considered the soul purely material and mortal. While Epicureanism did not rule out the existence of gods, it asserted that if they did exist, they were unconcerned with humanity.

The Roman poet Lucretius (c. 99–55 BC) agreed that, if there were gods, they were unconcerned with humanity and unable to affect the natural world. For this reason, he believed humanity should have no fear of the supernatural. He expounded his Epicurean views of the cosmos, the soul, mortality, and religion in *De Rerum Natura* (On the Nature of Things), which popularized Epicurus' philosophy in Rome. Disciples of Epicurus were essentially devotees of sensual enjoyment.

The meaning of 'atheist' changed over the course of classical antiquity. During the Roman Empire Christians were accused of being atheists for not worshiping the pagan deities and many were executed for their rejection of the Roman gods in general and Emperor-worship in particular.[2]

The Renaissance did much to expand the scope of free thought and sceptical inquiry. Individuals such as Leonardo da Vinci sought experimentation as a means of explanation, and opposed arguments from religious authority. He was one of several critics of the church during this period. But generally the Renaissance and Reformation eras witnessed resurgence in religious fervour, as evidenced by the proliferation of new religious orders and the emergence of Protestantism.

Criticism of Christianity became increasingly frequent in the seventeenth and eighteenth centuries, especially in France and England. Some thinkers who emerged from a Protestant tradition (such as Thomas Hobbes) espoused a materialist philosophy and scepticism toward supernatural occurrences, while the Jewish-Dutch philosopher Spinoza rejected divine providence in favour of naturalism. The philosopher David Hume developed a sceptical epistemology grounded in empiricism, undermining the metaphysical basis of natural theology.

The French Revolution took atheism and anti-clericalism into the public sphere. There was a restructuring and subordination of clergy with respect to the civil authority of the state. The enforcement of it led to anti-clerical violence and the expulsion of many clergy from France. The Napoleonic era institutionalized the secularization of French society, exported the revolution and inspired the founding of other republics.

Before the eighteenth century, the existence of God was so universally accepted in the western world that even the possibility of true atheism was questioned. According to this view, atheists were simply in denial. But the eighteenth century atheist Paul-Henri Thiry, asserted:

> The source of man's unhappiness is his ignorance of Nature. The pertinacity with which he clings to blind opinions imbibed in his infancy, which interweave themselves with his existence, the consequent prejudice that warps his mind, that prevents its expansion, that renders him the slave of fiction, appears to doom him to continual error.[3]

In the nineteenth century, atheists contributed to political and social revolution, facilitating the upheavals of 1848, the Risorgimento in Italy and the growth of an international socialist movement. Ludwig Feuerbach's *The Essence of Christianity* (1841) would greatly influence philosophers such as Engels, Marx and Nietzsche.

Atheism in the twentieth century found recognition in a wide variety of other, broader philosophies, such as existentialism, secular humanism, nihilism, anarchism, logical positivism, Marxism, feminism and the general scientific and rationalist movement.

Atheism and totalitarian regimes

The philosopher Ludwig Feuerbach and the psychologist Sigmund Freud (amongst many others) argued that belief in

God and other religious beliefs are human inventions, created to fulfil various psychological and emotional needs. Many Buddhists share this view. Karl Marx and Friedrich Engels, influenced by the work of Feuerbach, argued that belief in God and religion are social functions, used by those in power to oppress the working class. For such philosophers, psychologists and social theorists the concept of God implies the abdication of human reason; an abandonment of liberty has led to the enslavement of mankind.

The twentieth century also saw the political advancement of atheism, spurred on by the works of Marx and Engels. The Bolsheviks in Soviet Russia were inspired by an ideological creed that professed that religion weakened society and they resolved to eradicate it. After the Revolution in 1917 Orthodox hierarchy were summarily executed and children were deprived of any religious education outside the home. Increasingly draconian measures were employed to suppress religion. In addition to direct state persecution, the League of the Militant Godless was founded in 1925, resulting in churches being vandalized. While the Constitution of 1936 guaranteed freedom to hold religious services, the Soviet state under Stalin did not consider education a private matter; it outlawed religious instruction and waged campaigns to persuade people, at times violently, to abandon religion. By 1938, eighty bishops had lost their lives, while thousands of clerics were sent to labour camps.[4] Many Muslim mosques and Jewish synagogues were also shut down.

As well as the communist bloc countries of the Soviet Union, several other communist states (including China and North Korea) endorsed state atheism, deeming religion to be a subversive threat to the status quo. In 1967 Enver Hoxha's regime conducted a campaign to extinguish religious life in

Albania. By the end of that year over two thousand religious buildings were closed or converted to other uses, and religious leaders were imprisoned and executed. Albania was declared to be the world's first atheist country by its leaders, and Article 37 of the Albanian constitution of 1976 stated, 'The State recognizes no religion, and supports and carries out atheistic propaganda in order to implant a scientific materialistic world outlook in people.'[5]

Stalin (Russia), Mao (China), Pol Pot (Cambodia) and a host of others, all committed atrocities in the name of a communist ideology that was explicitly atheistic. Their bloody deeds were perpetrated in an attempt to create a new secular order, a utopia free of the curse of religion. This was not mass murder by people who happened to be atheists; atheism was a central part of their ideological inspiration.

Although since the fall of the Berlin Wall (1989) the number of actively anti-religious regimes has reduced considerably, the history of the twentieth century offers sobering lessons: The exclusion of God, religion and virtue from society leads ultimately to a poorer vision of humanity.

Demographic distribution

It is difficult to quantify the number of atheists in the world as respondents to religious-belief polls may define atheism differently. A 2005 survey published in Encyclopaedia Britannica found that the non-religious made up about 11.9% of the world's population, and atheists about 2.3%.[6] This figure did not include those who follow atheistic religions, such as some Buddhists.

A 2006 poll published in the Financial Times gives rates for the United States and five European countries. The lowest rates of atheism were in the United States at only 4%, while the rates of atheism in the European countries surveyed were considerably higher: Italy (7%), Spain (11%), Great Britain (17%), Germany (20%), and France (32%). These figures are similar to those of an official European Union survey, which reported that 18% of the EU population does not believe in god.[7] Other studies have placed the estimated percentage of atheists, agnostics, and other nonbelievers in a personal god as low as single digits in Poland, Romania and Cyprus. In Scandinavian countries the percentage of the populations describing themselves as atheists is very high (up to 85% in Sweden, 80% in Denmark, 72% in Norway, and 60% in Finland).[8] According to the Australian Bureau of Statistics 19% of Australians have 'no religion', a category that includes atheists.[9] Between 64% and 65% of Japanese are atheists or agnostics.[10]

Godless gurus

Many celebrities in contemporary society are atheists but there are others who have achieved celebrity status by virtue of the fact that they are exponents of atheism. They are part of a movement that has come to be known as New Atheism, in which the mood has changed from passive non-belief to something more dogmatic and aggressive. They advocate the view that religion should be countered, criticized and exposed by rational argument; it is a superstition and they are dedicated to its eradication.

Poisoned penmanship

Following the recent death of Christopher Hitchens (a conspicuous New Atheist voice) the obituaries described him as an articulate journalist, incomparable critic and masterful rhetorician. Hitchens was an intellectual with a world platform from which he advanced atheism. His works include *God is Not Great* and *The Portable Atheist.* Referring to Mother Theresa as 'a lying, thieving, Albanian dwarf' is typical of the poisoned penmanship he used to promulgate contempt for people who hold religious views. Hitchens is a harbinger of what is to come as aggressive atheism advances.

Such antipathy to a religious perspective of any kind has spawned pseudo-intellectuals who feel it is open season on people of faith. Many of these zealots are equally dogmatic in their opinions as those they criticize. But I have found that most of these devotees are profoundly ignorant of philosophical theology in the fields of ontology (that branch of metaphysics dealing with the nature of being) and epistemology (the philosophy of knowledge).

Richard Dawkins, author of *The God Delusion,* is probably the most well known advocate of atheism today, believing that science and religion are mutually incompatible. He is committed to the evolutionary theory of Darwin as a means of undermining religious belief.[11]

Some of these celebrity new atheists and their cult of devotees use the word 'fundamentalism' as a pejorative and convenient label to express contempt for people whose religious convictions shape their worldview. Such a broad definition includes suicide bombers and ordinary Christian worshippers. As such, they lack perspective and the nuances one might expect from intelligent debate. Ironically, these outspoken atheists have a form of evangelical zeal and a strident tone that has much in common with the 'fanaticism' they despise. They no longer speak like the besieged who have retrenched into defensive enclaves;

atheism is now a dogmatism that crushes the interrogative spirit and insists that its doctrinaire views are the only legitimate creed. As a belief system (for what it asserts in relation to the origin of the universe is, in fact, an unproven and un-provable theory) it is itself a form of orthodoxy which is intolerant of any disagreement. Those who do not subscribe to its views are deemed heretics and treated as outcasts who are ostracized and ridiculed. Some of the things they say about religion are so provocative that they constitute incitement to hatred, *de facto* if not *de jure*.

Several years ago I bought a book about atheism, written by an atheist. The Preface includes the following statement:

> This book is intended for a variety of different readers, including atheists looking for a systematic defence and explanation of their position, agnostics who think they might be atheists after all, and religious believers who have a sincere desire to understand what atheism is all about.[12]

As I belonged to the last category in this list I thought this will be helpful to me, but as I read the book I was surprised and disappointed to read Baggini's vitriolic attack on evangelical faith. He speaks of, 'The crass simplicity of this world view' and describes it as 'comforting idiocy'.[13] This is typical of the kind of attack one can expect from New Atheism. I felt cheated because the book was not what it promised in the Preface. I had, after all, a sincere desire to better understand atheism. Instead of a balanced dialogue the book rubbished belief in God, describing it as 'wishful thinking', 'self-delusion' and akin to believing in goblins and hobbits.[14]

Altruism, philanthropy and charity

Genuine faith has inspired altruism, philanthropy, and charity and acted as a stimulus in developing an enduring system of jurisprudence. There is a faith that is reasonable and welcomes intellectual inquiry and contributes positively to the debate on issues such as social justice, human rights and the environment. Faith has produced development agencies that work tirelessly and selflessly in underdeveloped countries. Nevertheless, these neo-atheists trawl through history for supporting data to underpin their atheistic presuppositions. They ignore the positive contribution of religion to the development of society, particularly in the field of doxological science (i.e. science conducted to the glory of God).

Many of them do not have an objective approach in accumulating and evaluating data. They are biased, subjective and much of their anti-religious diatribe is more philosophical in nature than scientific and many of these people are not competent in the field of philosophy.

Rogue's gallery

There are many influential atheists today but here is a sample of who's who in this rogue's gallery.

Daniel Dennett is a philosopher who has argued for materialistic atheism in everything from human consciousness to evolutionary biology. He has written, *Breaking the Spell* and *Darwin's Dangerous Idea*.

Stephen Hawking is one of the world's greatest theoretical physicists. His book, *A Brief History of Time*, had a phenomenal impact when it was first published in the late 1980s. In that work he raised the prospect of a self-creating universe. This theory has since developed at length. His consistent theme is the extraneousness of the God hypothesis. Another of his influential books is *The Grand Design*.

Steven Pinker is a cognitive scientist who deconstructs all elements of human thought that might be construed as pointing to a non-material origin. With a Harvard professorship and a steady stream of popular books arguing for a materialistic view of cognition, he has been a remarkably effective apologist for atheism. Some of his best known works are *How the Mind Works* and *The Blank Slate*.

Michael Shermer is a former evangelical Christian, promotes scepticism that eliminates any vestige of supernaturalism. Founder and publisher of *Skeptic* magazine, he is an indefatigable voice for atheism through popular books, highly visible debates and television interviews, and a monthly column with Scientific American. His books include: *Why People Believe Weird Things* and *The Science of Good and Evil.*

Steven Weinberg is a Nobel laureate physicist and deemed to be one of the great scientists of our time. He is also a remarkably good writer, as demonstrated in his popular books on physics, which advance an atheistic view of the universe. According to him, science's greatest cultural achievement will be to eradicate religion. His books include *The First Three Minutes* and *Lake Views: This World and the Universe*.

Paul Kurtz is a preeminent advocate of secular humanism, which eschews religion in the quest for human flourishing. He has been director of the Council for Secular Humanism, edited the Sceptical Inquirer, and founded Prometheus Press. His books include: *What is Secular Humanism*? and *Science and Religion*.

Lawrence Krauss is the darling of US television networks whom they frequently engage to discuss the relation between science and religion. A physicist with solid credentials as well as a ready pen, who has written many popular science books, Krauss has effectively used this platform to promote atheism. His books include, *Hiding in the Mirror* and *The Physics of Star Trek.*

Edward O. Wilson is the inventor of sociobiology and the inspiration behind contemporary evolutionary ethics. He started life as a Southern Baptist only to become an ardent supporter of evolutionary naturalism under the inspiration of Charles Darwin. A two-time Pulitzer Prize winner, he sacralizes nature and argues that it should replace traditional conceptions of God. His books include *Sociobiology and the Future of Life.*

P. Z. Myers is an associate professor of biology at the University of Minnesota. He was catapulted to atheist stardom through his popular (and outrageously blasphemous) blog '*Pharyngula*'.

John Brockman is the literary agent and publicist for all the leading atheist authors. Through his Edge Foundation he channels the energies and talents of his authors, advancing what he calls 'the third culture', an effort to integrate humanistic and scientific thought that excludes traditional religious belief. His books include, *This Will Change Everything* and *What We Believe but Cannot Prove.*

Philip Pullman is an Oxford-educated, best-selling author. He sees himself as 'undermining the basis for Christian belief'. Viewing C. S. Lewis's Narnia series as religious propaganda, he has written his *Dark Materials* trilogy as an atheistic foil. He has also written a fictional account of Jesus, *The Good Man Jesus and the Scoundrel Christ* representing Christ as a cynically manipulating deceiver.

Barbara Forrest is an active secular humanist who came to

prominence as the leading philosophical voice against the form of creationism known as intelligent design. Criticizing intelligent design as religious propaganda and as an attempt to insert God into educational curricula, she has been effective at making conceptual space for atheism. She has written, *Creationism's Trojan Horse.*

David Sloan Wilson is a biologist and anthropologist who argues for the pervasiveness of selection in the evolutionary process. In consequence, he sees religion itself as an adaptation that can motivate humans to cooperate and behave altruistically. At the same time, he denies that religion has any basis in transcendent reality. His books include, *Unto Others: The Evolution and Psychology of Unselfish Behavior* and *Darwin's Cathedral.*

Ray Kurzweil is an author, inventor and entrepreneur. He sees technology as fulfilling all aspirations previously ascribed to religion, including immortality. He argues that computing machines will soon outstrip human cognitive capacities, at which point humanity will upload itself onto a new, indestructible digital medium (an atheist version/vision of 'resurrection'). His books include, *The Age of Spiritual Machines* and *The Singularity is Near.*

The hiddenness of God

Without faith, God is hidden and even with faith there are times when God seems to be concealed. The idea of God's hiddenness is expressed in Scripture, for example, the lament of the Psalm, 'My God, my God, why have you forsaken me? Why are you so far from saving me, from the words of my groaning? O my God, I cry by day, but you do not answer, and by night, but I find no rest.' (Psalm 22:1–2). Isaiah also expresses this sentiment, 'Truly, you are a God who hides himself' (Isaiah 45:15). But both authors (David and Isaiah) knew God well. This merely reflects moments in their experience. God's hiddenness is not a valid excuse for non-belief.

One of the first philosophers to contemplate the problem of hiddenness was Anselm of Canterbury who in his *Proslogion* complains:

> I have never seen thee, O Lord my God; I do not know thy form. What, O most high Lord, shall this man do, an exile far from thee? What shall thy servant do, anxious in his love of thee, and cast out afar from thy face? He pants to see thee, and thy face is too far from him. He longs to come to thee, and thy dwelling place is inaccessible. He is eager to find thee, and knows not thy place. He desires to seek thee, and does not know thy face. Lord, thou art my God, and thou art my Lord, yet never have I seen thee. It is thou that hast made me, and hast made me anew, and hast bestowed upon me all the blessings I enjoy; and not yet do I know thee. Finally, I was created to see thee and not yet have I done that for which I was made.[15]

A person may be stubbornly blind to evidence of the divine, but the claim is that some non-believers have tried hard to believe in God. Schellenberg introduced the distinction between culpable and inculpable non-belief, where the latter is defined as 'non-belief that exists through no fault of the non-believer'.[16]

However, human beings possess an intuitive sense of God. This *sensus divinatis* (sense of divinity) means that the presence of God is universally perceived by all humans. Paul Helm explains, 'Calvin's use of the term "sense" signals that the knowledge of God is a common human endowment;

mankind is created not only as capable of knowing God, but as actually knowing him.'[17] Thus there is no inculpable or reasonable non-belief. Jonathan Edwards (the eighteenth-century American theologian) claimed that while every human being has been granted the capacity to know God, successful use of these capacities requires an attitude of 'true benevolence', a willingness to be open to the truth about God. Thus, the failure of non-believers to see 'divine things' is due to 'a dreadful stupidity of mind, occasioning a sottish insensibility of their truth and importance.'

Cognitive idolatry

Today's aggressive atheists demand that God should prove his existence. A detailed treatment of these kinds of demands, and their moral implication, is provided by Paul Moser who calls this 'cognitive idolatry'.[18] He defines idolatry as 'our not letting the true God be Lord in our lives' and instead committing to something other than God by pursuing a quest for self-realization on our own terms:

> Cognitive idolatry relies on a standard for knowledge that excludes the primacy of the morally self-transforming knowledge of God central to knowing God as Lord. It rests on an epistemological standard, whether empiricist, rationalist, or some hybrid that does not let God be Lord. Such idolatry aims to protect one's lifestyle from serious challenge by the God who calls, convicts, and reconciles. It disallows knowledge of God as personal subject and Lord to whom we are morally and cognitively responsible. It allows at most for knowledge of God as an undemanding object of human knowledge.[19]

Dangerous dogmatism

New Atheism is a form of dogmatism which could be described as scientific imperialism. Michael Novak reviewing books by Sam Harris, Daniel C. Dennett and Richard Dawkins writes: 'all three pretend that atheists "question everything" and submit to relentless, almost tedious, self-criticism. Yet in these books there is not a shred of evidence that their authors have ever had any doubts whatever about the rightness of their own atheism.'[20] Stephen Jay Gould criticized Richard Dawkins for having a 'Darwinian fundamentalism' and 'uncompromising ideology'.[21]

Harris has been criticized by some of his fellow contributors at *The Huffington Post*. In particular, R. J. Eskow has accused him of fostering intolerance towards faith, potentially as damaging as the religious fanaticism which he opposes.[22] Madeleine Bunting wrote in *The Guardian* that books by the so-called 'Four Horsemen' of the New Atheism (Dawkins, Dennett, Harris and Hitchens) are 'deeply political', sharing a 'loathing' of the role of religion in American culture and politics. Quoting Harris as saying, 'some propositions are so dangerous that it may even be ethical to kill people for believing them,' Bunting says '[t]his sounds like exactly the kind of argument put forward by those who ran the Inquisition.'[23] Quoting the same passage, theologian Catherine Keller asks, '... could there be a more dangerous proposition than that?'[24]

If there is no God

In Dostoevsky's novel, *The Brothers Karamazov* there is the famous argument that, if there is no God, all things are permitted: 'But what will become of men then?' I asked him, 'without God and immortal life? All things are lawful then, they can do what they like?'

In his Templeton Prize address Alexander Solzhenitsyn said:

> Over a half century ago, while I was still a child, I recall hearing a number of old people offer the following explanation for the great disasters that had befallen Russia: 'Men have forgotten God; that's why all this has happened.' Since then I have spent well-nigh fifty years working on the history of our revolution; in the process I have read hundreds of books, collected hundreds of personal testimonies, and have already contributed eight volumes of my own toward the effort of clearing away the rubble left by that upheaval. But if I were asked today to formulate as concisely as possible the main cause of the ruinous revolution that swallowed up some sixty million of our people, I could not put it more accurately than to repeat: 'Men have forgotten God; that's why all this has happened'.[25]

Well-functioning human beings are typically aware of actions as being right and wrong. Furthermore, this awareness binds them to certain obligations. A proposition such as, 'torturing babies for fun is wrong' is generally regarded as a statement of fact, a position known as moral realism.[26] The existence of God provides a better explanation for this than various alternatives.

Social organization strategies in the West (such as systems of jurisprudence) have evolved over time and are based on the transcendent ethical code of the Commandments. If morality is transcendental in nature then theism provides the best explanation for this. Thus, the existence of morality provides good grounds for belief in God. He made people in his image and morality reflects something of his nature. Thus morality is best explained within a theistic hypothesis; if God does not exist, then objective moral values do not exist. But objective values do exist and thus we must conclude that God exists.

Belief in God cannot be adequately explained in terms of psychological and sociological hypotheses. Although I believe there is sufficient evidence for the existence of God to warrant sincere investigation it must also be said that absence of evidence is not evidence of absence.[27] Faith is more than a shared neurological and cultural framework based on cognitive processes in the brain. Even if it were then it could be argued that those who don't possess it are cerebrally deficient. This runs counter to the widely held view of atheists that believers are stupid. Belief in God is one of the most powerful impulses in human development and a strong impetus to personal transformation and collective progress. There are countless examples of its transformational power and faith should be acknowledged as a constructive force that makes a positive difference in the lives of individuals and communities.

David and Goliath

It was noted earlier that in his confrontation with Goliath David possessed five noteworthy qualities: confidence in God, experience in defending the flock, a spirit grieved to hear the Lord's name being profaned, a courageous heart and a desire 'that all the earth may know that there is a God in Israel' (1 Sam 17:46). In closing it might be helpful to make some observations on those points.

What does it mean to have confidence in God?

Having sufficient confidence in God to enter such an arena is not the same as possessing self-assurance based on intellectual ability, level of education or aptitude for communication. Rather it comes from knowing who God is—a spiritual perspective which understands the relative proportion of things such as human wisdom in relation to the infinite wisdom of God. Knowing God comes from a meaningful relationship with the Lord which is cultivated (through prayer and reading Scripture) in times of intimate and dynamic communion. Such frequent encounters with God fortify the soul for battle.

What does it mean to defend the flock?

It is a pastoral duty not only to feed the flock but to also fend off predators. The welfare of God's people is well served by those who preach pastorally and prophetically. Christ-centred, Spirit-filled expository preaching of God's Word will minister to the mind as well as heart and will. Preaching that bridges the worlds of the ancient text and the contemporary context will have an apologetic emphasis, dispelling doubt, defending faith and creating a safe space for critical examination of relevant intellectual issues at all levels. Just as David refined his skill in the regular performance of his duty to the flock, so too the spiritual shepherds of today need to develop in their roles as defenders of their people.

What does it mean to have a spirit grieved to hear the Lord's name profaned?

Those who cultivate a close relationship with God will be possessed with something of the mind and heart of the Lord. Such was the case with Paul in Athens; Acts 17 records that he was 'greatly distressed to see that the city was full of idols' (v.16, NIV). Seeing as God sees will result in feeling as God feels. The next verse tells us how Paul responded to the situation:

'So he reasoned in the synagogue with the Jews and the devout persons, and in the marketplace every day'. How reminiscent this is of God's own gracious invitation to engage with those estranged from him: 'Come now, let us reason together, says the LORD: though your sins are like scarlet, they shall be as white as snow; though they are red like crimson, they shall become like wool' (Isaiah 1:18). Believers need to engage in this same kind of rational dialogue in both sacred and secular space so that spiritual/biblical discourse has an apologetic emphasis that addresses questions people are asking.

What does it mean to have a courageous heart?

Engaging in the embattling apologetics of New Atheism is a daunting prospect for most believers and 'fools rush in where angels fear to tread'. But having a courageous heart means preferring a potentially humiliating defeat rather than cowardly observing the Lord's name being traduced. David had a desire 'that all the earth may know that there is a God …' (1 Samuel 17:46). The apostle Paul said 'we do not wrestle against flesh and blood, but against the rulers, against the authorities, against the cosmic powers over this present darkness, against the spiritual forces of evil in the heavenly places' (Ephesians 6:12). Who would not be afraid of such a fight? But God has supplied the armour. In the very next verse Paul says 'Therefore take up the whole armour of God, that you may be able to withstand in the evil day, and having done all, to stand firm' (v.13). The word 'Therefore' emphasizes the necessity for spiritual weaponry in this war of worldviews. In vivid terms he explains that truth, righteousness, faith and the Word of God are necessary in this cosmic combat.

David stepped forward in the name of his God and

although the opposition was frightening to others, it was not overwhelming to him. A great victory was wrought that day which inspired the people of God and instilled fear in the hearts of those who were their enemies. Such exemplary qualities are needed today at a time when the deity is being publicly mocked. Let us do all that we can to champion the cause of the Lord today!

What does it mean to desire 'that all the earth may know … there is a God'?

The apostle Peter charged believers about the necessity of 'always being prepared to make a defence to anyone who asks you for a reason for the hope that is in you; yet do it with gentleness and respect' (1 Peter 3:15). This is not an instruction just for pastors, missionaries and those engaged in apologetics. This is what all believers must do and we need to consider our own role in encouraging atheism by our moral shortcomings and intellectual laziness. Those who profess faith in God need to reveal something of that divine nature and not conceal it or distort it. Let us love the Lord with all our hearts, souls and minds.

The believer's hope is a reasonable faith in the existence of God and must be presented as such in a spirit of humility. Christians must create a safe space for those with intellectual doubts to ask questions and find answers without recrimination. To respect other people's views does not necessarily mean that we agree with them. Making God known in contemporary culture will involve dialogue in the public forum as much as in the pulpit and pews. The secular humanist desire to write the obituary for religion is futile. It is not so much that God is back but rather that he has never gone away.[28]

Religion is experiencing resurgence in the twenty-first-century and this provides a new opportunity to make the true God known, not only through everyday interaction with friends, colleagues and neighbours but also preaching and teaching within the church, Christian publications and training seminars. The virtual community of our global village (with its social networks, websites and blogs) means that everybody has opportunity to speak out so that 'all the earth may know that there is a God'.

2

Militant Secularism

'... if the foundations are destroyed, what can the righteous do?' (Psalm 11:3)

In Western Europe and Northern Europe today mission is conducted in a post-Christian, postmodern and primarily secular society. Europe, once the continent from which the torch of evangelicalism was lit is now the spiritually darkest continent on the planet. A culture of secularism is gaining traction and those who conduct mission in such an environment face new challenges.

In the UK, Conservative Party co-chairwoman Baroness Warsi (the first female Muslim cabinet minister in parliament) has expressed the view that Britain is under threat from a rising tide of 'militant secularization' and warned that religion is being 'sidelined, marginalized and downgraded in the public sphere.' These sentiments were voiced in a speech at the Vatican and represent the growing fear amongst people of faith that their religious views are being intentionally attacked.[1] The speech was picked up by UK's *Channel 4 News* and the B.B.C. *Newsnight* program.[2] Sayeeda Warsi was on a two-day delegation of seven British ministers to the Holy See. This was the first time a serving minister of a foreign government gave an address to the staff and students of the Pontifical Ecclesiastical Academy. The visit marked the 30th anniversary of the re-establishment of full diplomatic ties between Britain and the Vatican.[3]

Unsurprisingly the British Humanist Association (BHA) described Warsi's comments as 'outdated, unwarranted and divisive'. Andrew Copson (chief executive of BHA) said: 'In an increasingly non-religious and, at the same time, diverse society, we need policies that will emphasize what we have in common as citizens rather than what divides us'.

Richard Dawkins was invited into the *Newsnight* discussion where he made a distinction between secularism and atheism. Dawkins rightly pointed out that many religious people favour the separation of church and state and that the founding fathers of America, who were fleeing religious persecution in England, enshrined this principle. What does all this mean? One thing is crystal clear; God, religion, secular humanism and atheism are newsworthy topics.

Ironically the Muslim peer (Warsi) said Europe needed to become 'more confident and more comfortable in its Christianity'. She said 'to create a more just society, people need to feel stronger in their religious identities and more confident in their creeds'. She went on to say that 'In practice this means individuals not diluting their faiths and nations not denying their religious heritages.'

But what if the establishment religion is a diluted and distorted version of Christianity which is liberal, pluralist and essentially nominal? What if the state is Muslim and enshrines the moral code of Islam in Shari'a Law or what if the dominant religion is Roman Catholicism or Hinduism?

A Muslim standing shoulder to shoulder with the Pope on this issue is typical of pluralism in contemporary culture. Warsi sees religion *per se* as a good thing. It does not seem to matter what religion. Clearly she sees religion as having a positive influence on society and that in her view is preferable to secularism. That is why she can adopt a position of co-belligerency with such peculiar allies as Pope Benedict XVI.

Warsi went on to say: 'You cannot and should not extract these Christian foundations from the evolution of our nations any more than you can or should erase the spires from our landscapes.' In the Republic of Ireland (for example) the spires of Roman Catholic churches are, for many, symbolic of the structures of domineering and abusive power in the social landscape and the dismantling of that institution is welcomed by many.

Is she correct in her assessment that 'militant secularization' is taking hold of society? She cites various examples saying: 'signs of religion cannot be displayed or worn in government buildings ... states won't fund faith schools'. Her comments come days after the High Court ruled that a Devon Town Council had acted unlawfully by allowing prayers to be said at meetings. Certainly there are a growing number of such issues being reported.

This is not the first time a senior Tory called for a revival of traditional Christian values. In December 2011 the Prime Minister David Cameron said the UK was a Christian country and 'should not be afraid to say so'.

Research conducted by Ipsos MORI in 2011 for the Richard

Dawkins Foundation for Reason and Science (UK) suggests that Britons who declare themselves Christian display a low level of belief and practice. The results are based on 1,136 responses from a face-to-face survey conducted with those who recorded themselves as 'Christian' in the 2011 Census. Even if one is sceptical about such dubious, agenda-driven and partisan 'research' and particularly wary about how such statistics will be used to further the aims of secular humanists, it does, nevertheless, give some insight to religious and social attitudes of UK 'Christians' in 2011. The findings suggest that almost three quarters of those polled agreed that religion should not influence public policy. It also found that 61% of Christians agreed homosexuals should have the same legal rights in all aspects of their lives as heterosexuals. And a further 62% were in favour of a woman's right to have an abortion within the legal time limit. There is nothing surprising here for evangelical Christians who are all too aware that many people who call themselves 'Christian' are in reality nominal adherents of mainstream denominations who do not have meaningful faith.

Warsi is certainly correct in her assessment of militant secularism that, 'at its core and in its instincts it is deeply intolerant.' The media who are fuelling the polemical fire which is warming the hearts of secular humanists neglected to report that Warsi said that: 'secularism is not intrinsically damaging. My concern is when secularization is pushed to an extreme, when it requires the complete removal of faith from the public sphere. So I am calling for a more open confidence in faith, where faith has a place at the table, though not an exclusive position.'

Without committing to an inter-faith agenda there has to be some dialogue which assists in building community relations and opposing bigotry. Such a strategy needs to be widened to include people of faith, secular humanists and atheists. The discussion is getting overheated and the masks of civility are beginning to slip, exposing mutual contempt in all its ugliness. The strident tone of secularism is undermining its own ability to market the concept to all of society. There is a huge religious constituency in Western society (far outnumbering the cohort of secularists, humanists, freethinkers, agnostics and atheists) and the way secularism is being promulgated, in anti-religious terms, reinforces the notion that this is a movement which seeks to disenfranchise people of faith. Suspicion and fear will thrive in an environment of ignorance and this in turn can only produce resentment and resistance. Is it possible for believers to subscribe to the aims and objectives of secularism without compromising spiritual integrity? Certainly the motives and methods of many secularists seem reactionary, radical and subversive and as such are unattractive to believers with more conservative views. Those who desire to conduct Christian mission in contemporary culture need to be cognizant of this new dynamic. Opposition to the gospel is getting more vehement.

Secularism as originally conceived (to protect religion from government interference and government from religious interference) is not necessarily a bad thing. But it has mutated into an anti-faith movement in contemporary society. With its agenda controlled by aggressive atheists it has been cast in a polemical context of embattling worldviews. As a consequence believers think that secularism is inherently wrong, perhaps without understanding the true nature of the concept as it touches on freedom of religion and the relationship between church and state. There should (in theory) be no bar to believers joining secular societies where they can make a positive contribution to shaping the process of secularization and acting as a restraint on its inherently anti-religious ethos. But secular societies are usually defined as 'humanist' and membership is restricted to 'non-religious' people. There is an important difference between humanism and secularism but the nuances of that distinction are not always understood or appreciated.

Those who would like to write the obituary of religion might have to wait a while longer. The supposed demise of religion is wishful thinking on the part of those who want to usher in a new era of secular humanism. The God debate is gaining momentum and anyone who wants to understand contemporary culture must first understand the role religion plays in it. Militant secularists will try to silence Christians but believers need to be unafraid and unashamed of the message of the gospel in our times.

There is certainly a process of secularization underway and it would be foolish to deny this but it is a myth to think that society is now predominantly secular or that a large minority of the public are secularized. Those who enthusiastically proclaim that the twenty-first century is the dawn of a new era of secularism (and that we are on the threshold of a new social order which will soon reflect this) are not just premature but delusional. A more measured hesitancy and caution in the debate is appropriate. On the contrary, the revival of religion evident in the rise of Christianity in Africa, Latin America, and Asia as well as the rapid expansion of Islam and the growth in minority religions and cults belies the notion of imminent *global* secularization.

Nevertheless *some* societies are growing more secular and this is true of Britain. But secular humanists have a disproportionate voice in relation to their membership (through publication and the media) which creates the illusion that they are a critical mass that will soon tip the balance in favour of secularization. This argument should not be swallowed hook, line and sinker because some would argue that secularization is a myth that needs to be debunked. In reality there is a noticeable resurgence in religion in the twenty-first-century and those who think religion is an endangered species are mistaken.[4]

Over the last few decades Europe underwent a simultaneous process of political fragmentation and unification. Many of the former Soviet Union's Eastern bloc countries asserted independence in the new post-Soviet environment and many of these countries underwent further fragmentation into independent states which subsequently joined the E.U. This kind of realignment is similar to what is happening in many parts of the world today with religion. There is a process of secularization underway but there is also a resurgence of religion and new strategic alliances are being formed.

What is secularism? Is society becoming increasingly secular? Is secularism inherently atheistic? These questions need to be addressed. An understanding of secularism will necessitate a definition of the concept which includes an outline of its aims and objectives. In tracing the philosophical roots and historical development of secularism a better understanding of the notion can be cultivated. From the divine right of kings in ancient times to the investiture controversy, the relationship between the Christian church and the state has been complex and controversial. Contemporary relationships between church and state and their particular manifestations in various countries around the globe are also varied and no less intricate or contentious. Whether it is the period from Constantine to

Charlemagne or the situation today in diverse societies it is important to understand the legal frameworks that define the parameters and shape the relationship between church and state.

What is secularism?

Secularism rightly understood is the separation of political and religious institutions so that government is free from the dominant (or domineering) influence of any particular religion. In other words secularism asserts that religion should not be privileged with regard to enacting legislation or formulating policy. Obviously this would have implications for funding criteria and consultation processes. Secularism guarantees freedom from the governmental imposition of religion upon the people within a state. This would be beneficial to Christians (and other minority religious groups) in Islamic states where Shari'a Law prevails and it would disenfranchise extremist groups such as the Taliban in Afghanistan who seek to impose their fundamentalist views on society.

Ideally secularism should be neutral about matters of belief. However there is a growing militancy among contemporary secularists which is inherently anti-religious. If many of a nation's citizens are religious then it seems inappropriate that the state would be anti-religious. This raises questions regarding the proper role of religion in society and what should be its relationship with the state?

The fundamental principle of secularism (that, in his whole conduct, man should be guided exclusively by considerations derived from the present life itself) is essentially rooted in humanism. Thus the secularist would contend that anything that is above or beyond the present life should be entirely overlooked. Accordingly secularists believe that whether God exists or not, whether the soul is immortal or not, are questions which at best cannot be answered.

The religious view is at variance with this as it holds the church is as earnest as secularists regarding the improvement of this life by scientific achievements and as eager for the fulfilment of all duties pertaining to the present life. But the present life cannot be looked upon as an end in itself, and independent of the future life. Knowledge of the material world, rightly understood, leads to knowledge of the spiritual world, and among the duties of the present life there are obligations which arise from the existence and nature of God, the fact of divine revelation, and the necessity of preparing for the future life.

Secularism perceives itself as interested in everything that touches the welfare of sentient beings. But many of its advocates are atheists who deny that humanity has a spiritual dimension. Perhaps the failure of some Christians to understand that the ultimate ecological ethic is rooted in God and the emphasis on the eschatological hope of the afterlife has de-emphasized temporal concern for the planet Earth. But great humanitarian endeavour and philanthropic interventions have been inspired by faith and sustained by faith groups. Secularism has evolved into a protest against what it perceives as theological oppression and ecclesiastical tyranny. In theory it upholds intellectual independence but in practice it is a despot that detests religion and desires its eradication.

Organizations

Groups such as the National Secular Society (UK) and Americans United campaign for secularism. In 2005, the National Secular Society held the inaugural 'Secularist of the

Year' awards ceremony. Its first winner was Maryam Namazie, of the Worker-Communist Party of Iran. Another secularist organization is the Secular Coalition for America. This body lobbies and advocates for separation of church and state as well as the acceptance and inclusion of secular Americans in American life and public policy.

There are many international, national, regional and local organizations that work to raise the profile of secularism in their countries and communities. These tend to include secularists, freethinkers, atheists, agnostics, and humanists under their organizational umbrella. Some student organizations, such as the Toronto Secular Alliance, try to popularize non-theism and secularism on campus. The Secular Student Alliance (USA) is an educational group that organizes and aids such high school and college secular student groups.

In Turkey, the most prominent and active secularist organization is the Atatürk Thought Association, which is credited with organizing the Republic Protests (demonstrations in the four largest cities in Turkey in 2007) where over two-million people, mostly women, showed their support of the secularist principles introduced by Mustafa Kemal Atatürk.

The Leicester Secular Society (founded in 1851) is the world's oldest secular society.

Assessment

Secularists see secularism as one of the most important movements in the history of the modern West, helping differentiate the West not only from the Middle-Ages and more ancient eras, but also from other cultural regions around the world. Their view is that the modern West is what it is largely because of secularism (meaning only its positive aspects).

Although secularism may be understood as simply the absence of religion, it is a philosophical system with personal, political, cultural, and social implications. Secularism desires to establish an autonomous political and social sphere which is naturalistic and materialistic, as opposed to a religious view where the supernatural and faith is affirmed. Thus its advocates argue generally for a sphere of knowledge, values, and action that is independent of religious authority. They desire to exclude religion from having any authority (perhaps even a voice) in political and social affairs. Supporters of secularism suggest that it (secularism) is vital for democracy, personal liberty, and even religious freedom. Secularism prescribes state neutrality in religious matters, but it is not morally or politically neutral.

Secularists support the separation of church and state, oppose religion or the religious being afforded privileges, which they see as others (non-religious) being disadvantaged. They believe that the reduced numbers attending church (usually mainstream denominations) show that people have chosen to give up faith. They say this underlines the unfairness of giving any special privileges or rights to faith groups. Secularists are particularly concerned about education. They think that religious schools are divisive and damage the prospects of a harmonious and diverse society.

In theory secularists are not against the right of individuals to have a religious faith but their stated aims seem akin to outlawing religion. They say that what they oppose is special treatment for religious beliefs and organizations but having cast themselves in the role of religious haters (along with aggressive atheists whose stated aim is the eradication of religion, à *la* Dawkins and co.) it is difficult for believers to trust them. They would contend that the protection already given by the law, including human rights legislation, should be sufficient to protect believers from assault or discrimination.

Some secularists seek to separate those bits of our present-day culture that originated in religion from the religions that inspired them (Christmas, for example). This reinforces the view of religious people that their cultural traditions are being marginalized and downgraded in a systematic attempt to sideline faith.

While most secularists are humanists and atheists, some new religious groups that compose a minority in a particular culture find secularism attractive because it would free them from the domineering and oppressive influence of the dominant religious culture. This is true of Christians in Islamic states where freedom of religion is often restricted and blasphemy laws and laws prohibiting proselytism inhibit evangelism.

A secularized public sphere

In Western culture (as well as some non-western cultures) society has become socially secularized. In many European countries, for example, the state has taken over the social roles of the church, leading to a generally secularized public sphere. The degree of separation varies from total separation mandated by a constitution to other less rigid structures. Thus while some countries have maintained legal recognition of an official state religion they are, nevertheless, largely secularized.

In the relationship between church and state the issue of freedom of religion is an important one. Just as religious minorities should have the rights of such freedom, so too secularists, humanists and atheists should be guaranteed the same privileges. A civilized society can be evaluated by how it treats its minorities. However, secularists, humanists and atheists should be aware that they are minority. The tail should not wag the dog!

With regard to religious freedom different countries can be placed on a continuum with liberal democracies on one end and authoritarian systems of government on the other end. Thus, there are varying positions in the international spectrum. Christians would argue for religious liberty for their fellow believers in Islamic states and secular/atheistic nations. Thus, to be entirely consistent, they ought to support religious liberty and free-thought in democracies that have a Christian tradition. Therefore, although believers may see the dangers of radical or militant secularism they should defend the right of free-thought and free speech, which is a cornerstone of liberal democracy. In fact Christians have an obligation to participate respectfully (which does not mean avoiding a robust critique) in the 'dialogue' about the origin, nature, identity and purpose of mankind. The believer has a right and a duty to contribute to how society is shaped. The believer has something important to say in relation to mankind's significance. The believer has a critical part to play in influencing legislation that influences ethical, ecological and economic issues and their interconnectedness. The believer can have and should have a voice that speaks of hope in a world of despair.

Nevertheless in the UK secularists lobby for the separation of church and state, the disestablishment of the Church of England and that there would be no official representation of religions in parliament, which would mean no bishops in the House of Lords. They want to ban prayers from parliament, council chambers, etc. They demand that no monies should be given to religious organizations. Generally they desire the abolition of any special privileges granted to religious organizations and the abolition of any special protection granted to faith groups. They lobby for the conversion of faith schools to community schools open to all pupils regardless of faith or lack of it. They contend that religious education should be non-denominational and multi-faith. They insist that education should present non-religious ways of looking at the world. Some secularists would prefer religious education to be replaced by citizenship lessons including only brief coverage of the basic tenets of world religions. Would this have implications in other subjects such as history and art?

In the USA secularists demand that the employment of chaplains in the army, navy, prisons, asylums, and all institutions supported by public money, should be discontinued. They also want the oath taken by witnesses in court to be abolished and replaced with a caution about the penalties of perjury. Essentially they desire that the entire political system should be conducted on a purely secular basis and this involves repealing all laws relating to Christian morality.

The American Secular Union and Freethought Association with many affiliated local societies aims for the separation of church and state and makes the following demands that churches and other ecclesiastical property shall be no longer be exempt from taxation. They insist that all public appropriations for educational and charitable institutions are of a sectarian character and should cease. They demand that religious teaching and the use of the Bible for religious purposes in public schools should be prohibited. They want to ban religious festivals, fasts, and days of prayer, including thanksgiving. They want all laws directly or indirectly enforcing Sabbath observance to be repealed. They want the entire political system to be conducted and administered on a purely secular basis.

Remove your helmets we want to throw rocks at you!

Secularists want the abolition of 'blasphemy' laws and contend that the law should not restrict reasonable and vigorous criticism of religion. They do not seem to be inhibited in this matter in Western society. They believe that the law should not prevent criticism that hurts religious feelings, but they do not seem to be in the least bit inhibited in this way either. Secularists support legislation to outlaw discrimination in employment on the grounds of religion (or lack of it). Christians favour such an approach to recruitment policy except where it might be a critical matter for the employer. But secularists oppose exemptions which religious organizations might seek. They see this as the state allowing discrimination. Secularists also want the abolition of special treatment given to religious broadcasting.

The problem

The problem with secularism is that it is essentially humanistic and as such atheistic. Secularists might argue that secularism is a philosophy to which believers can subscribe but in reality believers are not allowed membership of their societies because they have an anti-faith agenda. They do not want believers to have a place at the negotiating table whereby a healthy relationship between church and state, believers and non-believers, can shape the future together.

Secularism when it is interpreted as the right of the government to govern without religious interference and the right of religion to practice unfettered by government might be a good thing. But Dawkins and others like him have, ironically, done a great disservice to the cause of secularism by stating a commitment to the eradication of religion.

The materialistic worldview of secularists/atheists denies that there is any spiritual dimension to human beings. Many of them are aggressive and intolerant and their strident tone reveals a belligerent attitude rooted in a bellicose nature. They want to wrest the whip from religious power (as they see things) and apply it to the backs of the 'oppressor'. If they are allowed to succeed they will be as abusive of such power (in denying the right to freedom of religion) as the atheistic and totalitarian regimes of Russia, parts of Eastern Europe, North Korea and China. They share the same spirit of intolerance that possesses the regimes of Iran, Pakistan, Saudi Arabia and elsewhere. They would create a secular state where people of faith would be denied fair and proportionate representation. They present themselves as liberal and tolerant but in reality they behave like the thought police in totalitarian regimes.

The very foundations of European society are being radically undermined by secularism. The decision to refrain from any mention of God in its constitution is effectively a denial of its history. In both Western and Northern Europe (and to a lesser extent in North America) radical secularists want to gag God, straight-jacket believers and usher in a new order of relativistic and utilitarian morality. The extent to which they succeed in fulfilling these aims might well depend on the amount of scope believers allow for such a militant movement to manoeuvre its way to power.

3

Understanding Postmodernism

Understanding the contemporary context in which mission is conducted in the Western world will necessitate an understanding of postmodernism. A lot has been written in recent decades describing the phenomenon of postmodernism. But what is it? What are its essential features? How does it affect evangelism and engagement? In mission one is essentially involved in a work of translation whereby the ancient text of Scripture is contextualized in the culture where mission takes place. It is crucial, therefore to understand both the culture of the ancient world in which the text of Scripture was conceived as well as the contemporary culture where it is to be received. The world has certainly undergone radical change in terms of worldview. Postmodernism is a new and dramatically altered state of consciousness.[1]

The word postmodern is not just part of the academic jargon

of today. Although it emerged from literary and aesthetic criticism it has certainly become more generally used in communication.[2] But it is not entirely clear precisely what the term means. Daniel J. Adams has said that there are 'Few terms as commonly used, and just as commonly misunderstood as postmodernism.'[3] For some, such as Lawrence Cahoone postmodernism represents 'the defeat of modern European theology, metaphysics, authoritarianism, colonialism, racism, and domination.'[4] For others, postmodernism is a radical intellectual movement intent on subverting civilization. Furthermore, postmodernism has been described as 'a goofy collection of hermetically obscure writers who are really talking about nothing at all.'[5]

Charles Colson says 'Today, all the major ideological constructions are being tossed on the ash heap of history. All that remains is the cynicism of postmodernism, with its false assertions that there is no objective truth or meaning, that we are free to create our own truth as long as we understand that it's nothing more than an illusion'.[6]

Is this an accurate portrayal of postmodernism? Alister McGrath is correct in his statement that 'a full definition of postmodernism is virtually impossible.'[7] Cahoone suggests that it is a 'mistake to seek a single essential meaning' of postmodernism that is 'applicable to all the term's instances.'[8]

There are several postmodern perspectives in art (including film and music) architecture and so on.[9] David Ray Griffin indicates that there are various postmodern theologies.[10] The term postmodernism also pertains to some of the principal cultural and intellectual movements such as feminism, pragmatism, existentialism, deconstruction, and post-empiricist philosophy of science.[11] Postmodernism is associated more with what it rejects than with what it positively affirms.[12] As Adams says, postmodernism is a concept 'that has not yet discovered how to define itself in terms of what is, but only in terms of what it has just-now-ceased to be.'[13]

Any attempt to clarify the concept of postmodernism is further complicated by lack of consensus about how it ought to be defined.[14] Postmodernism has been classified in manifold ways: as an era,[15] a condition,[16] a state of mind or attitude,[17] and a philosophical movement.[18] As Griffin points out, postmodernism 'is used in a confusing variety of ways, some of them contradictory to others.'[19] Furthermore efforts to define postmodernism are considered, by some of its adherents, as an inimical desire to pigeonhole a concept that is inherently amorphous.[20] Finally, it is not always easy to clarify where modernism ends and postmodernism begins.[21] There is no agreement about when postmodernism began or when the term was first used.

Cahoone credits Rudolf Pannwitz as the first to use the designation in 1917. Pannwitz's usage delineates the nihilism of modern man as outlined by Friedrich Nietzsche.[22] Others credit Frederico de Oniz with initiating the term *postmodernismo* in 1934. Carl F. H. Henry says that John Cobb first coined the word, as it is currently understood, in 1964.[23] However, it must be said that postmodernism is generally understood to be a philosophical word that refers to a movement that started in France in the 1960s[24] and continued to be cultivated in the United States.[25]

Notwithstanding the difficulties of defining postmodernism some working definition is necessary. It can be said with certainty that postmodernism refers to the period 'after the modern world.'[26] McGrath says it is the 'general intellectual outlook arising after the collapse of modernism.'[27] It is a reaction to the modernism of Western civilization.[28] It is a counter-culture worldview that is inherently antithetical to the Enlightenment's confidence in universal rational principles.[29] As postmodern doctrine is generally taken to be true in our culture it is apt to refer to the present time as the postmodern era.[30]

Postmodernism is an influential worldview: 'Postmodernism is a new set of assumptions about reality', as Dockery asserts.[31] 'It impacts our literature, our dress, our art, our architecture, our music, our sense of right and wrong, our self-identity, and our theology.'[32]

As postmodernism is a reaction to modernism, a basic knowledge of modernism and pre-modernism is helpful for acquiring an understanding of postmodernism. As Millard J. Erickson states, 'If we would understand postmodernism, then, we must first understand the two periods that preceded it, namely, the pre-modern and the modern.'[33]

Pre-modernism as precursor of modernism

Postmodernism's more remote predecessor, the pre-modern period, is generally thought to refer to the pre-Enlightenment era incorporating the ancient and medieval periods.[34] What are the essential features this epoch? Erickson says the pre-modern world was characterized by 'belief in the rationality of the universe.'[35]

It was essentially dualistic so that not only was there the immediately identifiable natural world but there was also the less obvious, though nonetheless real, supernatural domain. If God created and sustained the universe then everything had a pattern and a purpose. Thus this dualistic rationality and spiritual order permitted humanity a privileged place in the hierarchical structure. Stanley J. Grenz notes, 'God stood at the apex, followed by the angelic hosts; humans found their place "a little lower than the heavenly beings" (Psalm 8:5) but above the rest of the created order.'[36]

Phenomena in the pre-modern world were perceived and explained by the purpose they served in teleological terms.[37] In theological terms that is the doctrine of design and purpose in the material world. In other words the pre-modern mind thought of the world as a reality designed by God for a particular purpose. This is particularly true in the Western world, where the great architect of the universe was thought to be the sovereign God superintending the affairs of history to the ultimate fulfilment of his will. Thus history was seen as a linear process moving inexorably toward an ultimate climax. Henry notes, the pre-modern age 'held that nature and history reflect God's immutable ordering of the cosmos. Its worldview elaborated a distinctive understanding of the nature and destiny of the human self in a meaningful and purposive universe created and ruled by God.'[38]

The pre-modern period held to a correspondence theory of truth. Thus assertions were deemed to be true if they accurately stated the characteristics of the real nature of what they sought to describe. The converse was also held to be true and so statements that did not accurately describe reality were understood to be false.[39]

Modernism as progenitor of postmodernism

It is generally accepted that the modern age spans the period of time from the Enlightenment to the late-twentieth century.[40] Oden dates it at exactly two hundred years from the overthrow of the Bastille in 1789 to the collapse of the Berlin Wall in 1989.

The modern era has both continuity and discontinuity with the pre-modern period.

One of the striking contrasts between the pre-modern and modern worlds is that the modern world was essentially humanistic. Humanism, as the name suggests, puts man at the centre of reality rather than God. In spite of the fact that many people believed in God, the deity was not viewed as the starting point for understanding the universe. Henry suggests that the modern world 'transferred to itself the attributes that had long characterized the traditional deity.'[41]

The philosophy of René Descartes made a significant contribution to this development. He is seen by some as the founder of modernism. He declared the cognitive domain of the human mind's conviction of its own existence as the place where understanding reality began. Thus there was a significant shift of emphasis from God to man.[42] As Richard Tarnas says, 'In effect, Descartes unintentionally began a theological Copernican revolution, for his mode of reasoning suggested that God's existence was established by human reason and not vice versa.'[43]

The modern period was also naturalistic. Some scientists practiced 'doxological science' where their work was performed to the glory of God. But most intellectuals 'gravitated toward naturalistic explanations of everything.'[44]

One of the essential features of the modern period was its central belief in the power of human reason.[45] They believed that human reason could lead to an objective understanding of knowledge and reality. This view is encapsulated in John Locke's statement 'Reason must be our last judge and guide in everything.'[46]

The modern world was primarily optimistic and as such it was convinced of the inevitability of progress. It put its faith in pedagogical progress. Learning, science, and technology would help solve most of the problems facing the world. Thomas Oden refers to this belief as 'technological messianism.'[47] The modern mind believed in the ability of man to deliver the utopia to which he aspired. This belief rested on a more fundamental presupposition that had faith in the inherent integrity of knowledge. It assumed a direct correlation between knowledge and improvement.

The modern era was also distinguished by Foundationalism. That is the view that 'the world rests on a foundation of indubitable beliefs from which further propositions can be inferred to produce a superstructure of known truths.'[48] Whether these foundations were self-evident truths or sense data, it was on the basis of such foundations that one could understand reality.[49] For Descartes these primary and absolute principles were lucid and definite ideas. For David Hume they were sense experience.

The modern period was one of epistemological certainty. D. A. Carson says 'the assumption for many thinkers in the period of modernity was that certainty, absolute epistemological certainty (and not just a psychological feeling), was not only desirable but attainable.'[50]

Finally, another essential feature of the modern period is its confidence in metanarratives to explain reality. Metanarratives are universal stories or accounts of reality that show how things really are.[51] Cahoone states that metanarratives are 'philosophical stories, which legitimate all other discourse.'[52] They demonstrate how knowledge and experience are interconnected and how they may be explicated. Jean-Francois Lyotard asserts that belief in metanarratives was the most essential feature of modernism.[53] Religions, including Christianity, are seen as metanarratives as are philosophies and ideologies such as Nationalism and Marxism.

The passing of modernism

Modernism is in a serious tailspin and the inexorable outcome will be its ultimate demise.[54] McGrath notes, 'Although a number of writers still maintain that modernism is alive and active, this attitude is becoming increasingly rare.'[55] Anderson says that modernism has taken a serious fall and he asserts that 'Humpty-Dumpty is not going to be put back together again.'[56] He argues that any attempt to do so is 'ultimately self defeating.'[57]

This does not mean that every aspect of modernism has ceased to exist. Oden observes:

> It would be wrongheaded to infer that every aspect of modern consciousness is dead or that all social and political achievements of the last two centuries are lost. Modernity is not dead in the sense that all its repercussions and consequences are over, but in the sense that the ideological engine propelling the movement of modernity is broken down irreparably'.[58]

Oden argues that many good aspects of modernism are still extant in literature, aesthetics, architecture, music, politics, civil liberties, medical advancements and new technologies.[59]

Differences between modernism and postmodernism

There is in postmodernism a loss of confidence in the ability of reason to deliver the utopia that it seemed to promise. There is also a denial of the objectivity of knowledge. Knowledge is subjective and, therefore, relative and this involves a rejection of absolutes. Confidence in the inevitability of progress has been displaced with cynicism. Foundationalism has been rejected and metanarratives have been cast aside as discredited worldviews. Language has come to be understood as a human construct. Tolerance is the spirit of the age and the acceptance of philosophical and religious pluralism reflects this.

Loss of confidence in reason

The modernist mind believed in the power of reason. The modernist, therefore, had a faith in reason to deliver an objective understanding of knowledge and reality. That conviction and confidence which characterized modernism has been displaced with a disillusioned cynicism. McGrath says, 'There has been a general collapse of confidence in the Enlightenment trust in the power of reason to provide foundations for a universally valid knowledge of the world, including God.'[60]

D. A. Carson observes a certain 'irony' in this trend, 'The modernity which has arrogantly insisted that human reason is the final arbiter of truth has spawned a stepchild that has arisen to slay it.'[61]

Rejection of the objectivity of knowledge

Modernism's belief in the objectivity of knowledge has come to be viewed as a discredited theory. Thus postmodernism denies the objectivity of knowledge because it asserts that all knowledge is determined by cultural and social factors. In the words of James B. Miller 'In the postmodern context, all knowledge is viewed as cultural artefact.'[62]

Postmodernism asserts that all knowledge is theoretical and

the idea of impartial, empirical facts is a modernist myth. Thus the cognitive capacity of reason is an inadequate tool for objectively evaluating the world. Tarnas notes, 'Human knowledge is the historically contingent product of linguistic and social practices of particular local communities of interpreters, with no assured 'ever-closer' relation to an independent ahistorical reality.'[63]

Anderson's story of the three umpires gives us an understanding of the postmodern perspective on reality. He talks about three umpires discussing balls and strikes. The first umpire said, 'There are balls and there are strikes, and I call 'em the way they are.' The second umpire said, 'There are balls and there are strikes and I call 'em the way I see 'em.' The third umpire declared, 'There are balls and there are strikes, and they ain't *nothin'* until I call 'em.' According to Anderson, the first umpire represents a pre-modern view of reality, while the second represents a modern perspective. The third umpire is 'a postmodern radical.'[64]

Absolutely no absolutes

Richard Rorty says, 'Tradition in Western culture ... centres around the notion of the search for Truth.'[65] This 'truth' is 'something to be pursued for its own sake.'[66] One of the consequences of the loss of confidence in reason and the denial of objective knowledge is a rejection of absolutes, especially the notion of absolute truth. The failure of reason to find objective reality has led to a crisis in confidence which has given birth to a cynical denial of absolute truth. Anderson notes, 'Few of us realise that even to hold a *concept* of relative truth makes us entirely different from people who lived only a few decades ago.'[67]

According to postmodernism the idea of absolute truth is an oppressive tool used by the powerful to exploit the weak.[68] The modernist perspective of absolute truth has led to the justification of the oppression and exploitation of others. Christopher Norris says, 'Postmodernism derives much of its suasive appeal from the notion that truth-claims are *always* on the side of some ultimate, transcendent, self-authorized Truth which excludes all meanings save those vouchsafed to the guardians of orthodox thought.'[69]

Belief in the universal and absolute nature of truth is seen as absurd in the postmodern perspective. The notion of universal truth and its exclusive claims is questioned and thought to be arrogant and intolerant. Anderson outlines the effect of this:

Once we let go of absolutes, nobody gets to have a position that is anything more than a position. Nobody gets to speak for God, nobody gets to speak for American values, and nobody gets to speak for nature.[70]

In addition to denying the concept of absolute truth, postmodernism asserts that 'all religion reflects a historically conditioned bias.'[71] Those with Christian convictions are less likely to face logical refutations of their beliefs than dismissal of them. Previously (in the modernist world) logic might be employed to refute the claims of Christianity. Postmodernists, however, do not contend in the same cognitive domain. Rather they dismiss Christianity's unique and universal claims as antiquated and irrelevant. The notion of transcendent truth is displaced or trivialized by relative truth.

Loss of confidence in the inevitability of progress

Modernism placed its confidence in science and education to deliver a better world. Two world wars and numerous other conflagrations in which there have been acts of genocide, continuing famine, poverty, pollution and other calamities, together with racism and terrorism have demonstrated that progress is not the inexorable outcome of advances in science and education. The postmodernist, therefore, rejects what Oden calls 'the smug fantasy of inevitable historical progress.'[72]

Postmodernism acknowledges that the modern era witnessed significant medical and technological breakthroughs but says that it has also brought 'unparalleled potentiality for the demolition of humanity and the planet.'[73] Henry says 'The twentieth-century—the century of scientific progress—brought with it, among other debacles, World War I, World War II, Marxist totalitarianism, Auschwitz, the increasing poisoning of the planet, and bare escape from nuclear destruction.'[74] Nuclear, chemical and biological weapons of mass destruction threaten humanity. Thus postmodernists view many of modernism's technological advances as 'a threat to planetary life and survival.'[75]

Postmodernism not only rejects the idea of inevitable progress it also denies the modern faith in the inherent integrity of knowledge. It does not accept that there is a correlation between man's knowledge and munificence. Grenz notes, 'In the postmodern world, people are no longer convinced that knowledge is inherently good.'[76] There has been a shift therefore, from the optimism that characterized the modern period to a pessimism that is the hallmark of postmodernism. Oliver says postmodernism 'can reflect cynicism in a world regarded as increasingly chaotic and out of control.'[77]

Rejection of foundationalism

The view that there is a perpetual substructure to knowledge (foundationalism) has been critiqued and jettisoned by the postmodernist.[78] Henry observes, 'the rejection of foundationalism' is the unique 'epistemic premise' shared by all postmodernists.[79]

Foundationalism, which bases reality on universal truths and principles has been substituted by non-foundationalism. This is a 'widespread attempt to continue philosophy without recourse to the kind of foundationalism found in classical modern philosophers.'[80] Non-foundationalist philosophers (in the school of Wittgenstein, Heidegger and Rorty) dispute that philosophy can accomplish Cartesian certitude.[81] Thus philosophy may have pragmatic advantages but it cannot convey universal validity.

Adams notes that non-foundationalism seriously affects theology because it 'seeks to disassociate theology from objective foundations such as Scripture, creeds and confessions, and ecclesiastical tradition.'[82] With non-foundationalism, 'theology arises out of the need of the community within the ever-changing contexts of culture and history.'[83] If theology emerges from communal exigencies then Scripture, creeds, and church tradition cannot be a satisfactory foundation of theological activity.

Rejection of metanarratives

Metanarratives endeavour to support and clarify the nature of reality. Postmodernism rejects metanarratives as manipulative and exploitative. Thus Jean-Francois Lyotard says that postmodernism is best defined as 'incredulity toward metanarratives.'[84]

Postmodernism rules out metanarratives because it discards all forms of 'totalization' and any form of striving toward rational coherence.[85] It does not permit a reality that is coherent and intelligible if it articulates an argument in a manner consistent with modernist absolute assumptions. So the use of metanarratives to explain reality is seen as both groundless and hazardous. Thus Phillips and Ockholm state: 'Postmodernism repudiates any appeal to Reality or Truth. The very attempt to propose totalizing metanarratives that define and legitimate reality are denounced as oppressive'.[86] Postmodernism does not permit metanarratives that claim to explicate reality because for it absolute reality does not exist.

Language viewed as a human construct

Kevin J. Vanhoozer argues that in the recent past there were 'hard and fast lines between philosophy and literature.'[87] This differentiation has become indistinct in the postmodern period, as language has come to be seen as a crucial constituent in how reality is understood. Horace L. Fairlamb notes, 'Postmodernism is the time for which language is the game'.[88]

Thus in the postmodernism period language is understood as a social construct whose significance is not inherent in reality. Seminal postmodern authors such as Jacques Derrida and Michel Foucault have reasoned that language is capricious and notional and does not actually resonate any extraneous linguistic laws.[89] Language does not correspond to an objective 'other' and texts are seen as constructs that neither describe nor define reality.[90] Language is a continuous system of artificial sign systems.[91]

There is a connection between postmodernism and deconstructionism.[92] Deconstruction is primarily about unpacking the constructions or explanations of language. Vanhoozer says 'It is about dismantling certain distinctions and oppositions that have traditionally guaranteed to philosophy its superior place among the humanities.'[93] Essentially, therefore, deconstruction centres on the difficulty of linguistic representation.[94] As such it is a challenge to what Derrida calls 'logo-centrism.' This is 'the belief that there is some stable point *outside* language—reason, revelation, Platonic ideas—from which one can ensure that Deconstruction theory asserts that texts have no extra-linguistic basis or referent. As such the intended meanings of the author are deemed irrelevant to the interpretation of a text. If there are no legitimate interpretations of texts it follows one's words ... correspond to the world.'[95] Logo-centrism, therefore, rests on the presupposition that one can speak truly.[96]

Postmodernism asserts that any interpretation may have equal validity or, on the other hand, they may be considered equally meaningless.[97] This has clear implications for secular and sacred textual analysis as the nature of hermeneutics and exegesis is fundamentally altered. Henry states:

> Texts are declared to be intrinsically incapable of conveying truth about some objective reality. One interpreter's meaning is as proper as another's, however incompatible these may be. There is no original or final textual meaning, no one way to interpret the Bible or any other text.[98]

Language in postmodern theory is merely a functional tool.[99] There cannot be, therefore, statements that are asserted to be true, in propositional terms, because it is not possible to prove or disprove them. It is merely a matter of linguistics. Our cognitive comprehension, then, is merely a matter of individual perception and no understanding is absolute.[100]

Pluralism

Pluralism is a phenomenon that predates postmodernism. Various religions and cultures have always lived in close proximity. Henry observes 'Postmodernity approves pluralism as a necessary and desirable cultural and philosophical phenomenon.'[101]

Pluralism contends that all religions have equal validity. Therefore no individual belief system is superior.[102] Hence it is tolerant of most religions. It abhors any religious system that makes exclusive claims concerning truth. Oliver says 'The postmodern attitude … rejects the idea that a rational belief system can claim authority over all others.'[103] Thus the postmodern author, David Hall, states, 'Dogmatism, totalitarianism, and narrow intolerance are all directly connected with unjustified claims to final truth.'[104] Philosophical pluralism was not a feature of the modern period, as Anderson notes:

> A mere couple of centuries ago, most societies recognized a single official reality and dedicated themselves to destroying its opposition. You could get burned at the stake for suggesting that there might be more than one version of reality. Today, in some intellectual circles, you can get into trouble for suggesting there might be only one.[105]

Conclusion

From a Christian perspective postmodernism presents new challenges. One might think that the tyranny of rationalism is over but it is not. In reality those who have become disillusioned with the idea that science can deliver the utopia it seemed to promise have not necessarily lifted the 'embargo' on the potentiality of the existence of God. Or where they have cast off the yoke of rationalism many have just capitulated to New Age philosophy. While at the same time the advocates of scientific messianism continue to press ahead on the assumption that the Enlightenment project is not yet finished. So the embattling apologetics of modernism continues on one front while the new skirmish of postmodernism develops on another.

This is the context in which mission is conducted today in Western culture. Understanding this is a necessary first step in formulating an effective apologetic strategy. Is it feasible to communicate the absolute truth of the gospel as authoritative revelation in a postmodern world? Is it possible to present the unique and universal claims of Christ without those claims being viewed as an oppressive metanarrative? Can one hold to the inspiration, authority, inerrancy and canonicity of Scripture in a post-Christian, postmodern society? The answer to these questions is a resounding 'Yes, yes, yes!' Not only can we do this, we must. In a world that has lost its way the clarion call of the gospel is needed more than ever. How that can be done best is another matter and one which calls for creative and courageous rethinking the mission paradigm in the light of emerging challenges. In any way forward Christ must be central. The north star of Christian truth is obscured by clouds of confusion but it will always be in the ascendancy.

Certainly the postmodern mind is more relational than rational and so the Christian must engage in cultivating relationships. Tolerance is the spirit of the age but tolerance is not necessarily a loving response where challenge might be more appropriate. We want to connect with postmodern people but that might involve confronting them. The Christian cannot capitulate to the notion that there is no absolute truth. Seeing and communicating the relevance of revelation is needed. This will demand a new apologetic emphasis in the communication of the gospel.

As Christians we tend to place strong emphasis on knowledge of the Scriptures. This is right and good. But we also need to understand our culture. After all we do not just teach the Bible, rather we teach people the Bible. Knowledge and expertise in a subject area does not necessarily make one a good teacher. In order to be able to teach Johnny one needs to understand Johnny. So it is with the postmodern. If we are to communicate effectively with postmoderns we need to understand them. In a sense all Christians are missionaries in a foreign culture. It can be frustrating when we encounter obstacles. But it can be rewarding when those apparent 'obstacles' become opportunities for dialogue. Often in our engagement with others we will find that 'problems' become 'possibilities' if we remain sensitive to the leading of the Lord and compassionate about those to whom we are seeking to relate.

We must never lose confidence in the power of the Word of God to bring conviction of sin and lead to repentance and salvation. The writer to the Hebrews clearly states that 'the word of God is living and active, sharper than any two-edged sword, piercing to the division of soul and of spirit, of joints and of marrow, and discerning the thoughts and intentions of the heart' (Hebrews 4:12).

In a world that is becoming increasingly sceptical of ultimate truth claims and where preaching practitioners are becoming disillusioned we need some guidelines about communicating with postmoderns. However, the church must not abandon preaching as a means of communicating truth. The apostle Paul instructed the younger Timothy to 'preach the word; be ready in season and out of season; reprove, rebuke, and exhort, with complete patience and teaching (2 Timothy 4:2). Nevertheless the timeless Word of God must be communicated in a timely manner. It must be proclaimed whether it is fashionable or not. The Christian message has not changed but its potential recipients have. Thus we need to understand the assumptions, beliefs and values of our culture if we are going to engage them.

Finding common ground is only the starting place for dialogue, it ought not to become the resting place for Christian community. It is the Christian duty to lead people out of that area of intersection and into the reality of spiritual (biblical) truth. The true Christian church can offer the belonging and community that people crave if it is willing to try to understand the postmodern mind.

The allure of the world has always been seductive and so we must present the message of the gospel with freshness, relevance and meaning. This might involve taking risks, but without compromising the truth. People are yearning for the sacred. They want to experience the transcendent and are attracted to mystery.

The postmodern mindset is sceptical, cynical, rejects the idea of objective, absolute truth and is suspicious of authority. One might well wonder if the homiletic task is feasible in the face of such challenges. I firmly believe that expository preaching of God's Word is crucial to the well-being of the church and an essential component in Christian communication of the gospel message. By taking a more inductive (as distinct from deductive) approach to the presentation of the truth we are assisting postmoderns on a voyage of discovery where the transcendent mystery of spirituality can become a vital, dynamic encounter with the living God. Thus we are asking them to discover for themselves rather than accept what we say. We need to have a respectful dialogue that enables postmodern people to discover identity, purpose, meaning, significance, hope and belonging. We don't want to dilute the message to make it more palatable but we do need to break it down so that it is more accessible.

We have a sacred duty to preserve the body of divinity entrusted to us and to ensure that it is passed on intact to the next generation. It is crucial that we are not distracted in passing on the baton in this great relay race.

The postmodern crisis of confidence in reason actually presents an opportunity for the entrance of faith because belief no longer needs to be proven. Postmoderns have faith in many things that are intuitively felt and this is sufficient. The same can be said with regard to the rejection of the objectivity of knowledge. We don't need to convince the postmodernist that the Christian faith is true in an objective sense. Rather it can be verifiable experientially. The postmodern idea that there are absolutely no absolutes is self-referentially defeating and inherently contradictory. Postmoderns admit exemptions to this such as 'justice' and this gives leverage to the believer to seek to add the Christian faith as another exemption. Postmoderns have rightly lost confidence in the inevitability of progress. Science has failed to deliver the utopia it promised and the potential for transformative community can be presented in alternative worldviews, including the Christian faith. People have failed to understand the depravity of human nature and so postmodernists have become disillusioned with the idea that science has all the answers. Here there can be a point of agreement with believers. Postmodernists reject metanarratives as manipulative. But the Bible can be presented as liberating narrative and our own stories (or petit-narratives) give access to its redemptive message. Language has come to be viewed as a human construct but Scripture can be presented as transcendental. Christian confidence in the authority of Scripture needs to be presented with humility so that it is not seen as authoritarian.

Pluralism is a symptom of the malady that afflicts religion and it is essentially syncretistic. Pluralism thrives in an atmosphere where people reject the idea of absolute truth. Thus the pied piper is leading many on the procession of an inter-faith agenda that will ultimately end in grief.

Postmodernists are concerned about the environment and here is an outstanding opportunity to present the truth that the ultimate ecological ethic is rooted in the idea of God as creator. The cosmic Christ can restore people to right relationship with God, their fellow human beings and the environment.

Because postmoderns are more relational than rational they will be more attracted to experiential encounters with God. A good starting place for dialogue therefore is to echo what the psalmist says: 'Oh, taste and see that the LORD is good! Blessed is the man who takes refuge in him!' (Psalm 34:8).

4

The Church Community in Contemporary Culture Evangelism and Engagement

'He who loves his dream of a community more than the Christian community itself becomes a destroyer of the latter, even though his personal intention may be ever so honest and earnest and sacrificial' (Deitrich Bonhoeffer)[1]

There is a movement 'within' the church that is disillusioned with the existing model and methods of traditional church practice. I am not just referring to a restless few who dislike conservative mainstream denominational churches. I am not just referring to people who want to move away from church buildings with pews, elevated pulpits and stained-glass windows. The same attitude is adopted with regard to churches with more modern buildings and more contemporary styles of worship. I am referring to what is known as the missional church.

What is the church? What is its nature and purpose? What is its role in this world? What is its relationship to the wider community? What are its sacred and secular responsibilities? What is a Christian? What is the gospel? What is mission? What is evangelism? In our eagerness to engage with contemporary culture these questions tend to be neglected. But they come into focus if we try to unite in inter-church collaboration on evangelism. Without broad consensus any such endeavour will be problematic. But we also need a clear understanding of the answers to these questions within our own church community.

Church communities are being drawn in to the vortex of unhelpful and unhealthy alliances ostensibly for the sake of evangelism and engagement. These problematic partnerships lead to confusion and compromise. I am concerned that people with evangelistic antennae are picking up this signal on their radar and embarking on a route to nowhere. We need to rethink the mission paradigm in the light of emerging challenges. We need to keep mission central to church life. We need to be in tune with the rhythm of God's heartbeat. But we need biblical perspectives on mission theology as a prerequisite to identifying the way forward. Why? Because there are new directions in mission and it is important to examine these new departures. I want to take the missional church (the most significant new direction in evangelism and engagement) as a case study and offer a critique of this emerging phenomenon by asking whether it is a menace or catalyst.

The important question to be addressed is whether or not God is at work in this recent phenomenon. Some will say it's the new reality and we better get on board before the ship leaves shore. We cannot simply endorse something just because it is a reality, we must be more discerning and test the spirits. For this we will need some criteria for evaluating a work of the Holy Spirit.

Is the missional church a menace? It is perceived by some as a threat to the welfare of the church. Is it a dangerous development? It seems to me (as a father of three) that new life has a nuisance element to it inasmuch as it disrupts life as it has been heretofore. Certainly the missional church is a catalyst insofar as it is precipitating change. The question I want to address is: 'Is this change a good thing?' It is a development which has implications not only for missiology but also for Christology and ecclesiology.

The 'attractional' church is understood as a church with a building that is used for regular worship services, prayer meetings, Bible studies, Sunday school, youth group meetings and a host of other programs and activities. It is argued (by missional church advocates) that in this postmodern culture the 'attractional' church is outmoded. It has been so named because of the idea that the church's missional stance is futile. They see it as ineffective (unsuccessful) because it is based on the hope that people will be attracted to our pews by our preaching and programs. It might be likened to lighthouses which were once manned and useful but have become irrelevant in a world where seafarers have sophisticated navigation technology based on global positioning systems.

The new movement in evangelism and engagement advocates what it calls 'incarnational' communities. These communities are essentially mission-focused, seeker-centred alternatives to the attractional church model. The locus of mission is re-centred so that instead of expecting un-churched people to come to us we are exhorted to go to them. Clearly there is much merit in taking such an approach. The exponents of this new way would advocate launching lifeboats rather than building lighthouses as a mission strategy.

So what? At first glance it might sound like nothing more than a different way of fishing for souls. But it is not. This is not a movement that advocates a different way of doing church or merely an attempt to put mission at the centre of church life. If we stay with the nautical analogy for a moment they would say that doing church differently is like re-arranging the deck chairs on the Titanic. So they see existing attractional church models (our churches) as doomed structures and they are sounding the bell to abandon ship. But are they entering uncharted waters in crafts that will withstand the fury of the raging seas?

There is some concern that some people in this new movement do not have the theological competence to pilot these flimsy vessels. But some of its leaders have advanced theological training and are directors of global networks and are quite organized in their approach to the dissemination of this new thinking through publication, consultation and training. One has to admire the energy of these radical activists. We can be defensive and rigid and reject this new order but that would be as unwise as unquestioningly embracing it. What is needed is an honest, open-minded critique of this movement rather than a gut-feeling response rooted in a predisposed antipathy to anything perceived as novel or trendy.

Has the attractional church passed its 'best before' date? According to the leading exponents of the missional movement it is time to shut our doors and walk away before the sun sets on the institutionalized church form.

God can and does work in surprising ways and unexpected places as happened in the charismatic movement of the 1960s and 1970s in Ireland and elsewhere. By and large the evangelical community kept its distance because it was problematic and messy. With hindsight we can see that it was a movement where the Holy Spirit was active. It was perceived as a problem but maybe it was an opportunity to provide leadership and discipleship to seekers. I'm not saying Christians should have got involved then and I am not sure how we could be involved with some new directions in evangelism and engagement now. But we do need to think about the dynamics of our relationship with the missional church.

According to missional church literature this movement is seeing people being converted, lives being changed, a searching of the Scriptures and evidence of a new love for God and for one another. Some will say that surely this is to be welcomed and that God does not need our permission to act in unexpected ways. The argument might be offered that, sadly, the Christian establishment is often dragged reluctantly into acknowledging God's work outside its own restricted circles.

Once upon a time

I once read a story about a lifeboat station on the Eastern Coast of the United States.

> It had begun when some of the locals with sailing experience became concerned about the number of ships that got into trouble in their waters. So they clubbed together and bought a lifeboat. Then they built a boathouse to keep it in. Over the years many lives were saved and there were countless instances of remarkable bravery. Often when the men were out on a rescue,

> the women would gather at the boathouse, comforting one another as they waited anxiously for news of their husbands. They discovered they worried less if they kept busy, so they put up curtains on the boathouse windows and generally smartened the place up. They persuaded their husbands (when not out on rescues) to put in a little kitchen and some comfortable chairs. Over the years the boathouse became a much more comfortable place to wait. In fact it became so comfortable that the men and their wives used to meet there sometimes when there was no rescuing to be done. Sometimes they brought friends who had never been out in a lifeboat in their lives. Some of the friends moored their yachts nearby. Gradually the character of the lifeboat station changed. One day there was a furious storm and a ship got into trouble just a little way along the coast. The people were all very concerned but no one went out to help. Why? The lifeboat station had become a yacht club.[2]

Many people are now saying that our churches have ceased to be rescue stations for the lost and have become comfortable clubs for the saved.

In fairness to the missional church, which is seeking to create incarnational communities, it must be said that they are well meaning, sincere, hard-working, and dedicated to achieving their goals. They rightly understand that there is a problem with regard to reaching the un-churched. They correctly understand that dwindling church attendance and declining numbers of church adherents is a perplexing trend. But because they are evangelists they think that everything in the church should centre on evangelism. I think all believers would want to place huge importance on evangelism but in a balanced way. People with evangelistic antennae have a tendency to develop tunnel vision. The church needs people with these gifts but some blinkered individuals who do not have a panoramic view of the church think that evangelism is all that really matters. I have no doubt that many zealous but theologically naïve individuals are attracted to emerging situations. But I believe the more discerning churches will pick and mix the best and most innovative approaches and this is to be encouraged.

What is church?

When it comes to understanding the missional church it is important to examine the biblical basis for Christian community. We all agree that a church is not a building in which Christians meet for worship. Rather the local church consists of a fellowship of believers who gather to worship God. If we do not understand the biblical basis for Christian community we will be terribly confused about the nature of true fellowship. An obvious concern about the new directions in evangelism and engagement which need to be addressed is that 'fellowship' with unbelievers is more a kind of camaraderie which does not constitute true unity of the Holy Spirit.

Many church leaders will agree with the missional church's diagnosis concerning the condition of the attractional church in the twenty-first century. But it is their prognosis and prescription that causes some concern. It is important for every generation to find ways of communicating the gospel to its culture but there is a danger that in seeking to be relevant we cross a line that ought not to be crossed.

Seeker-centred or seeker-sensitive?

An occupational hazard for evangelists and church planters is that they become seeker-centred (as distinct from seeker-sensitive) and cross the line between contextualization and syncretism. Contextualization is about finding ways of explaining and exhibiting the gospel that can be understood within a particular cultural context, without compromising the integrity of the message or the messenger. Syncretism occurs when the desire to be relevant transcends all other motives and both message and messenger become integrated into the prevailing cultural context. Syncretism occurs when Christians adapt, either consciously or unconsciously, to the prevailing worldview. It is the reshaping of Christian beliefs and practices so that they reflect those of the dominant culture. In this process Christianity loses it distinctiveness.[3] Syncretism is frequently birthed from a yearning to make the gospel appear relevant. The church attempts to make its message attractive to outsiders and as these adaptations become regularly assimilated they become an integral part of the church's life. When significant changes in worldview take place the Christian community, swept along by the ebb and flow of cultural currents, begins to lose her moorings.[4]

There has been a significant paradigm shift best summarized by the word 'postmodernism', as discussed in the previous chapter. Some church people are wondering if it will come into the church. The reality is that it is well embedded in the church. Many churches have gone beyond the process of contextualizing the gospel in Western culture and have married themselves to these core values of society. One writer cautions: 'While Christian witness must be savvy concerning the realities of the postmodern condition in order to make the historic Christian message understandable and pertinent to denizens of the contemporary world, this does not mean that we should become postmodernists in the process.'[5]

Radical developments

There are many radical developments in how church is practiced today. We are going to see much more of this kind of thoroughgoing recalibration in the next decade. The orientation toward missional and incarnational communities is not merely a rediscovery of the values and vision of the ancient faith communities found in the book of Acts. We must be careful not to disregard centuries of subsequent church history (including the Reformation) as if they are entirely irrelevant. That would be like throwing the baby out with the bathwater and that is a calamitous thing to do. Has our failure to address mission in a holistic way partly contributed to new departures in evangelism and engagement?[6]

The missional church is not a counter-cultural movement; it is in fact the opposite. Certainly they react to the consumerist, materialistic and therapeutic values of modernist churches that have developed too cosy a relationship with the prevailing cultural norms. There is a real danger that they will lose their distinct identity as Christians.

The missional church contends that traditional Christian identity is perceived as unattractive to seekers. It charges the church with creating self-serving institutions that are not connecting with community. It would say that the attractional church has merely created holy huddles which are no-go zones for unbelievers who do not feel they belong to these 'clubs'. They say that we have retrenched into our private enclaves. The accusation that we live a kind of neo-monastic existence is nonsense and this myth needs to be dispelled. Most of our people are connected to the real world in one way or another.

Missional church people integrate themselves into various communities and sub-cultures and intentionally conceal their spiritual identities until they have built what they call, 'meaningful relationships'. I feel there is something inappropriate and dishonest in this kind of subterfuge. I think Christians are called to be conspicuous in this world, not chameleons who adapt to the surrounding environment. We should not be disingenuous about our intentions. Christians are to be *in* the world but not *of* the world. D. L. Moody said, 'The ship is meant to be in the water but God help her when the water gets into the ship'. It is an obvious truth which states an important principle of Christian living.

The missional church claims to be involved in creating places of inclusive belonging where God's kingdom can be experienced. This sounds good until what that actually means is spelled out. Certainly Christians should be creating places of welcome but we should not adopt an 'end-justifies-the–means' approach to winning souls. The church is the bride of Christ and should remain pure and uncompromised.

Some new directions in evangelism and engagement are manifestations of a myopic movement which appeals to the disaffected and trend-orientated. Any critique of their motives and methods is viewed with suspicion and deemed to be judgmental. They dismiss people who present a different theological perspective as those who, 'know too much, talk too much and judge too much.'[7] This is both unfair and unhelpful.

The missional church criticism of the attractional church is rooted in the observation that there are so few conversions. They say churches are, 'musty, fussy, clubby, judgmental, mean, punishing, ungenerous … '[8] It is an unfair generalization to have the faithful and fervent work of so many pastors, elders, deacons and church members denigrated in this way. Yet we must examine ourselves to see if there is an element of truth in this.

However, I think the missional church tend to see 'growth' in narrow terms, as an increase in numbers. But growth in a church context is not just about people coming to faith but also about people growing to maturity as individuals and also growing together in unity and love as a community and numerical growth may be part of this process.

Schismatic squabble

Differences about how evangelism and engagement are to be conducted have the potential to give rise to schismatic squabbles. I don't want to contribute to polemical 'debate' but new directions have potentially dangerous undercurrents and I think it would be negligent not to flag this. Our desire to engage with contemporary culture must have safeguards against being ensnared by it. Otherwise many who start out meaning well might end up watching Oprah, Larry King or Dr Phil for spiritual guidance.

What are we to make of pastors leaving churches to become baristas and barmen in the belief that in so doing they will be more effective witnesses for Christ? I suggest that people who do this were never ideally suited to pastoral ministry. Rather they were church planters and evangelists. I wish them well but hope their new mission outpost situations will stay connected to local church communities.

For the missional church connecting with sojourners is paramount. They establish communities which permit anybody, irrespective of belief or behaviour, to belong. It appears to have a disregard for doctrine and tradition and argues that we should set aside our apologetics and theology and include those outside the kingdom. Church communities must be places of benevolence and blessing. We must extend a warm and genuine welcome to all. However, the theological and biblical reality is that one does not belong to Christ until and unless one has repented of one's sin and confessed Christ as Saviour. We should not pretend that people belong when in fact they do not. That would be deceptive and unwise. It is like allowing people to come to our homes and dine with us. We can have a great deal of interaction but they are not members of our family.

Some new directions in mission tend to have an end-justifies-the-means approach to involving non-believers in church ministries. This has resulted in incidents such as stoned and drunk musicians playing at their gatherings and the unconverted teaching Bible stories to children. Boundaries are blurred and nobody in their communities is bothered by this.

Because society has lost interest in 'organized Christendom' there is a desire to offer it a radical alternative. An important question, therefore, is whether or not this 'alternative' is authentic to the ideals of Scripture.

The missional church seems to have lost confidence in the efficacy of preaching to accomplish God's purposes. Maybe they have been exposed to poor models of preaching and sadly there is much of that about. I believe that preaching Christ in a postmodern culture is not only feasible but imperative. The missional church argues that people won't change by listening to preaching. I wonder why Jesus preached. Jesus was first and foremost a preacher. The Nazareth Manifesto identifies preaching as central to his ministry.[9] If we want to model him we cannot dismiss preaching. Even by their own admission the missional church says that, 'Christology determines missiology, and missiology determines ecclesiology.'[10] The whole notion of church is being systematically deconstructed and radically redefined.

To boldly go where no man has gone before

The missional desire to spend time with the un-churched is admirable. They see themselves as pioneers who are taking risks in going, 'where no man has gone before'. For them the fulfilment of the Great Commission to 'go' is not merely about outreach evangelism programs, rather it is about living among and belonging. But we must love the found as well as the lost. To what extent (if any) have we contributed to the sense of disaffection which is giving rise to this movement by inserting extra-biblical proscriptions, written and unwritten, (about issues like alcohol, smoking, styles of dress etc.) as conditions of membership in constitutions and codes of conduct.

It is difficult to get the balance right between being a community which confronts the godless values of the cultural norms and being an inclusive community. The missional church is calling for a revolution in inclusive community in which the masses will want to participate. The distaste for present forms of church is evident in the words of Hugh Halter, 'The typical message has been to be good, stop sinning, go to church, and wait for God to come back. Yuck. It's too simple.'[11] Surely it is right to stop sinning. Sin is grievously offensive to God and to cease sinning is an indication that the person has newness of life. This is what God wants and expects of converts. Is it not right to go to a place where like-minded people assemble to worship God as a community of believers? Did not the early church have an eschatological hope that radically altered how it lived?

The missional church believes that through benevolent action in the community, spiritual dialogue will ensue and so they openly admit that they would prefer do something useful (like picking up litter in the community) on Sunday morning instead of going to church. They will randomly cancel their gatherings so that they can do something alternative to 'worship'. But the kingdom of God is not about winning the 'Tidy Towns' competition! Some churches have involved their youth in making a positive contribution to the community by clearing up litter. This kind of activity can be very positive and can open doors of opportunity to conversations about how our faith motivates us to do good deeds. The problem is in conducting such benevolent acts as *alternatives* to church worship services. The missional church does not seem to care much if people attend their Sabbath gatherings. They encourage people to spend their Sunday mornings being with sojourners. Perhaps the missional church is attractive because one does not have to forsake much or believe much in order to belong to it.

The missional church talks about *apprenticing* disciples as more authentic than *cognitive* discipleship. But Jesus taught his disciples for three years and the Great Commission instructs us to 'teach' all that Christ has taught. This is clearly part of the discipleship process. Maybe the discipleship process is best done through supervised hands-on experience supplemented with teaching.

In his trenchant analysis of the cultural corruption weakening the church's thought and witness, David Wells argues that evangelicals have blurred the distinctions between Christ and culture, and have largely abandoned their traditional emphasis on divine transcendence in favour of an emphasis on divine immanence. In doing so, they have produced a faith in God that is of little consequence to those who believe. He says, 'there is a profound sense in which the church has to be "otherworldly".'[12]

Nobody is saying that everything in existing structures and the prevailing *modus operandi* is sacrosanct. We must be open to the idea of reviewing our structures to see if they hinder or help our goals. But all of this must be done in the light of Scripture. In this new movement church becomes a discovery zone for participating sojourners where the desire to be relevant leads to convictions being diluted. We must be careful about how we proceed so that what is harmful can be rejected and what is helpful can be retained as we seek to advance in evangelism and engagement.

Evaluating criteria

Are there any criteria that can be used to evaluate contemporary approaches to mission? What is a genuine work of the Holy Spirit? One would certainly hesitate to make unfair accusations or derive inappropriate conclusions about any activity which might be authentic. John MacArthur has presented material condensed, adapted and excerpted from Jonathan Edwards's, 'The Distinguishing Marks of a Work of the Spirit of God'.[13] This MacArthur/Edwards article identifies five distinguishing characteristics of the Holy Spirit's work, based on an analysis of 1 John 4:1–8. These are helpful in determining whether or not emerging trends are a true work of God. MacArthur says that a genuine work of the Holy Spirit exalts the true Christ, opposes Satan's interests, points people to the Scriptures, elevates truth and results in love for God and others. Let us examine the new phenomenon in the light of this standard.

First, we must ask if the missional church upholds a Scriptural view of Christ. Clearly the doctrine of the incarnation must be affirmed. The missional church subscribes to this truth in asserting that Jesus is the Son of God.[14] This community of believers (and I think that is, generally, what they are) genuinely desires to lead people to Christ. Christ is revered (perhaps sentimentally) in this new movement.

Nevertheless there is something imaginary about the Christ they extol. I have already asserted that Jesus was a preacher. The missional church makes a distinction between 'Galilean' Christians and 'Jerusalem' Christians. The Galilean Christians are those who interpret the Bible through the life of Jesus. The Jerusalem Christians are more doctrinal. This bias toward the Galilean way is quite subjective. They see Jerusalem people as idolaters of the Bible who have overly intellectualized spirituality. They have reduced the Bible to the gospels and argue that if we only had the gospels Christianity would look very different today. But we have the entire canon of Scripture because God wanted to reveal more than what is disclosed in the gospels. Their tendency to ignore, reject or devalue any Scripture that is not directly spoken by Jesus is potentially heretical.

Second, a distinguishing mark of a work of the Spirit of God is that it will oppose Satan's interests. Satan desires that people remain in a sinful condition and succumb to the lusts of the flesh. The missional church is not entirely indifferent to sinfulness but its attitude to sin is lax. I am not saying they are dens of iniquity. They claim to create an environment in which the conscience can become sensitive to the truth in relation to sin. But in the absence of preaching about the dreadfulness of sin they have created an environment which is casual about sin.

A third mark that distinguishes a work of the Spirit of God is that it points people to the Scriptures. The missional church does not induce a high a regard for the whole counsel of God. As already mentioned they tend to be red-letter people rather than biblical people. In other words they put a higher value on the words of Christ than on the words of other authors of Scripture. This distorts revelation.

A fourth feature of a work of the Spirit of God is that it elevates truth. Certainly, the missional church makes people more aware of the central gospel truths. They may be effective in leading people to faith but fall short of leading them to maturity in Christ.

The fifth and final mark that distinguishes a work of the Spirit of God is that it results in love for God and others. The missional church loves the lost and it is to be highly commended for this. They profess to love God and I don't doubt their sincerity in this regard. Nevertheless, the God they profess to love is eviscerated of much of the divine nature as a sin-loathing God.

The missional church is not heretical but it is a movement which has potentially harmful effects. Nevertheless, in spite of reservations about and objections to its 'unorthodox' irregularities and potential hazards it cannot be dismissed as a work of Satan. Must it, therefore, be embraced as a work of the Holy Spirit? From past experience (consider the history of revival movements) it is clear that the Spirit of God can work even in the midst of much that might be deemed 'problematic'.

We should be very reluctant, therefore, to condemn a work in which the Holy Spirit might be involved and we should have a similar sense of hesitancy about contributing to the polarization of differing Christian communities. But we must test the spirits and where we find deficiencies and dangers we must be diligent in alerting others to the potential pitfalls.

The way forward

One's ideas about mission are shaped by one's theology. Much has been written in recent years about mission, which focuses on methodological approaches to engaging contemporary culture. Many of these works boldly propose new ways of engaging with contemporary culture. We must be concerned about keeping mission central to church life and identifying a way forward in the labyrinthine complexity of postmodern society.

The trendy literature suggests that the 'attractional' model of the church of Christendom is outmoded. It is an influential body of work which contends that what is needed now is a 'missional' and 'incarnational' Christian church. But these works tend to be primarily focused on how to engage in mission rather than putting in place a theological foundation which would underpin the missionary enterprise. What is needed is a biblical perspective on mission theology which informs and shapes our understanding, approaches and methodologies in facing the unfinished task of, 'making disciples of all nations'. This will not only safeguard and strengthen mission but will also provide a means of evaluating trends which seek to influence future directions in mission activity.

Postmodernism presents a new frontier situation. We must have a missionary impulse to bear witness to the gospel. Certainly we must adapt to the new environment but without compromising. We live with the tension of seeking ways of contextualizing the gospel without capitulating to culture. As the current cultural context is emerging we are in uncharted waters and navigating our way will require experienced and savvy people at the helm.

Paradigm shift

It is generally acknowledged now that a paradigm shift has taken place. This 'cultural sea change' has contributed to significantly widening the gulf between church and culture.[15] This is not necessarily a bad thing because the Western church has had too cosy a relationship with the prevailing culture. We now have to talk not about 'culture' but 'cultures' because we live in what might be called a 'pluriverse' rather than a 'universe'. In this kaleidoscopic cultural context we are all influenced by a variety of cultures in diet, dress, art, architecture, music and the media. Secularization, cultural and religious pluralism, globalization, advances in technology have all impacted on the church's role in society. It is not just city centre churches that have this *mélange* of cultures but rural churches as well. It is in response to such challenges that new directions and departures in evangelism and engagement have emerged.

Navigating this emerging missiological landscape will involve experimenting with approaches to ministry that will challenge present understandings of what it means to be the church today. These challenges are new opportunities to engage in innovative forms of communication and dialogue. Should we consider this taking place in unconventional spaces, often referred to as 'the third place'? This would mean inhabiting places outside church buildings that are also inhabited by non-Christians. The missional church thinks in terms of shared space rather than sacred space. They see our commitment to buildings as an absurd loyalty akin to the captain going down with the sinking ship. Evangelists and theologians must work together like architects and engineers in constructing a new order which is both attractive and safe.

Being church today

So, what does it mean to be the church today? It is about participating in a way of life. It means an understanding that we are the gathered community of God's people. We gather around Christ and a body of divinity, indwelt by the Holy Spirit, united as blood-brothers. We can create all sorts of artificial communities but the church is an organism, not an organization. It is a living, dynamic and organic entity of the redeemed.

The missional church challenges believers to leave their private enclaves and comfort zones and infiltrate unorthodox and even profane places. But discernment is needed. Some will reject the call out of hand as an invitation to compromise which can only result in Christians being contaminated. Others will rush in 'where angels fear to tread'.

When visiting a city it is helpful to find the map that says, 'you are here' accompanied by a big arrow pointing to the spot, or to get your bearings with a smart phone. We can navigate from there. With regard to evangelism and engagement there is a sense in which the landscape does not change and the map does not change but we need to know where we are and re-orientate the map so that we can head in the right direction.

Evangelism is not an elective element of the spiritual life. These new approaches to evangelism and engagement have far-reaching implications because they are not proposing prioritizing mission within existing church structures. It is not about churches giving more time to mission or conducting outreach more often. It is not about preaching more about mission or having more missionaries come and speak in the local church. It is not about more time being given to prayer for mission. It is, rather, a 'complete reorientation of the church, a reshaping of its life, a rediscovery of mission as the activity around which everything else is coordinated.'[16]

Emerging phenomenon

In the West we are now living in what may be called the post-Christendom era. Many people are no longer interested in what the church has to offer. Paradoxically, in postmodern culture there is a new openness to spirituality. In this situation, where the church, in its present institutionalized form is perceived as irrelevant, growing numbers of Christians are engaging in more innovative missionary activity. But the stories gathered from these emergent church projects give rise to some concern about the future direction of mission. These spirited experiments are primarily motivated by a desire, within the church, to be more relevant to society in the twenty-first-century. This relatively new movement is not comprised merely of armchair theorists. Rather this is a radicalized and organized cohort of activists who are effectively disseminating their message, recruiting adherents and replicating missional communities in Western society.

The missional church is an expression of the emerging church phenomenon. It deemphasizes what it perceives as 'divisive' doctrine by emphasizing the primacy of relationship. This is characteristically postmodern. They also elevate God's (almost indiscriminate) love for mankind over his essential holiness. By raising unity above truth, the missional church creates an atmosphere where peace is the *summum bonum*, that is, the supreme good from which all others are derived.

The missional church is essentially rooted in contemporary culture and this fact may be the cause of its own demise. Philosophies that are driven by culture are inexorably destined to disappear in time. As Os Guinness warned, 'He who marries the spirit of the age soon becomes a widower.'[17]

The greatest threats to the health of the church are liberalism on the one hand and legalism on the other. The *avant-garde* are the adventurers and innovators who pioneer new approaches and departures. They are more likely to gravitate to liberalism than legalism. The missional church mentality is compatible with this instinct. The rearguard, however, is comprised of those whose instinct is conservative and whose desire is to protect and preserve the status quo and as such they are more likely to gravitate to legalism. I think we all have a default mode in this regard.

Faith should not be inert and unchanging, rather it should be dynamic and vibrant. Our experiences of life must inspire reflection and our interaction with others who hold different views ought to stimulate honest appraisal and reappraisal of our own opinions and positions. Daniel Migliore says:

> ... theology must be critical reflection on the community's faith and practice ... not simply a reiteration of what has been or is currently believed and practiced by a community of faith. It is a quest for truth, and that presupposes that the proclamation and practice of the community of faith are always in need of examination and reform ... When this responsibility is neglected ... the faith of the community is invariably threatened by shallowness, arrogance and ossification[18]

Those with a risk-taking disposition want to face the white-water rapids in a canoe. Those with a conservative bias would prefer to take a trip in a barge on the canal. It is unlikely that those with a risk-taking disposition and those with a conservative bias will enjoy a journey together. The disposition of the reformers at the time of the Reformation was not conservative. This may be a surprise to those who revere the reformers as establishment heroes. We must cherish a past that is not only connected to the present but also connected to the future.

At the outset I asked if the missional church was a menace or a catalyst. I believe it is both. The words of Mr Spock might be applied to the missional church: 'It's life, Jim, but not as we know it'.

Our theoretical presuppositions about mission and our theological rationale for mission should be determined by the Word of God. We must allow Scripture to speak for itself as the missionary manual rather than impose our views upon it. Eric Wright says:

> Nothing can be more important than to ensure that our missionary presuppositions reflect the principles of Scripture. This will not be true if theology is ignored, because theology brings us face to face with the principles, parameters and priorities that God has revealed.[19]

Mission must be a Christ-centred intentional process of communicating the gospel in word and deed. An informed biblical missional view goes beyond the frequently quoted commissioning passages to a more comprehensive perspective from Genesis to Revelation. Nevertheless the missionary mandate is about living out the Great Commission with the passion of the Great Commandment (to make disciples and love God and neighbour). Christ's followers are to take the gospel to all peoples (nations and ethnic groups) irrespective of class, culture or creed. This demands conviction, commitment and courage in the face of the objections of pluralism and the hostility of anti-Christian fundamentalisms. Christians must avoid the pitfall of theological liberalism which perceives evangelism as proselytizing. Christians must also avoid the snare of religious legalism which is nurtured in separatist enclaves.

Our God is a missionary God. The Bible is a missionary book. The church is a missionary institution. Christ's mandate is a missionary mandate. The Great Commandment (to love) is to be the regulating principle of all mission activity. Contemporary culture presents many opportunities for the entrance of the gospel. So each church must find ways of having meaningful interaction with those outside the church. But this must be done without capitulating to the prevailing culture.

The missional church may be over zealous in its approach and naïve in much of its activity but it has led to some innovative ways of engaging with culture. However, its central problem is its overemphasis on pragmatism. A. W. Tozer identified this issue as far back as 1955 when he said, 'Religious pragmatism is running wild among the orthodox. Truth is whatever works. If it gets results it is good.'[20]

Eric Wright suggests that, 'the most pragmatic thing we can do in the long run is to teach what God has revealed, trust his revealed methods and try to apply them in dependence on the Holy Spirit':[21]

> Our involvement in the world comes about in a variety of natural and intentional ways. One of the most obvious is in the workplace (though, for pastors this might be a problem because our world is inhabited by Christians). There are other areas where the Christian may come into contact with the world,

such as sports, cultural pursuits, social activities, volunteering, educational programs and local/national politics.

Scripture refers to anyone involved in any form of government as 'God's servant' (Romans 13:4). God has ordained the powers that be (Romans 13:10). Clearly the Christian individual may, in good conscience, be involved in politics. The Old Testament character Daniel walked with God and occupied a senior position in the Babylonian/Persian civil service. Another Old Testament character, Joseph, was directly involved in the government of Egypt. Clearly, therefore, God's people are not forbidden to be involved in society. Some Christians have spearheaded important social reform, such as William Wilberforce, with the abolition of slavery.

There are many practical and positive ways in which we can let our light shine. Our good deeds give credibility to the gospel message which we proclaim. The Christian is to be concerned for good works as well as good words. If we are to model the master we must realize that he was compassionate and went about doing good (Acts 10:38).

But there is a difference between humanitarianism and Christian mission. Therefore, we need to ensure that we engage in more than philanthropy. The essential difference is the gospel message of salvation. Christian mission ministers to the soul of humanity and its greatest need: that of a Saviour. We must distinguish between the calling of the Christian citizen to engage in social and political action and the mandate of the church. Nevertheless, in certain contexts, the gospel has unavoidable political implications.

Jesus could have gained enormous popularity if he had been willing to respond to the people's political agenda but he resisted. We must do likewise by resisting such temptations and being alert to the danger of being used to further the world's agenda, even when aspects of that agenda are good causes. History abounds with sad examples of the church being hijacked in this way. Para-church organizations which started out with an overtly Christian mission have drifted from their formative ideals and have become virtually secularized. Examples of this are, The Salvation Army and the Y.M.C.A.

One of the major dangers facing the Christian church in contemporary culture is religious pluralism. The missionary frontier is the line which separates belief from unbelief. That means that it is also the line between false and true religion where cherished beliefs are challenged, contradicted or even, when necessary, condemned. With regard to the latter, the practice of sati in the Indian context was identified, by William Carey, as morally wrong and William Wilberforce was instrumental in the abolition of the slave trade.

It is important that the Bible should be respected, in any shaping of things to come, because it is the authoritative source of our understanding of evangelism and engagement. The church's mission is about presenting the unique and universal claims of Jesus and that runs counter to the pluralist agenda. The church's mission is about calling people to repentance, faith and community relationship. We are partners in this great work in progress. Consider the challenging words of the well known hymn:

Facing a task unfinished[22]

Facing a task unfinished
That drives us to our knees
A need that, undiminished

Rebukes our slothful ease
We, who rejoice to know Thee
Renew before Thy throne
The solemn pledge we owe Thee
To go and make Thee known

Where other lords beside Thee
Hold their unhindered sway
Where forces that defied Thee
Defy Thee still today
With none to heed their crying
For life, and love, and light
Unnumbered souls are dying
And pass into the night

We bear the torch that flaming
Fell from the hands of those
Who gave their lives proclaiming
That Jesus died and rose
Ours is the same commission
The same glad message ours
Fired by the same ambition
To Thee we yield our powers

O Father who sustained them
O Spirit who inspired
Saviour, whose love constrained them
To toil with zeal untired
From cowardice defend us
From lethargy awake!

Forth on Thine errands send us
To labour for Thy sake.

5

What About Those Who Have Never Heard The Gospel?

'Shall not the Judge of all the earth do what is just?' (Genesis 18:25).

At a meeting of Christian leaders recently somebody asked me, 'what about those who have never heard the gospel?' I quoted a verse from Genesis, which I find helpful in addressing this question, 'Shall not the Judge of all the earth do what is just?' (Genesis 18:25). He asked, humorously but earnestly, 'has anybody got a better answer?' There was no time to engage in further discussion on the matter as the meeting had come to an end and I had pressing engagements elsewhere. However, this question remained in my mind for several days afterwards and I felt an obligation to attempt to answer it as best I could. I suspect that many Christians carry those kinds of questions around for years without fully engaging with them or adequately answering them. Its relevance to mission is obvious. In seeking to be faithful to the mandate to 'make disciples of all nations' we are faced with this perplexing question.

Ultimately God alone will determine the answer to this question. His inscrutable decrees are beyond human comprehension. Nevertheless we can explore the question to find clarity and affirm confidence in the holy, just and merciful God who bears witness to his existence in his creation and in the very psyche of humanity.

Christians who ask this kind of question want to know the answer, not just to satisfy their curiosity, but to remove impediments to their faith. Then in turn they want to be able to answer such questions because they desire to share their faith with non-Christians. This kind of question is often encountered in an adversarial dialogue where it is posed as an objection to faith. All believers are obliged to try to communicate their faith to others. This involves taking the instruction of Peter seriously, 'always being prepared to make a defence to anyone who asks you for a reason for the hope that is in you; yet do it with gentleness and respect' (1 Peter 3:15). However, this question has been asked for centuries and stubbornly remains as a tough question. Nevertheless Christians should not ignore it. Believers must try to address it.

So, what about people who have never heard the gospel? The short answer to that question is that it is not ultimately our responsibility. Yes, we must certainly do all that we can to make the gospel known, not just in our own locality but also throughout the world but ultimately God will do what is right and just. Isaiah said '… for that which has not been told them they see, and that which they have not heard they understand'

(Isaiah 52:15). God is able to save without our assistance. He deigns to use us but in fact he does not need to use us. He could entrust this work to angels. Nevertheless he has commissioned us with the task of bringing the good news to all nations and expects us to be his witnesses.

Acts 13:38 says, 'All who were appointed for eternal life believed' It does not say 'All who believed were appointed for eternal life'. Yet this is a common distortion of Scripture today. Scripture makes it clear that salvation is God's choice (Romans 8:29–30) and that this choice was made 'before the foundation of the world' (Ephesians 1:4). Salvation is a work of the Holy Spirit. We are instruments that God deigns to use and even delights to use in leading people to faith in Christ. Nevertheless salvation is his work and his choice. It is comforting to know that nobody will be excluded from salvation because we failed in our duty to bring the message of the gospel to them. This is not an excuse for complacency about sharing the message of the gospel. Because we do not know whom God has chosen, we witness to all without prejudice and trust he will lead us to the ones whose hearts will be receptive and responsive to the good news of the gospel. We cannot neglect our duty in this regard because we are commissioned with the task of making disciples of all nations (Matthew 28:20).

Questioning the integrity of God

People ask this question for different reasons. Some people, particularly believers, ask this because they are genuinely hoping to find an answer. It is also a typical question asked by sceptics. Some non-Christians, especially atheistic types, raise it as an objection to faith. For this latter group the question is really a red herring and as such can be misleading. For them it is really a statement which could be interpreted to mean, 'Your "gospel" can't be the truth because there are many people in the world who have never heard it.' They are not hoping to be answered. Rather they are hoping to deny the validity of the gospel's universal claims.

It is helpful to remind such people that they are accountable for themselves and how they respond to the message of the gospel. It is important to try to answer both groups as compassionately and comprehensively as possible. But it is also important to bear in mind that such a question cannot be comprehensively answered on the doorstep. A considered answer will take time and it might be a good idea to invite the person to come to a talk/discussion on this topic. If the person is a genuine seeker who is trying to overcome an obstacle to faith he will be willing to attend such a talk. If he is just trying to trip you up, he will have no interest in attending such a discussion.

Is God unfair?

Jesus was born in Bethlehem and lived and ministered in the relative obscurity of Palestine two-thousand years ago. Some people might wonder how such a limited revelation of God can be the universal standard by which the world (prior to and after the events of the incarnation and Calvary) will be judged. They ask if this can be an adequate revelation to all humanity in every age and geographical location. They say surely God cannot hold people accountable if they have never heard of Jesus. What is being implied here is that God is unfair.

This notion of God's unfairness is compounded by the view that heaven is reserved for an elite and tiny minority of the entire populace, which consists wholly of Christ's disciples.

On one occasion Jesus was asked a direct question about how many would be saved:

> And someone said to him, 'Lord, will those who are saved be few?' And he said to them, 'Strive to enter through the narrow door. For many, I tell you, will seek to enter and will not be able … And people will come from east and west, and from north and south, and recline at table in the kingdom of God' (Luke 13:23–29).

In his answer Christ focused on the way of salvation. Some will emphasize that this passage suggests a minority citizenship in heaven. But it should be noted that Jesus talks here about people coming from east, west, north and south for the great banquet of the redeemed in heaven. This tells us that there will be people from every part of the world numbered amongst those who will be saved. This is consistent with other passages of Scripture. For example, in the book of Revelation John says of the Lamb, 'by your blood you ransomed people for God from every tribe and language and people and nation' (Revelation 5:9). So, according to the Bible there will be people from every nation, language group and ethnicity in heaven.

Furthermore Scripture asserts that this group is a vast multitude:

> After this I looked, and behold, a great multitude that no one could number, from every nation, from all tribes and peoples and languages, standing before the throne and before the Lamb, clothed in white robes, with palm branches in their hands, and crying out with a loud voice, 'Salvation belongs to our God who sits on the throne, and to the Lamb!' (Revelation 7:9–10)

Notice that the number is so vast that it could not be counted. Christians have been active in this world for two millennia disseminating the gospel so that the extent of God's work is not as restricted as sceptics might suggest.

Jesus ministered primarily (but not exclusively) to Jews and he said that many Gentiles (non-Jews) would inherit the kingdom of God. On one occasion a Roman centurion in Capernaum appealed to him about his servant who was paralyzed and suffering. Jesus offered to go to the centurion's house and heal the servant. But the centurion professed that he was unworthy to have Christ visit his home and then he asked Jesus to, 'only say the word, and my servant will be healed'. The account in Matthew goes on to say, 'When Jesus heard this, he marvelled and said to those who followed him, "Truly, I tell you, with no one in Israel have I found such faith. I tell you, many will come from east and west and recline at table with Abraham, Isaac, and Jacob in the kingdom of heaven".' (Matthew 8:10–11). Here Jesus uses the word 'many' and the phrase 'east and the west' is a general idiom which means 'from all over the world'.

The character of God

God is good, gracious and merciful to all people. There is ample evidence in Scripture to support this view. The psalmist says, 'The LORD is gracious and merciful, slow to anger and abounding in steadfast love. The LORD is good to all, and his mercy is over all that he has made' (Psalm 145:8–9). Jesus said of his heavenly father, 'For he makes his sun rise on the evil and on the good, and sends rain on the just and on the unjust' (Matthew 5:45). What may be observed from these verses is that God's love is gracious, merciful, abundant, steadfast and vast in scope. It is not restricted to a small elite group of people from a particular period in history. Rather it spans all time and all places and includes all peoples. This, of course does not mean that everyone will be saved.

Scripture affirms that God does what is right in all matters (Genesis 18:25). The rebellious do not have a right understanding of God. But those who are born again of the Holy Spirit know that what the Scriptures attest concerning him is true, 'his work is perfect, for all his ways are justice. A God of faithfulness and without iniquity, just and upright is he' (Deuteronomy 32:4). Another psalm says, 'He will judge the world with righteousness, and the peoples with equity' (Psalm 98.9). So, when this is applied to those who have never heard the gospel it is clear that there will be nothing unfair in God's dealing with such a group of people.

The universal revelation of God

There is universal revelation of God in nature. The psalmist says, 'The heavens declare the glory of God, and the sky above proclaims his handiwork' (Psalm 19:1). The created order is itself a testimony to God's existence. The starry sky, the snow-capped mountain peak, sunset and the awesome majesty of the sea all proclaim God's existence. Nature is like a sermon from God and this voice is heard everywhere on the planet. Nobody can, therefore, claim to be exempt from the reality that there is a God to whom we are all accountable. But there are many who deny the existence of a creator. There are many who suppress the truth. These people are without excuse. The apostle Paul, writing to Christians in Rome said:

> For the wrath of God is revealed from heaven against all ungodliness and unrighteousness of men, who by their

> unrighteousness suppress the truth. For what can be known about God is plain to them, because God has shown it to them. For his invisible attributes, namely, his eternal power and divine nature, have been clearly perceived, ever since the creation of the world, in the things that have been made. So they are without excuse. For although they knew God, they did not honour him as God or give thanks to him, but they became futile in their thinking, and their foolish hearts were darkened. Claiming to be wise, they became fools (Romans 1:18–22).

There is evidence not only of God's existence but also of God's goodness through his providential care. Paul and Barnabas at Lystra said that God, 'did not leave himself without witness, for he did good by giving you rains from heaven and fruitful seasons, satisfying your hearts with food and gladness' (Acts 14:17).[1]

Those who have never heard the message of the gospel and never had opportunity to read the Bible, which is God's *special* revelation, still have God's *general* revelation in creation and providence. Not only that but people also have the witness of their own God-given consciences which enables them to understand the difference between right and wrong behaviour:

> For when Gentiles, who do not have the law, by nature do what the law requires, they are a law to themselves, even though they do not have the law. They show that the work of the law is written on their hearts, while their conscience also bears witness, and their conflicting thoughts accuse or even excuse them on that day when, according to my gospel, God judges the secrets of men by Christ Jesus (Romans 2:14–16)

Nobody will be saved through observance of the law because nobody has ever fully kept the law, except Christ. The law teaches us that we need mercy and grace and when we humbly turn to God in that frame of mind he can read the heart and he will do what is right. So certain aspects of God's existence and character are evident to all and therefore people are accountable to God for what they do with that knowledge.

God speaks to humanity in many ways—through Creation and conscience for example—but this does not mean that such revelation will necessarily lead to salvation. Nevertheless it is one of God's means of communicating with his created beings. If people habitually ignore their God-given consciences they become calloused and stand condemned before God (Romans 1:20f). But this passage teaches that creation and conscience bear the stamp of God and serve the purpose of arousing wonder and awe for the creator, thereby stimulating a sense of reverence which in turn should compel an open heart and mind to seek God. Those who truly seek the Lord will find Jesus, God's very special and unique revelation of himself. Conscience lets us know the difference between right and wrong and how much we are in need of grace and mercy. This should drive us to call out for salvation.

Extra or ordinary evidence

Some people say that if God spoke personally to them then they would be willing to believe. Consider the parable of the rich man and Lazarus:

> There was a rich man who was clothed in purple and fine linen and who feasted sumptuously every day. And at his gate was laid a poor man named Lazarus, covered with sores, who desired to

> be fed with what fell from the rich man's table. Moreover, even the dogs came and licked his sores. The poor man died and was carried by the angels to Abraham's side. The rich man also died and was buried, and in Hades, being in torment, he lifted up his eyes and saw Abraham far off and Lazarus at his side. And he called out, 'Father Abraham, have mercy on me, and send Lazarus to dip the end of his finger in water and cool my tongue, for I am in anguish in this flame.' But Abraham said, 'Child, remember that you in your lifetime received your good things, and Lazarus in like manner bad things; but now he is comforted here, and you are in anguish. And besides all this, between us and you a great chasm has been fixed, in order that those who would pass from here to you may not be able, and none may cross from there to us.' And he said, 'Then I beg you, father, to send him to my father's house—for I have five brothers—so that he may warn them, lest they also come into this place of torment.' But Abraham said, 'They have Moses and the Prophets; let them hear them.' And he said, 'No, father Abraham, but if someone goes to them from the dead, they will repent.' He said to him, 'If they do not hear Moses and the Prophets, neither will they be convinced if someone should rise from the dead' (Luke 16:19–31).

Christ makes it clear that the ordinary revelation of Scripture is sufficient evidence and that those who think that extraordinary evidence, such as somebody returning from the dead, will be more convincing are, in fact, wrong. There is a warning in this story for anybody who would not heed the written Word of God. Even Christ's disciples who had witnessed Jesus bringing people back from the dead and many other signs and wonders were slow to believe. He said to the two disciples whom he met on the road to Emmaus, 'O foolish ones, and slow of heart to believe all that the prophets have spoken!' (Luke 24:25).

God's voice

Genesis chapters 1–9 describe the origin of the human family. The early communications between God and Adam, and then the children of Adam down through Noah would have contained enough information for these people to be saved. This information could have been passed down through all of Noah's sons. These early generations would not have had a precise knowledge of the gospel as we know it today.

Hebrews chapter eleven lists many faith-heroes (both men and women) of the Old Testament. Most of these people, identified as examples of faith, would not have had the precision of gospel teaching we have today. They believed specific promises of God which related to his activity in history in Israel.

A detailed theological understanding of the gospel evolved over a long period of time.[2] The progressive nature of revelation is relevant in addressing this question because many heroes of faith did not actually have a precise understanding of the gospel message *per se*. Therefore it is not necessary to salvation to have a theologically refined and comprehensive understanding of what we call the 'gospel message'. As God added more Scripture, the cognitive content of the gospel became more detailed. But Old Testament people were saved by faith in God as saviour, without a significant amount of detail on 'how', though it was always linked to blood sacrifice and what that represented in terms of atonement. Generally the messianic content of the gospel was probably not very clear until the Davidic Kingdom.

Considering the question 'What about those who have never

heard the gospel?' will bring us outside our comfort zones. The one essential that needs to be borne in mind at all times is that salvation is by grace alone, through faith alone, in Christ alone.

The Old Testament saints were saved by faith in God as Saviour. Christ is present in all the Scriptures in type and shadow. But none of the types are perfect and shadows are broad outlines which by definition are not delineated in great detail. Certainly the law convicts of sin and the need for a Saviour and functions as a signpost that leads to Christ.

Jesus said, 'Abraham rejoiced that he would see my day. He saw it and was glad.' (John 8:56).). It is clearly stated here that Abraham had a preview of Christ's ministry. Presumably this refers to the promise God gave to Abraham that his seed would become the channel of divine blessing to all nations through the redemptive work of Christ (Genesis 12:3). Isaac represented to Abraham the seed through which God would fulfil his promise. The miraculous birth of Isaac, his unquestioning trust in his father, his willingness to become a sacrifice to fulfil the command of God and his deliverance from certain death all seem to point forward to the coming incarnation, death and resurrection of the promised Seed.[3] All of this proves the point that God can and does work in mysterious ways. Although God communicates primarily through the specific revelation of his Word the Holy Spirit is neither mute nor powerless to prevail upon the hearts of people and quicken them to repentance and faith if he so chooses.

Undoubtedly the heroes of faith were looking for a better country, which is the same hope as New Testament believers. They were not saved by any means other than by the redemptive work of Christ of which Isaiah and other

Old Testament servants of the Lord spoke, prophetically. Nevertheless there was much more that was not clearly defined.

There are many people in Scripture who had a sense of God even without the Old Testament canon of Scripture. Some of these people did not belong to the covenant community of Israel and, therefore, did not have detailed knowledge of God as given in the revealed Word. Although Abraham was descended from Noah he was living in a pagan land (Ur of the Chaldeans) when he heard God speak to him. The Lord opened the eyes of Balaam and communicated with Nebuchadnezzar, the king of Babylon.

Nevertheless the book of Job is the oldest book in the Bible and Job has a sophisticated theology, even though it was written before God spoke to his people through the prophets. In the New Testament the magi that came and worshipped the infant Jesus were foreigners and Gentiles. Abel, Enoch and Noah are all identified as examples of faith in Hebrews chapter eleven. Yet none of these men had the Scriptures. They were part of the unfolding narrative which became the Scriptures that revealed God's redemptive plan.

There are hundreds of biblical references to God communicating through visions and dreams, mostly to prophets and kings, but not exclusively (note the magi and Cornelius).[4] Angels can be used to deliver messages from God, and although the gospel is primarily the ministry of people, angels are not precluded from preaching in some cases, 'Then I saw another angel flying directly overhead, with an eternal gospel to proclaim to those who dwell on earth, to every nation and tribe and language and people' (Revelation 14:6). God is certainly able to get the message of the gospel to people in remote locations and to those who are in false religions. God can break through the hedonistic, atheistic, secular and materialistic worlds that people inhabit and redeem people from these empty ways of life through faith.

Perhaps the reference to Revelation 14:6 should not be taken as an angel literally preaching (given the symbolic nature of Revelation) although the wording of the opening phrase, 'Then I saw another angel …' implies there are some other cases. But the good news of the conception and impending incarnation was announced by the angel Gabriel. In fact the gospel was first proclaimed by 'the angel of the Lord':[5]

> And in the same region there were shepherds out in the field, keeping watch over their flock by night. And an angel of the Lord appeared to them, and the glory of the Lord shone around them, and they were filled with fear. And the angel said to them, 'Fear not, for behold, I bring you good news of great joy that will be for all the people. For unto you is born this day in the city of David a Saviour, who is Christ the Lord. And this will be a sign for you: you will find a baby wrapped in swaddling cloths and lying in a manger'. And suddenly there was with the angel a multitude of the heavenly host praising God and saying, 'Glory to God in the highest, and on earth peace among those with whom he is pleased!' (Luke 2:8–14)

An angel of the Lord directed Cornelius to seek out Peter in order that he could encounter the message of the gospel.

God can and indeed still does (in extraordinary situations) communicate with people in dreams and through visions.[6] There are many stories (especially, from India and Africa and other parts of the developing world) of people who were converted by direct personal encounters with God. These people had no chance of having somebody share the message of the gospel with them because of the remoteness of their villages or the obscurity of their language or the hostility of their community. Nevertheless God broke through all the barriers to enable them to find faith in the true God and to reject the false gods of their culture. God led them through many obstacles to find the fellowship of true believers. Their testimonies are powerful evidence that God can and does still draw people to himself in extraordinary ways.

It is interesting to consider Paul's words to the Athenians when he spoke in the Areopagus:

> 'Men of Athens, I perceive that in every way you are very religious. For as I passed along and observed the objects of your worship, I found also an altar with this inscription, "To the unknown god." What therefore you worship as unknown, this I proclaim to you. The God who made the world and everything in it, being Lord of heaven and earth, does not live in temples made by man, nor is he served by human hands, as though he needed anything, since he himself gives to all mankind life and breath and everything. And he made from one man every nation of mankind to live on all the face of the earth, having determined allotted periods and the boundaries of their dwelling place, that they should seek God, in the hope that they might feel their way toward him and find him. Yet he is actually not far from each one of us, for "In him we live and move and have our being"; as even some of your own poets have said, "For we are indeed his offspring." Being then God's offspring, we ought not to think that the divine being is like gold or silver or stone, an image formed by the art and imagination of man. The times of ignorance God overlooked, but now he commands all people everywhere to

> repent, because he has fixed a day on which he will judge the world in righteousness by a man whom he has appointed; and of this he has given assurance to all by raising him from the dead.'

It is clear that the Athenians wanted to cover all their options. They had an altar to 'the unknown God' as a kind of insurance against offending deity. The way Paul connected with them is a masterstroke of communication. But it should be noticed that Paul tells these pagan people that God had in the past overlooked their ignorance. God overlooks such ignorance amongst those who have never heard the message of the gospel. This does not mean that everybody will be saved.

Millions of first generation Christians have been converted on the slightest knowledge of the gospel. They have no theological understanding. Perhaps all they know is that Jesus loves them. They come to know much more gradually as they read Scripture, pray, listen to sermons, attend Bible studies and have fellowship with other like-minded believers. It may sound like heresy but a person does not need a comprehensive knowledge of evangelical theology to be converted. Most new converts (first generation people who have never been to Sunday-School or a church that is truly Christian) would be unable to satisfactorily explain the message of the gospel if asked to do so at the very early stages of their post conversion experience.

Usually salvation depends on a person's exposure to the New Testament message of the gospel but this may not always be so. The early chapters of Paul's letter to the Romans indicate that a certain degree of moral purity is theoretically attainable by those who seek to live to please God and adhere to the promptings of conscience. But nobody attains a level of moral purity sufficient to attain salvation by either abstaining from sin (in thought, word and deed) or by performing good deeds or by adhering to religious rituals. God looks at the heart. Thankfully he does not look at the head because there can be much theological confusion there. Some Christians who have a very refined theology seem to think that people who do not believe exactly what they believe cannot be saved.

God's inclusive plans

God's plan of redemption always included individuals outside of Israel. We see this with Rahab, the heathen harlot, who was grafted in to God's purposes. It is worth developing this point because it is helpful to our understanding of the heart of God

Rahab lived in a house built into the walls of Jericho. The two spies sent by Joshua lodged there with her. When this became known it was reported to the King of Jericho who sent word to Rahab to turn over these enemies of Jericho. She disobeyed the king and concealed them under drying stalks of flax on the roof. When the city of Jericho and all its inhabitants was destroyed, Rahab, her parents, possessions and relatives were spared. Thereafter she lived in Israel and she is mentioned in three of the New Testament books. In Matthew she is listed in the genealogy of Jesus, 'Salmon the father of Boaz by Rahab, and Boaz the father of Obed by Ruth, and Obed the father of Jesse' (1:5). She was woven into God's grand scheme. In Hebrews we are told that it was, 'By faith Rahab the prostitute did not perish with those who were disobedient, because she had given a friendly welcome to the spies' (11:31). In this chapter she, once a heathen prostitute, is listed with the great patriarchs and heroes of faith.

But we should also bear in mind that Abraham too was once a pagan and was also a flawed character that lied to a king, claiming that Sarah, was his sister (not his wife). He did this because he feared what the king might do to him in order to be with Sarah. This shows Abraham lied and behaved in cowardly manner. This incident took place after he was called by God! I mention this because the notion that the believer's life is one of sinless perfection needs to be dispelled.

In James also Rahab is identified along with Abraham, 'And in the same way was not also Rahab the prostitute justified by works when she received the messengers and sent them out by another way?' (James 2:25). Placing the two characters side by side in this way brings some theological truths into focus. Abraham was renowned for his lifelong faith whereas Rahab's notoriety, by contrast, reveals an act of faith set against the backdrop of a life of sin. In this we are being taught that no matter how meagre, faith in God leads to justification before God. Even the weakest faith must bear fruit in works, not to earn salvation but as evidence of that reality. Rahab is mentioned to demonstrate that infamous people without distinguished pedigree are as acceptable to God as those of notable lineage. As Scripture tells us; 'God shows no partiality' (Galatians 2:6).

Rahab obviously believed that God was with Israel. Furthermore that faith was demonstrated in the way she played a part and risked her life to hide the spies sent by Joshua. She helped them to escape by sending them on a route that was more likely to assist them in evading capture. In this we see the transforming power of faith demonstrated in new attitudes and actions. God honoured that faith as he always does. It is also evident from her actions that she preferred the glory of God and the good of his people to the preservation of her own country. Some may be inclined to think of her as a traitor who committed a treasonous act against her own people by collaborating with the enemy. Certainly she betrayed her country but in doing this she showed a new allegiance.

In considering Rahab we have made the point that God had gracious dealings with people outside Israel. We could equally well convey the same message by considering Ruth, a Moabite woman, who became the great grandmother of King David. Ruth's husband, Boaz, was the son of Rahab. So not only is Rahab listed in the genealogy of Jesus but so too is Ruth, in the same verse cited earlier (Matthew 1:5).

Ultimately God's plan is that people of every tribe and nation would become beneficiaries of his great grace. God is merciful to the undeserving.

A lesson in Jonah

Consider the situation of the Ninevites, recorded in Jonah chapter three. Jonah preached impending destruction on that great city and called for repentance. The people repented and destruction was averted. Here were a pagan people, outside the covenant community, who were infamous for their idolatry and brutality. They heard a message from God, delivered through the reluctant prophet Jonah and responded appropriately. In one sense this event does not fit with our investigation because we are seeking to address the question, 'what about those who have never heard the gospel?' Clearly these people heard a call for repentance (would we call it a gospel message today?) but what is interesting about this scenario is that their knowledge of 'the gospel' would have been very limited. We could say that theirs was merely a secular deliverance whereby calamity was temporarily averted (they were eventually destroyed) but that is sidestepping the issue. It is clear that God was compassionate and forgave their wickedness in the face of genuine repentance as evidenced by their fasting from food and drink and the wearing of sackcloth and ashes. The point is that God accepts a very basic understanding if it is genuine. The pagan Ninevites heard a message preached which called for repentance and they responded positively to it.

The fact that a relationship with God does not depend on intelligence or education is clear in the way children can enjoy this relationship. God does not choose us on the basis of our intellectual ability. Paul made this abundantly clear to the church at Corinth:

> For consider your calling, brothers: not many of you were wise according to worldly standards, not many were powerful, not many were of noble birth. But God chose what is foolish in the world to shame the wise; God chose what is weak in the world to shame the strong; God chose what is low and despised in the world, even things that are not, to bring to nothing things that are, so that no human being might boast in the presence of God. And because of him you are in Christ Jesus, who became to us wisdom from God, righteousness and sanctification and redemption, so that, as it is written, 'Let the one who boasts, boast in the Lord' (1 Corinthians 1:26–31).

Very little doctrinal or theological knowledge is required for salvation and, it would seem also that a great deal of 'error' is allowed. All Christian denominations as well as Christians of a non-denominational hue have misunderstandings and a degree of ignorance, although some might like to think otherwise.

Pagan sailors

Consider the pagan sailors who accompanied Jonah on his perilous sea voyage. The book of Jonah is a revelation of the largeness of the heart of God. There is a process of spiritual enlightenment taking place among these men. God's dealings with them is woven into the fabric of the story because it serves to illustrate the thematic purpose of the book by demonstrating that God is not a limited, local, tribal deity.

In chapter one it is recorded, 'Then the mariners were afraid, and each cried out to his god' (Jonah 1:5). Initially there is a manifestation of their crude paganism but eventually these men come to some knowledge of God. Belief in the immortality and accountability of the soul is fundamental to all religions. A. W. Tozer said, 'Religion, so far as it is genuine, is in essence the response of created personalities to the creating personality of God.' The sailors were genuinely afraid of losing their lives and while Jonah was in a deep sleep below deck they were busy tossing the cargo into the sea in order to save the vessel from sinking. However, when Jonah is aroused and he confesses that he is an Israelite and that he worships the God who made the sea, they are terrified. The phrase 'exceedingly afraid' in verse 10 refers, not merely to physical fear, but to a deep religious awe. Verse 14 says they cried out to 'the Lord', not *a god*, not *the gods* but that they called upon Jehovah, the covenant God of Israel. Then verse 16 speaks of their *sacrifice* and *vows* to Jehovah. In this act they are binding themselves to lives of covenant obligation. Whether they kept these promises or reneged on them is another matter. What does matter is that here are all the essential ingredients of true heart religion, which began with a reverential awe of the living God.

These were experienced sailors who were not afraid of a few

waves. They were well used to sailing in squalls and swells. But on this occasion they hear the very structure of the ship creaking and realize that the vessel is in imminent danger of sinking. They are certain that there is a connection between the heaving tempest and somebody on board. We could say they were merely superstitious but in truth were they not correct? What we learn about these men from this incident is that they are inherently religious. Matthew Henry said, 'The root of religion is the fear of God reigning in the heart, a reverence of his majesty, a deference to his authority and a dread of his wrath.' They want to know who is guilty of provoking God. They cried out to *the Lord.* This shows that they acknowledge that there is a supreme being who stands above their lesser 'gods'. Furthermore they acknowledge the relationship between the pleasure and displeasure of this God and the physical world. They recognize that this God controls the elements of the world. They exhort Jonah: 'Arise, call on your god!' Thus they accept that this God is accessible through prayer. So here you have the essential ingredients of a religious constitution. At a minimum we can allow that there is evidence of a fundamental theism, albeit in the midst of superstition and error. Yet God is at work in their activity as much as he is in the activity of the storm.

These men, at a time of crisis, are drawn to God and in their distress they call out to God for salvation. Although their primary concern is to be rescued from this storm and as such they are seeking a temporal salvation. Could this also be said of the inhabitants of Nineveh, that they too desired and only experienced temporal salvation? Although the Lord may communicate through visions and supernatural means it is the exception not the rule.

In many Western societies today the appearance of prevailing secularism may be deceptive because some societies still retain a sense of the reality of God. There is in such societies a residual theism and despite religious superstition and error this fundamental belief in God can be an opening for the entrance of the true gospel. In a metaphorical sense we might say there are times of crises when storms are raging and people become afraid that the creaking timbers of their ship (i.e. the institutions in which they trust) will not survive in such tempestuous waters.

The frightening implication of the storm in Jonah is that it is a result of Jonah's disobedient refusal to fulfil the charge entrusted to him. People in our society are being tossed about like corks in violent storms of confusion so we need to fulfil the commission assigned to us. We must be awake and alert and bear testimony to our God. One might say it is difficult to comprehend how Jonah could sleep in circumstances like this but perhaps the church today is slumbering at a time of crisis in the world when the very destruction of the planet is threatened by man's greed and reckless disregard for the stewardship of ecology:

The way of salvation

And it happened that while Apollos was at Corinth, Paul passed through the inland country and came to Ephesus. There he found some disciples. And he said to them, 'Did you receive the Holy Spirit when you believed?' And they said, 'No, we have not even heard that there is a Holy Spirit.' And he said, 'Into what then were you baptized?' They said, 'Into John's baptism.' And Paul said, 'John baptized with the baptism of repentance, telling the people to believe in the one who was to come after him, that is,

> Jesus.' On hearing this, they were baptized in the name of the Lord Jesus (Acts 19:1–5).

Here were 'disciples' who were not even aware of the existence of the Holy Spirit. There are isolated peoples of the world today who have an imprecise understanding of the means of salvation or other doctrines but they are nevertheless adherents of the truth inasmuch as they know it.

Consider some key verses such as John 14.6 where Jesus said, 'I am the way, and the truth, and the life. No one comes to the Father except through me' or Acts 4:12 where Peter and John proclaim, 'And there is salvation in no one else, for there is no other name under heaven given among men by which we must be saved.' These statements are unequivocally true. Furthermore the name 'Jesus' is the most precious name for followers of Christ. But the reality is that many people before Christ's incarnate existence, and even since his first coming, have never heard of Jesus. Indeed many people have heard of Jesus but their understanding of his nature and work is distorted because it is part of a religious system that disseminates misinformation about Christ. Yet the Bible makes these statements and it also tells us that, 'there is one God, and there is one mediator between God and men, the man Christ Jesus' (1 Timothy 2:5). This is undoubtedly true. There is no other mediator, just as there is no other name by which salvation comes. This needs to be spelled out. Mohammad cannot save, Krishna cannot save, Mary (the mother of Jesus) cannot save or mediate between God and man. The 'saints' of the Roman Catholic Church cannot mediate salvation. No other so-called 'deity' can save.

Nevertheless, these verses do not teach that the recipients of God's grace need necessarily know the name 'Jesus'. Many Old

Testament saints would not have known the name Jesus. Yet Acts 4:12 specifically says that there is no other 'name' whereby people can be saved. This seems to suggest that the name Jesus is undeniably critical to salvation. But 'name' was normally used to mean, 'on behalf of', 'in the cause of' or 'by the authority of'. Thus to speak in the name of Rome, for example, would mean to speak on behalf of Rome, in the cause of Rome or by the authority of Rome. Therefore in Acts 4:18, when the Sanhedrin charged Peter and John not to speak in the 'name' of Jesus they were effectively trying to gag them so that they would not speak 'on behalf of Jesus', 'in the cause of Jesus' or 'by the authority of Jesus'. They are effectively being commanded not to try to win adherents to this cause.

So, when Peter and John say that there is, 'no other *name* under heaven given among men by which we must be saved' it really means that there is no other *authority* by which people can be saved. It is possible then for the heart to cry out to the 'authority' in heaven without knowing the name Jesus. Importantly, however, this verse teaches that it is futile to call upon or trust in any other person, religious leader, religious system or 'deity'. To do so will only take people to the wrong address; to someone or something which cannot save. There is no mystical meaning in the name 'Jesus' itself.[7] That after all is a title that describes his work. Elsewhere in Scripture Jesus is called the 'Son' (Hebrews 1) or the 'Word' (John 1:1; Revelation 19:13). So Acts 4:12 does not necessarily mean that the appellation 'Jesus' is essential to salvation because other designations are acceptable.

Other religions

Without capitulating to the false notion that 'all roads lead to heaven' it can be admitted that one can find traces of personal faith in the major monotheistic religions where concepts of grace and moral judgment can exist. It is certainly not given the kind of emphasis that we as evangelicals would want but it can be a starting place in a journey that might lead to Jesus.

Most Christians readily accept that there are concepts of moral judgment in Islam but might wonder if there are really concepts of grace in Islam.[8] According to Abu Huraira, Muhammad once said that 'None amongst you can get into Paradise by virtue of his deeds alone … not even I, but that Allah should wrap me in his grace and mercy.'[1]

Some false religions present God as the creator. Such religions emphasize that people should live lives that are pleasing to God. Such religions present the notion of divine judgment (including heaven and hell). So there is some element of truth even in some false religions. They might have some understanding of the origin, purpose and destiny of mankind. They have an ethical standard comparable to the Ten Commandments. There are many observations in these works that might (in spite of grievous error and downright heresy) stimulate a spiritual curiosity that could turn people towards the one true God.[2] Because this is part of the argument of those with an inter-faith agenda we evangelicals tend to dismiss it outright. But there can be in these commonalities a fertile place for the true gospel of Jesus to take root, germinate and bear fruit in salvation.

But I would not want to give the impression that people throwing themselves on God's mercy in response to natural revelation necessarily leads to salvation. The heavens declare the glory of God and as such preach a sermon. If I was to give that sermon a title I would call it: 'God exists'. As such natural revelation proclaims the creator but not the redeemer. There is a great chasm between theism and faith in the Lord Jesus as Saviour, but it could be the start of a journey that leads to Christ if a person's heart is open.

Multitudes of Jews who, in Old Testament times, turned to God in repentance, brought the prescribed sacrifice, and threw themselves on God's mercy. It was not that they earned that mercy by their repentance or obedience, or that an animal sacrifice could ever atone for their sin. Rather, their repentance and faith (the result of God's work in their lives) opened the way to the grace, mercy and forgiveness which he always longed to extend to them, and which was to be made forever available by Christ's death and resurrection.

We can reasonably hope that the God of all mercy can work in the lives of the misguided followers of other religions. The Holy Spirit can enable such people to come, in some measure, to realize their sin and need for forgiveness. Even in the midst of darkness, misunderstanding and error people can come to cast themselves on the mercy of God.

The story of Cornelius recounted in Acts is a fascinating insight to this issue. Is not this, perhaps, the meaning of Peter's words in the house of Cornelius: 'Truly I understand that God shows no partiality, but in every nation anyone who fears him and does what is right is acceptable to him' (Acts 10:34–35)? This does not mean that the person who endeavours to be religious and strives to be moral will earn salvation, for the whole Bible denies this possibility. But it does mean that the people who realize something of their sin or need, and throw themselves on the mercy of God may find that mercy. Such people have a sincerity which is demonstrated in their lives and this is a sign of the inward prompting of God's Spirit, especially in the case of one who has never heard the gospel. Without fully understanding it they can encounter the grace of God mediated through Christ's death at Calvary.

Nevertheless Cornelius was an upright and God-fearing man of good reputation and an angel of the Lord directed him to one who could bring the message of the gospel to him. Consider this passage from Acts:

> Now while Peter was inwardly perplexed as to what the vision that he had seen might mean, behold, the men who were sent by Cornelius, having made inquiry for Simon's house, stood at the gate and called out to ask whether Simon who was called Peter was lodging there. And while Peter was pondering the vision, the Spirit said to him, 'Behold, three men are looking for you. Rise and go down and accompany them without hesitation, for I have sent them.' And Peter went down to the men and said, 'I am the one you are looking for. What is the reason for your coming?' And they said, 'Cornelius, a centurion, an upright and God-fearing man, who is well spoken of by the whole Jewish nation, was directed by a holy angel to send for you to come to his house and to hear what you have to say.' So he invited them in to be his guests. The next day he rose and went away with them, and some of the brothers from Joppa accompanied him. And on the following day they entered Caesarea. Cornelius was expecting them and had called together his relatives and close friends. When Peter entered, Cornelius met him and fell down at his feet and worshiped him. But Peter lifted him up, saying, 'Stand up; I too am a man.' And as he talked with him, he went in and found many persons gathered. And he said to them, 'You yourselves know how unlawful it is for a Jew to associate with or to visit anyone of another nation, but God has shown me that I should not call any person common or unclean. So when I was sent for,

> I came without objection. I ask then why you sent for me.' And Cornelius said, 'Four days ago, about this hour, I was praying in my house at the ninth hour, and behold, a man stood before me in bright clothing and said, "Cornelius, your prayer has been heard and your alms have been remembered before God."'

Many people, in other religions have been soundly converted to Christ before they realize exactly what has taken place. They have a dynamic relationship with God but no understanding of doctrine or theology. I have known some people who were converted and reading the Scriptures and they thought they were the only people in the world who had this kind of unique experience of God. They were genuinely surprised and delighted to learn that there were communities of believers who loved the Word of God and relied upon it in all matters of faith and practice and used it for comfort and counsel and as a means of learning more about God.

I am the pastor of a Baptist church which consists entirely of first generation converted Roman Catholics and what I have described above is the testimony of one of our members. Also my wife was soundly converted long before she knew what that really meant. She had been attending charismatic prayer meetings and Bible studies and was saved! She had a living, dynamic relationship with God and eventually that led her away from the Roman Catholic Church into fellowship with like-minded believers who had more in common than a shared experience; they had a shared theology which was based on the Scriptures and bear testimony to the fact that salvation is by grace alone through faith alone in Christ alone. There can be a period of continuity with the old religion and one would hope sufficient insight to eventually bring about a radical discontinuity with wrong understandings and false practices. But in the absence of anybody to teach them this process may be retarded.

It is something like youth worker practitioners who after many years on the job go on to study sociological theory in this field. They then come to a better understanding of what they already know. The theoretical frameworks enable them to appreciate the bigger picture. They begin to see the interconnections and how theory can clarify the historical origins, purposes, aims and objectives. They see templates and paradigms. They were always part of a network of interconnected agencies and providers. They always understood their particular roles in either raising awareness, compensating for lack of educational attainment in education, providing recreation, disseminating information, addressing poverty issues, strategizing for social action to effect political change and so on. But perhaps they did not have the professional terminology, theoretical insights, and ability to analyse the qualitative data or the skills required to access and assess the quantitative information. Nevertheless they were youth workers who were actually doing the job. Theological competence and doctrinal awareness enhance our understanding of faith and God and although very important in our spiritual development they are nonetheless not essential to salvation.

This illustration of a youth worker coming to understand theory is like the Christian who grows in knowledge. This is not to equate salvation with intellectual comprehension but to show that where salvation has taken place theological knowledge will greatly enhance this person's understanding of that experience.

Most people are not theologians

Evangelical Christians who come to the Republic of Ireland as missionaries tend to suppose that because they have come to a Catholic country that Catholic people understand what they are supposed to believe. This is not true. Most Irish Catholics are ignorant of Catholic teaching. It is a cultural tradition more than a theology. I have often joked that Free Presbyterians from Northern Ireland know infinitely more about Roman Catholic teaching than most Roman Catholics in the Republic of Ireland. The same is true for many Jews and Muslims inasmuch as their respective religions may be erroneous but that does not mean that individual adherents who were born into those cultures know and practice those teachings in every detail.

Rejecting Christ

Scripture, however, makes it clear that not believing in Christ, not obeying him or rejecting Christ will incur the wrath of God and thereby all who reject Jesus will forfeit eternal life, 'Whoever believes in the Son has eternal life; whoever does not obey the Son shall not see life, but the wrath of God remains on him' (John 3:36). Rejecting the truth is a not merely about expressing or actively demonstrating hostility to Christ, it is also about indifference to the truth. However it is not about ignorance of the truth. A caution is needed here because many people whom we might suspect as having rejected Christ may have merely rejected the phony images of Christ presented to them. Many non-Christian sceptics and atheists have rejected a caricature of Jesus.

Those who reject Christ will be damned not just because they reject Jesus but because of their original and actual sin. Their rejection of the free offer of salvation is symptomatic of their heart's true, condition.

It must be borne in mind that God does not want people to perish, 'Have I any pleasure in the death of the wicked, declares the Lord God, and not rather that he should turn from his way and live' (Ezekiel 18:23). A few verses later in the same chapter God says, 'For I have no pleasure in the death of anyone, declares the Lord God; so turn, and live' (18:32).

The Scriptures are available in the vast majority of languages today but in cases where they are not available or where a person has not had access to Scripture we may be sure that God knows how individuals would have responded if given the opportunity to do so.[3]

Heaven will be populated, with people from all nations, tribes, and languages. God's judgment is completely fair and his kindness is communicated (and operative) to all. God reveals himself to humanity through several non-linguistic forms (especially creation and conscience). God deals with people according to the information they have, particularly with regard to how they respond to the truth. Some will reject it, others will resist it, but some will receive it. God's moral judgment is based on motives and deeds (which is a very fair standard for everyone) but salvation is ultimately his choice, made before the foundation of the world. All of God's overtures to man, and the acceptance of imperfect people into a living relationship with the morally pure God, are based on the penalty-removing sacrifice of God the Son on the Cross. God is perfectly good and just in all his dealings with humanity. He is patient in delaying judgment and has made provision for forgiveness through the death of his Son.

So we can leave the matter confidently in the hands the Lord knowing that he elects those whom he has chosen before the foundation of the world. He is just, holy, gracious and merciful and all his decisions are right and good.

Nevertheless the Christian has a sacred duty to diligently seek the lost by sharing with them the good news of the gospel of Christ so that they can join in God-centred worship, thereby giving glory to God as creator and redeemer. Though not every believer is a God-gifted evangelist all believers are called to be witnesses. Jesus said, 'But you will receive power when the Holy Spirit has come upon you, and you will be my witnesses in Jerusalem and in all Judea and Samaria, and to the end of the earth' (Acts 1:8). They were the last words Christ spoke on earth, his parting words to his disciples. His last words should be our first concern. These words have a very special significance. The last words spoken by a person on earth have great importance. We tend to think often about the last words of loved ones. Such words constitute a kind of last will and testament. If we love the person who spoke those words then we try to ensure that their last expressed wish is carried out. Love motivates us to do this.

Romans 10

One passage of Scripture crucial to this discussion is to be found in Paul's letter to the Romans:

> … if you confess with your mouth that Jesus is Lord and believe in your heart that God raised him from the dead, you will be saved. For with the heart one believes and is justified, and with the mouth one confesses and is saved. For the Scripture says, 'Everyone who believes in him will not be put to shame.' For there is no distinction between Jew and Greek; for the same Lord is Lord of all, bestowing his riches on all who call on him.

> For 'everyone who calls on the name of the Lord will be saved.' How then will they call on him in whom they have not believed? And how are they to believe in him of whom they have never heard? And how are they to hear without someone preaching? And how are they to preach unless they are sent? As it is written, 'How beautiful are the feet of those who preach the good news!' But they have not all obeyed the gospel. For Isaiah says, 'Lord, who has believed what he has heard from us?' So faith comes from hearing, and hearing through the word of Christ (Romans 10:9–17).

This discourse refers to the principle of faith established in the Old Testament. The law calls for obedience and performance of the will of God. Here Paul cites Leviticus 18:5. But observance of these statutes and ordinances cannot in themselves bring life because of human weakness and imperfection. The Pharisees demonstrate that in fact such literal and external observance leads to self-deception and pride. But the law presupposed a heart attitude of loving obedience (Deuteronomy 30:6–10) rather than a legalistic attempt to attain righteousness by self-effort. This is faith.

In this passage Paul speaks of the content of the gospel message as something to be 'confessed' as well as 'believed'. The statement 'Jesus is Lord' is the earliest creedal confession of the church (Acts 2:36; 1 Corinthians 12:3). Paul cites Joel 2:32 and this calling on this Lord is the echo within the human heart of the call of God himself, according to his gracious purpose (Romans 8:28–30). God will hear the cry of any who call upon him for salvation. The Lord of Joel is the Lord Jesus Christ (compare verses 9 and 13). The whole thrust of this passage is to direct people away from a legalistic and merely external observance of the law in hope of attaining righteousness and to direct them to turn in faith to the Lord.

Paul then turns from the responsibility of the seeker after salvation to the responsibility that believers have in God's plan of salvation. He emphasizes the believer's role in reaching the lost by stressing that it is the believer's duty to present Christ as worthy of confidence and trust. Paul emphasizes the fact that faith is based on knowledge. One must hear the gospel before one can be expected to receive it or reject it. The gospel message must be communicated. Paul talks of it being communicated by word of mouth to the hearing of others. Of course that is one means of communication that does not necessarily preclude others, such as reading the Bible or other Christian literature. This too can lead to salvation. If we were to insist that the message of the gospel must be orally transmitted (encoded) and aurally received (decoded) then we exclude deaf people from salvation and that would be absurd. We are saved to serve and our paramount duty is to bear witness to the saving power of Jesus.

So Paul is saying that faith depends on hearing and understanding the message. That message is about Christ's redemptive act as an atoning sacrifice for all those who repent and believe and trust in that finished work for salvation. This is the way the Lord has ordained for the dissemination of the gospel message.

Because we are addressing the question: 'what about those who have never heard the gospel?' we have been forced to speculate, but within the constraints of Scripture. Some may feel uncomfortable with such an approach but I trust I have not strayed beyond the revelation of the Word that we, as believers, know must govern us in all matters of faith and practice.

Ultimately we are trying to answer something very difficult and mysterious and troubling. If I have given exceptions too much prominence it is only because I am addressing this thorny question. Though God in his sovereignty may do as he pleases we know his *modus operandi* is outlined in the above passage from Romans. For our part we must insist that one is saved by grace, through faith in the Lord Jesus Christ.

Developing a theology of evangelism

In Romans chapter one Paul said that the gospel is the power of God for salvation. The gospel has transformative power. It is God's way of radically changing a person's life. God is sovereign in salvation. We cannot save anybody and are not, therefore, responsible for the eternal destiny of someone else. But we are responsible for obeying the Lord's instruction to be his witnesses. It is the moral responsibility of the Christian to obey the Lord and to seek to do his will. Indeed, obedience is one measure of our love, since Jesus once said: 'If you love me, you will keep my commandments' (John 14:15).

We ought to look for opportunities to share the gospel with anybody who will listen. We are searching for anyone who will talk with us about spiritual matters, come to a home Bible study or accept our invitation to attend church. But in another sense we are searching for those whom 'God chose to be saved, through sanctification by the Spirit and belief in the truth' (2 Thessalonians 2:13). As we do not know who these people are, we witness to all without reservation.

Since we do not know who God's chosen people are and as they don't have a 'C' (for 'Chosen') tattooed on their foreheads we are to witness to all who are willing to listen. Like the sower Jesus spoke of in Matthew chapter thirteen, we are to scatter the seed of the gospel everywhere we can, even though we know that only some of it will fall on good ground (Matthew 13:3–8). Like the fisherman Jesus spoke of in that same chapter, we are to cast as wide a net as possible (Matthew 13:47–50).

Many scriptures attest that salvation is God's choice (e.g. Romans 8:29–30; Ephesians 1:4–6, 11). Furthermore, Scripture tells us when that choice was made, 'he chose us in him before the foundation of the world' (Ephesians 1:4). The doctrine of predestination is clearly taught in Scripture. W. R. Godfrey says:

> The contemporary evangelical church has become largely Arminian, often as a result of anti-doctrinal bias rather than careful theological reflection. The historic Augustinian doctrine of predestination remains biblically and theologically compelling.[4]

In Romans 9:14 Paul asks the question 'Is God unjust?' The resounding answer exclaimed by the apostle is 'Not at all!' If unconditional election is not being taught in Romans chapter nine, why raise and answer this question? Obviously Paul is anticipating objections to this teaching and addresses the issue. He is addressing a charge that presupposes he will be understood as teaching unconditional election. If Paul were teaching universal election or divine election without that unconditional element, nobody would raise a question about God's fairness. The issue of the injustice of God never arises in the Arminian theory because salvation is seen as a judicious foreordination.[5]

Verse sixteen directly addresses the Arminian issue. It does not, therefore, depend on man's desire or effort, but on God's mercy. Man is free to make choices but that freedom is limited by his fallen nature. He has only his perverse rational powers to guide him to follow his depraved inclinations.

Arminianism is a man-centred theory whereas Calvinism is a God-centred perspective. Election is not merely a ratification of man's decision. As John Owen put it, 'Christ did not die for any upon condition, if they believe; but he died for all God's elect, that they should believe.' What is truly amazing in election is not that God chose only some but that he chose any!

Since the fall of Adam man in his lost and sinful condition is at enmity with God. His fallen and rebellious nature is so corrupted that he has neither the desire nor the inclination to seek after God. Salvation, therefore, must, of necessity, come from God's gracious initiative. Calvin said, 'God … wrote the names of his children in the Book of life before the creation of the world; but he enrols them in the catalogue of his saints only when, having regenerated them by the spirit of adoption, he impresses his own mark upon them.'

The election of a soul to salvation does not depend on any virtue in the individual. A person is elected to salvation in accordance with God's sovereign purpose by his eternal and inscrutable decree. It is based on the goodwill and pleasure of God alone. As to when God's choice was settled, we uphold Calvin's view that, 'The election of God is anterior to Adam's fall.'

The reason why some are rescued while others are passed over is a mystery to the rational mind that seems to breach our understanding of the notion of justice. To some, God may appear to be capricious and even callous. But there is nothing whimsical or arbitrary in God's choice. Election is not the random and indifferent action of a despotic God. Rather it magnifies his grace. Grace has often been presented as God's unmerited favour to the undeserving but that is a definition that fails to explain fully the true nature of grace because grace is, rather, God's unmerited favour, not to the undeserving, but to the hell-deserving! The reprobate, therefore, receive what they deserve and the seriousness of sin is stressed in their eternal punishment.

It is right to be unequivocal and unashamed of this glorious truth as the authentic teaching of Scripture but it is ugly when there is a haughty spirit where humility would be more appropriate. The keynote for a befitting attitude to the profundity of predestination may well be taken from Paul's great doxological statement: 'Oh, the depth of the riches of the wisdom and knowledge of God! How unsearchable his judgments, and his paths beyond tracing out! "Who has known the mind of the Lord?"' (Romans 11:33–34). However, we must assert this truth in love, not only to affirm our own faith but also to establish others in a truly biblical understanding of election. Spurgeon said that some medicine is better swallowed than chewed: 'In the same way there are some things in the Word of God which are undoubtedly true which must be swallowed at once by an effort of faith, and must not be chewed by perpetual questioning.'

Rightly grasped, the doctrine of unconditional election should be a stimulus to evangelism. Understanding election ought to inspire rather than inhibit evangelism. We have a duty to desire all men to be saved and this attitude will inform and motivate our evangelism. In praying for all to be saved and preaching to all that they must be saved we leave their election to God's eternal and inscrutable discretion. We must bear in mind that God has appointed preaching and evangelism as the means by which he will accomplish his saving purposes. Our understanding of election should not restrict our preaching. This is a crucial matter and it seems strange that an appreciation of this truth can have the effect of gagging gospel preaching.

Iain Murray addresses this issue: 'While Reformed Confessions may begin with statements on the doctrine of God and divine decrees, that is not where preachers and teachers need to begin in addressing men about salvation'.[6] He points out that in the apostolic and evangelistic preaching of Acts no mention is made of the doctrine of election but that the epistles emphasize this truth. He then says: 'In accordance with this approach, Calvin, in the later editions of his Institutes, moved his treatment of election to follow teaching on justification. He recognized that Scripture generally introduces the doctrine of election to show believers the security and certainty of their salvation ...'[7]

Evangelism should be motivated primarily by a concern for the glory of God and obedience to Christ's commission (Matthew 19:20). It ought to be a spontaneous outworking of our gratitude for God's grace. It must be inspired by a concern for the eternal destiny of souls.

Nevertheless there is no time to waste. We should not procrastinate by putting off getting actively involved in fulfilling Christ's mandate to be his witnesses. We must share the gospel by preaching and other means. That is the message that Jesus came into the world to save sinners. That he is the Lamb of God who was slain as a sacrifice for sin. We must lift Christ up and call on people to repent, believe and confess Christ as Saviour and Lord. This is undoubtedly the desired response to preaching. We preach Christ exclusively and witness to the truth of his unique and universal claims. Our preaching of the gospel is part of the eschatological activity of the Kingdom inaugurated in Christ. The greatest need of the human soul is met by embracing the Christian gospel. No other message offers the hope and assurance of salvation. It is, therefore both important and urgent that the Christian gospel be disseminated throughout the world. To this end we must do all that we can to support that work by going to those who have never heard, by giving to the work of mission, by sharing the gospel in word and deed. We ought to engage in frequent and fervent prayer (private and corporate) for those who work in mission that the seed of the Word of God may find fertile soil, germinate, take root and bear fruit to the glory of God.

6

Identifying the Way Forward Keeping Mission Central to Church Life

Political parties produce manifestos. In these ambitious documents they publish their aspirations and policies. An understanding of their position and purpose may be gleaned from their manifestos. Such documents usually contain promises whereby political parties inform the public what they will do if elected. These statements spell out their intentions and the course of action they will adopt if/when elected to government. So the manifesto sets out the agenda for the future direction. It states what the party (or individual/independent candidate) want to achieve and how they intend to go about it. In the *Communist Manifesto* (1848) Karl Marx and Friedrich Engels, social scientists, authors and political theorists developed a philosophy known as communist theory. The *Communist Manifesto* set out a plan which proposed that the capitalist system of private ownership would be replaced by a communist society in which capital would be communally owned. It shaped the vision of communism as a movement. As such it was a seminal and influential document. Karl Marx called religion 'the opium of the masses'. What he meant is generally misunderstood. It was not religion *per se* he was talking about, rather he was referring to the kind of religion that fails to address social issues. It was a stinging but justifiable criticism, aimed at those who professed faith in Christ but did not speak out against the oppression of the weak by the powerful.

When Jesus stood up to read the Scriptures in the synagogue at Nazareth he read words from the Old Testament book of Isaiah:

> The Spirit of the LORD is upon Me,
> Because He has anointed Me
> To preach the gospel to the poor;
> He has sent Me to heal the brokenhearted,
> To proclaim liberty to the captives
> And recovery of sight to the blind,
> To set at liberty those who are oppressed;
> To proclaim the acceptable year of the LORD (Luke 4:18–19 NKJV)

He then sat down to teach, as was the custom. These words are known as 'The Nazareth Manifesto'. They are a public statement setting the agenda for his ministry. Jesus came to his hometown of Nazareth and to the synagogue to great acclaim.

People were amazed, 'All … marvelled at the gracious words which proceeded out of His mouth' (Luke 4:22). But the story of Jesus returning to his hometown is instructive. The warmth of the welcome he received soon turned to anger. Jesus becomes an object of hate and focus of the people's rage. What was it that turned the people against Jesus and so very quickly? Why did they so decisively reject the prophet whom they had so enthusiastically welcomed? It is in this very passage of Scripture that Jesus said, 'no prophet is accepted in his own country' (v.24). The church has a prophetic ministry, to speak and act as God wants. But there is resentment of and resistance to this kind of message. For Christ on that occasion the outcome was quite sinister because the people to whom he was speaking (namely, the devout adherents of the religious establishment) tried to kill him.

What did he say that was so offensive? The mood changed when Jesus began to tell them that God loves those outside their own religious community. They had reduced God, in their thinking, to a local, tribal deity who doted on them alone. The people loved Jesus until he started to talk about how God loved foreigners too. The thought that God's favour could be extended in this way was offensive to them. They were privileged citizens and they were not going to share the rights of citizenship with outsiders. Perhaps the wealthy loved Jesus until he started to talk about loving the poor because that would cost more than they were willing to pay. The difficulty comes when Jesus challenges us to reach out to those on the edge. This stretches our thinking and our emotional and financial resources. That kind of preaching is uncomfortable to those who don't want to look beyond the boundaries of their own community and self-interest.

But the Spirit of the Lord desires to operate through the church in establishing and extending the kingdom of God. So we must do all that we can to keep mission central to church life. The way forward begins by knowing what mission is all about. A necessary first step, therefore, is helping people to understand that mission is more than evangelism. Unpacking that might mean helping people to unlearn what they have received (or assumed) and labelled and dismissed as the 'social gospel'.

What is mission?

The church's mission is rooted in the *Missio Dei*; that is the calling of Israel to be a light to all nations: 'I will make you as a light for the nations, that my salvation may reach to the end of the earth' (Isaiah.49:6).[1] Christ's commission to his disciples says that they were to be his witnesses to the ends of the earth and the end of time (Matthew 28:18–20; Acts 1:8). Mission expresses the biblical idea of being sent. This is conveyed in the words of Jesus, 'As the Father has sent me, I am sending you' (John 20:21). Eric Wright offers a helpful definition of mission:

> By mission I mean the total calling of the church as it reflects the eternal purpose of God. This involves an upward activity—worship, thanksgiving, intercession, fellowship with God. It also involves an inward aspect—the organisation of individual believers into local churches, their edification or discipling, their care and comfort, their mutual fellowship and training. Finally, it involves an outward activity—witnessing or evangelism, concern and care for the needs of the community, and particularly missionary outreach, a commitment of the resources necessary

> to plant churches among the unreached in the community and among all the peoples of the earth.[2]

Though evangelism is central to mission, mission is more than evangelism. Evangelism is about proclaiming the gospel message and inviting people to believe in Christ for salvation. Mission is a broader term that incorporates the idea of Christian social responsibility. Christians need to co-operate in prayer, planning and participation in the evangelization of the whole world. That work will necessitate a holistic approach to the spiritual, physical and psychological needs of people struggling to survive in adverse political, social, economic and environmental conditions.

Some Christians want to define mission as evangelism because this is their limited theological understanding of mission.[3] Others are in situations that are geared toward evangelism and 'change' is just too much to think about. Many feel that evangelism will be diluted in a wider mission agenda. Largely, in the West (though not exclusively so) the evangelical church is oriented toward evangelism and mission in broader terms is just too daunting to contemplate. It is difficult to get these kinds of churches to consider mission because as far as they are concerned their members already have enough commitments in attending church on Sundays, the mid-week prayer meeting and Bible study, teaching in Sunday school, leading worship, preaching and outreach (usually defined as sharing the message of the gospel and distributing literature that shows the way of salvation). This is essential and vital work and must be continued but it must not be *either* evangelism *or* mission rather it must be mission with evangelism at its core. There are a number of dimensions to missiology.[4]

First and foremost, mission must bear witness to the truth of the gospel, 'that Christ Jesus came into the world to save sinners' (1 Timothy 1:15). This is an apostolic gospel that is doctrinally defined by Scripture, to lead people to faith and wholeness in Christ. This will involve evangelism, including a reasoned defence of the faith (apologetics), and pre-evangelism. Pre-evangelism is about removing obstacles that hinder the proclamation of the gospel. A farmer does not plough a field that is full of boulders. These objects must be removed prior to ploughing and planting seed. Bearing witness to the truth as it is in Christ is both verbal and visual. There is a message to be proclaimed; a message which can be *heard* but there is also a necessity to live in such a way, as individuals and as a community of believers, so as to make it possible for this message to be *seen* as it is lived out in the transformed lives of redeemed people living in harmonious relationship.

This involves demonstrating what it means to be a redeemed, transformed and transformative community. In a sense it is not only about *doing* mission but *being* mission. Mission is not the *raison d'être* of the church. But the church is a community that bears witness to God's glorious grace made manifest in a new order. Mission, in this sense, demonstrates what it means in practice to be a people of integrity, peace and hope in a world that is corrupt, distressed and despairing. Part of the church's mission is to bear testimony to the practical reality of God's unmerited grace by being a people who exercise forgiveness and looking out for the needs of others in the family of God by sharing the resources God has given. The church must work toward the elimination of prejudice and suspicion within its own multi-ethnic communities before it can expect to be heard on this matter by others outside its precincts. In a postmodern age the church must exercise influence not as a domineering or controlling power but rather as a servant. In this way the church is to be both a sign and an agent of God's purposes.

This brings us to the second dimension of mission, namely, the church's role as a servant. Mission must be motivated by genuine compassion. The church must not engage in aiding others only as a means to a greater end. Mission must have no ulterior motive. The church has a role to play in working in development programs with victims of natural catastrophes (drought, flood, famine) and the consequent diseases associated with such phenomena.[5] The church can play an important role in advocating for peaceful solutions to local, national and international conflicts. It can function in the midst of conflict as an agent of practical aid.

Poverty has many forms. It is obviously the lack of food, shelter and clothing. The church's response must address these issues. But poverty is also about lack of opportunity arising out of poor health or poor education. Therefore, mission will include literacy and other educational programs, particularly health education. This is about addressing disadvantage. Many people in the third world have no opportunity to go to school, for reasons of finance, gender (girls), lack of infrastructure and so on. Many, even in the developed world, drop out because they are facing issues in the home or school environment. Here, there is a need for special programs to compensate early school leavers for their lack of educational attainment.

Mission will not neglect those with physical or mental disability. The church also has a particular responsibility to create a society which ministers to the needs of the elderly and vulnerable. Many people today are suffering from stress, anxiety and depression. Suicides arising out of such feelings are all too frequent, especially among the young. One does not necessarily have to have medical expertise to assist those who are mentally afflicted.[6] There are so many opportunities for service that there is no excuse for a church not being active in mission. Each local church must look to the needs of those in the wider community. Where can it serve? God is close to the broken-hearted (Psalm 34:18) and he wants his people involved in binding up their wounds (Psalm 147:3). Whether it is comforting those who are bereaved, working with children at risk or families in tension all can be done to the glory of God as mission. There are ministries to rehabilitate offenders against the law, ministries working with alcoholics, drug addicts and chronic gamblers. This is where the rubber hits the road in terms of mission impacting on society. Mission means reaching out to those who are marginalized, alienated, rejected and despised. The church must minister God's grace to those who need it most.

Thirdly, mission means doing all that can be done to ensure that justice prevails in society. The church has been rightly vocal on many social issues of concern such as promoting and defending family values. It has been articulate on matters such as divorce, abortion and experimentation on early human life. It has not been silent with regard to sexual issues such as fornication, adultery and homosexuality. It has voiced its objections to pornography and the exploitation of women and children. All of this is good in itself but the church is called upon to do more by way of advocating alternatives to economic policies that are likely to increase homelessness. Many people are badly educated, undernourished and unemployed because of greed and exploitation. A society where racism has not been eradicated is underdeveloped. It may be materially wealthy but it is socially and spiritually poor. Why has the church failed to successfully challenge the inexorable build-up of weapons of mass destruction and the increasing arms trade between rich and poor nations which is contributing to the misery of so many? Frankly it is because of a failure to realize that there is a social dimension to the gospel. The church is guilty of privatizing faith and detaching it from these issues. Vested interests have won out over virtuous interests.

Ensuring that justice prevails in society also involves the equitable distribution of the wealth of material resources so that ordinary people can benefit from their national wealth. Thus mission is about contributing to the creation of a society where material resources are understood as part of God's creation. These resources should not be pillaged and plundered by the elite for the accumulation of vast profits. Sadly not only have Christians stood idly by as this exploitation took place but many have actively participated in it. Why is it left to secular activists to engage in raising conservation awareness and working toward the elimination of pollution when the ultimate ecological ethic is rooted in God?[7] Mission will necessitate renouncing greed. The church needs to do all that it can to promote a more restrained enjoyment of material goods by all in such a way that future generations will find life sustainable on earth.

Obviously no local church can engage in *all* of this kind of activity but each church can engage in *some* aspect of it and in so doing its corporate witness will be greatly enhanced. This catalogue of issues is not meant to overwhelm us with the daunting prospect of tackling all of the world's social ills, rather it indicates the almost inexhaustible opportunity to put matters on the agenda and to get involved in cutting edge missional activity.

Thus to pray, 'Your kingdom come', means preaching the gospel to the poor. To pray, 'Your kingdom come', means ministering to the broken-hearted. To pray, 'Your kingdom come', means leading those who are spiritual captives to freedom in Christ. To pray, 'Your kingdom come', means leading the spiritually blind to behold the Lamb of God who takes away the sin of the world. To pray these words means speaking out on behalf of the oppressed. It means working toward a fairer and more just society. To pray these words is not passive. Prayer of this kind is transformative and it enables those who pray in this manner to continue the work of his kingdom.

The church is called to be a prophetic community. Those who work in the cause of the kingdom will encounter the opposition (or at least a lack of sympathy and support) of those who want to protect their own interests. Who has the courage for this sort of mission? Certain sections of the Christian community might well ask if they are fulfilling his mission in this regard. God has invited the church to join him in this great project. As the saying goes, 'familiarity breeds contempt'. Is the Christian community so familiar with this manifesto that it fails to fully realize its radical nature? There are varying degrees of commitment to fulfilling the details of such a manifesto which indicate that if there is not contempt for it then there is complacency about it. God invites the Christian community to play its part in his kingdom enterprise. It needs to make his manifesto its manifesto!

The Nazareth manifesto declares a bias for the poor that the church should never lose sight of. What is good news for the poor if it does not include the alleviation of poverty? The

Christian community cannot turn a blind eye to the miserable conditions under which three quarters of the world's population live their lives. To talk about the redistribution of wealth and the sharing of the world's resources and the elimination of poverty not only sounds unattainable but it also sounds like communism to Christians who have vested interests in the structural inequalities of the economic world.

There is an obligation not only to dare to imagine a radical alternative but to work toward the achievement of such a reality. The utopian dream may not be achievable but there is a duty to seek to eradicate the dystopian nightmare of those enslaved to poverty and all its attendant social evils. The church should work toward a politics of peace and ethical economics.

Spiritual education must be part of the strategy in keeping mission central to church life. Many Christians are unaware of the reality of poverty in this world and will want to respond when informed. We need to be more diligent in finding ways whereby they can give practical expression to that heartfelt desire. But more fundamentally those engaged in the theological training of ministers have a great responsibility to ensure that they convey the message that: 'Missionary theology is not an appendix to biblical theology; it belongs at its very core. No doctrine of God, Christ or the Holy Spirit has been expounded completely according to the Bible until it has established the triune God as the God of mission.'[8]

It is one of God's communicable attributes that he reaches out to redeem the lost. God is a God of truth and mission is about calling people out of false religion, false philosophy and godless ideologies and 'isms'. God is a God of holiness and mission must bear witness to this by warning of the final judgment. God is patient and because he is patient judgment is delayed while his mission is being fulfilled. God is a God of goodness and grace, who is 'rich in mercy' (Ephesians 2:4). Mission must reflect this attribute of God. Because God is love (1 John 4:8, 16) mission will be a loving intervention in the lives of people who need to hear the story of God's love and experience the practical application of that love in acts of kindness and care. God is sovereign and the outworking of his sovereign purposes involves his people engaging in mission. His sovereignty ensures that the outcomes of our missionary endeavours in partnership with him will be in accordance with his will.

God is triune. The Father sent the Son on a mission to redeem the lost. The Son, in turn sent his disciples to extend and complete the mission he commenced. The Holy Spirit enables and assists in the work of mission by bringing conviction of sin. Engaging in mission is being involved in the fulfilment of God's will. Mission is about the restoration of right relationship with God which was lost in the Garden of Eden. Christians are privileged ambassadors engaged in this work of reconciliation. Mission is not only intrinsically connected to the person and work of Christ but also to the person and work of the Holy Spirit whose ministry involves executing the decrees of the Father in this world. The incarnation is a missionary event, for Christ came into the world to save sinners. The gospels record the commencement of Christ's missionary activity. The book of Acts documents the continuation of that mission and the book of Revelation emphasizes the culmination of that mission.

The names of Christ identify his missionary nature. 'Jesus' means Saviour. 'Emmanuel' emphasizes his incarnational missionary journey. 'Master' refers to his missionary message. The 'I am' statements of Christ proclaim his missionary purpose: the shepherd, the door, the living water, the bread of life, the way the truth and the life, the resurrection and the life, the light of the world.

God is a communicating God and there is a gospel message to be communicated. Eric Wright says:

> The central activity of missions is the communication of the gospel. Although Christ healed, cast out demons, raised the dead and fed the hungry, these activities gave way more and more in his second and third years of ministry to teaching. Indeed, the Spirit revealed to John at the beginning of his Gospel that communication was so central to the mission of Christ that one of Christ's most important names is 'Word'. 'In the beginning was the Word, and the Word was with God, and the Word was God.' (John 1:1) ... God has been eternally committed to communication and that communication centres on the incarnate Christ.[9]

Mission today

Today's world cannot be neatly divided into Christian and non-Christian regions. Certainly it has to be acknowledged that the '10/40 Window' remains as a challenge to mission. This is a geographical area which refers to regions of the eastern hemisphere located between ten and forty degrees north of the equator. It has the highest level of socio-economic challenges and least access to the Christian message and Christian resources on the planet. The '10/40 Window' concept brings into the church's radar an area of the world, with great poverty and lack of access to Christian resources. This area encompasses Saharan and North Africa as well as almost all of Asia. Roughly two-thirds of the world's populations live in this region. It is populated by people who are predominantly Muslim, Hindu,

Buddhist, Animist, Jewish or Atheist. Many governments in the '10/40 Window' are formally or informally opposed to Christian work of any kind within their borders. Understandably many Christians want to prioritize mission in this region.

The apostle Paul liked to, 'boldly go where no man has gone before'. He said: 'I make it my ambition to preach the gospel, not where Christ has already been named, lest I build on someone else's foundation, but as it is written, "Those who have never been told of him will see, and those who have never heard will understand."' (Romans 15:20). Such opportunities still exist today but not everybody can avail of them. Not everybody is called to be a 'professional' missionary. Nevertheless we all have a part to play in mission. From a pastoral point of view keeping mission central to church life is essentially about enabling people to identify areas where they can serve in mission. It is about equipping them to fulfil these roles effectively. All believers must be witnesses of the gospel in word and deed. Nobody is exempt from this. People are fearful of participating in mission because they feel under-skilled. Some may be reluctant to be involved in mission because they are ashamed of the gospel and don't want to be associated with, 'that bunch of fundamentalists'. Serious self-examination is required from every believer as a necessary prerequisite to putting mission at the heart of the church.

Theory and practice

A former Prime Minister of Ireland, Dr Garret Fitzgerald, was noted for his great intellect. He is reported to have once said, 'That is all very well in *practice* but how does it work out in *theory*?' Whether he actually said this or not I cannot say for certain, but most people are prepared to believe it. All who remember him are amused by the possibility that it could actually be true because he was a theorist. On one occasion he wore a brown shoe and a black shoe in public. When this was pointed out he made some feeble excuse about it still being dark when he left home and how he didn't want to put on the light which would have disturbed his wife, who was still sleeping. This added to the generally accepted view that he was brilliant but a little out of touch with reality. I wonder if our churches have become like academic academies where learning takes place about mission but evangelism is left to the evangelism team and mission is left to the 'professionals' who occasionally visit our congregations to give power-point presentations, share a brief word from Scripture, tell stories and make subtle financial appeals.

It is easier, in a church context, to arouse interest in mission than it is to stimulate participation in the task of reaching the lost world. Many Christians meditate on and study truth but appear detached from the practical realities of engaging with contemporary culture. Mission is not just a component of the curriculum of Bible colleges and theological seminaries.[10] Mission must be upheld as a core value in the church today. Engaging effectively with our culture will involve a holistic approach to mission because mission involves the whole purpose of God for humanity, including spiritual salvation. This means that Christian mission should encompass issues related to ecology, health, education, social justice (including poverty, race and gender issues) and a host of other issues which intersect with people's lives and concerns.

In every community there are many people who suffer from depression, stress, anxiety and loneliness. Many people experience suicidal thoughts and sadly for some those thoughts are translated into action, often resulting in their deaths. The church must minister to these people. We must bear testimony to the fact that we are a redeemed and transformed community of people living in harmonious relationship with God and each other. We must offer benevolence, blessing and belonging to people who need help and kindness and meaningful relationship.

The world is a global village and no local church ought to be ignorant of or indifferent to the reality of poverty. It is not enough to say we care. Real compassion acts out the love of God in service and sacrificial giving.

The U2 lead singer, Bono, once walked on a stage at a gig and started clapping his hands at intervals of three seconds. He proclaimed to the audience that, 'every 3 seconds someone dies of hunger on this planet'. A witty reply came back from the crowd: 'Then stop clapping your hands, you sadist!' I know some people who were at that event and they felt that Bono was spoiling their party. I wonder if we are like that in the church. Do we resent being presented with statistical data about the reality of poverty? Do we resist the challenge of participating in mission? We are called and commissioned to be partners with God in this project and we need to see it as a privilege and an exciting adventure.

Global village[11]

Here is a peek into the disturbing reality that we find so uncomfortable. If you could fit the entire population of the world into a village consisting of one-hundred people, maintaining the proportions of all the people living on Earth, that village would consist of sixty Asians, eleven Europeans, fourteen Americans (North, Central and South) and fifteen

Africans. There would be fifty women and fifty men. There would be thirty-three 'Christians' (many of whom would be nominal Christians) and sixty-seven non-Christians. Would it surprise you to know that one person would possess 40% of the wealth? In this global village which depicts the reality of world poverty seventeen would be illiterate. Only seven would have a college degree. Twenty-two would own or share a computer. Fifteen would be undernourished. One would be dying of starvation. Looking at the world like this helps us understand the reality of poverty.

But, consider the following. If you woke up this morning in good health, you are better off than one million people, who won't live through the week. If you have never experienced the horror of war, the anguish of prison, the pain of torture or been close to death from starvation then you are better off than five-hundred-million people! If you can go to your place of worship without fear that someone will assault or kill you then you are more privileged than three-billion (that's right) people. If you have food in your fridge, clothes on your back, a roof over your head and a place to sleep, you are wealthier than 75% of the world's population. If you currently have money in the bank or in your wallet or a few coins in your purse, you are one of eight of the privileged few in the world. If your parents are still alive and still married, you are a rare individual.[12]

Such daunting challenges can immobilize us or inspire us. So we need a universal vision but with a particular focus. Nevertheless the question must be asked: 'what are we doing about it?' If the answer to that question is, 'nothing', we are in serious trouble as individuals and as churches. Listen to what Jesus has to say about this:

> When the Son of Man comes in his glory, and all the angels with him, then he will sit on his glorious throne. Before him will be gathered all the nations, and he will separate people one from another as a shepherd separates the sheep from the goats. And he will place the sheep on his right, but the goats on the left. Then the King will say to those on his right, 'Come, you who are blessed by my Father, inherit the kingdom prepared for you from the foundation of the world. For I was hungry and you gave me food, I was thirsty and you gave me drink, I was a stranger and you welcomed me, I was naked and you clothed me, I was sick and you visited me, I was in prison and you came to me.' Then the righteous will answer him, saying, 'Lord, when did we see you hungry and feed you, or thirsty and give you drink? And when did we see you a stranger and welcome you, or naked and clothe you? And when did we see you sick or in prison and visit you?' And the King will answer them, 'Truly, I say to you, as you did it to one of the least of these my brothers, you did it to me.' Then he will say to those on his left, 'Depart from me, you cursed, into the eternal fire prepared for the devil and his angels. For I was hungry and you gave me no food, I was thirsty and you gave me no drink, I was a stranger and you did not welcome me, naked and you did not clothe me, sick and in prison and you did not visit me.' Then they also will answer, saying, 'Lord, when did we see you hungry or thirsty or a stranger or naked or sick or in prison, and did not minister to you?' Then he will answer them, saying, 'Truly, I say to you, as you did not do it to one of the least of these, you did not do it to me.' And these will go away into eternal punishment, but the righteous into eternal life. (Matthew 25:31–41)

Frequently when we partake of the Lord's Supper we read

or recite a passage of Scripture from Paul's first letter to the Corinthians:

> For I received from the Lord what I also delivered to you, that the Lord Jesus on the night when he was betrayed took bread, and when he had given thanks, he broke it, and said, 'This is my body which is for you. Do this in remembrance of me.' In the same way also he took the cup, after supper, saying, 'This cup is the new covenant in my blood. Do this, as often as you drink it, in remembrance of me.' For as often as you eat this bread and drink the cup, you proclaim the Lord's death until he comes. Whoever, therefore, eats the bread or drinks the cup of the Lord in an unworthy manner will be guilty concerning the body and blood of the Lord. Let a person examine himself, then, and so eat of the bread and drink of the cup. (1 Corinthians 11:23–32)

We use this to remind us of our security in Christ and to celebrate the New Covenant. We use it to see what we are doing that is wrong. But there are sins of *omission* as well as *commission* and failing to do good things is sin: 'So whoever knows the right thing to do and fails to do it, for him it is sin' (James 4:17). What would happen if we were to read the passage from Matthew 25 (cited above) at the Lord's Table as an aid to self-examination in the light of Scripture? Probably some well-meaning soul would try to offer an antidote to the 'guilt-trip' by saying, 'There is therefore now no condemnation for those who are in Christ Jesus' (Romans 8:1). There would probably be a sigh of relief from all those who feel that this lets them off the hook. But that verse from Romans does not excuse our apathy in a world of inequalities and injustices and suffering and greed. Christ is saying that his true disciples will be those who care for the destitute. Not just care about them but actually provide practical care. The fruit of true discipleship will be evident in practical ways. How concerned are we really about people's physical wellbeing?

Furthermore how concerned are we about the eternal destiny of those in our world, especially those in our immediate community? There is a story about parents who overheard their five-year-old daughter, Sarah, telling her little friend about Jesus. Sarah told her friend that if she believed in Jesus and prayed he would forgive her sins and she would go to heaven. The little girl was convinced and prayed and then asked, 'Will my mommy go to heaven too?' Sarah replied, 'Yea, if she believes in Jesus, but if you don't want her there don't tell her about Jesus!' I have no doubt that if you tell this story to a group of Christians they will enjoy the humour. But it begs the question: are we telling people about Jesus?

The best way to keep mission central to the life of the church is for the leadership to get in tune with the rhythm of God's heartbeat. Mission is the metronome (the device ticking at a selected rate to mark time for musicians) that helps us measure the pace of progress in God's purposes. In conducting the affairs of the church we must employ diverse gifting to engage harmoniously in producing the majestic melody of mission, to the glory of God.

7

The Rhythm of God's Heartbeat Biblical Perspective on Mission Theology

Our theoretical presuppositions about mission and our theological rationale for mission should be determined by the Word of God. We must allow Scripture to speak for itself as the missionary manual rather than impose our views upon it. Eric Wright says:

> Nothing can be more important than to ensure that our missionary presuppositions reflect the principles of Scripture. This will not be true if theology is ignored, because theology brings us face to face with the principles, parameters and priorities that God has revealed.[1]

Understanding the rhythm of God's heartbeat is about being in tune with his heart and being in touch with what he is doing in contemporary culture. Being missional minded is about seeing as God sees, feeling as God feels and acting as God acts. The heart of God demonstrates that he is a missionary God, seeking to reach a world separated from him.

The apostle John said, 'For God so loved the world, that he gave his only Son, that whoever believes in him should not perish but have eternal life' (John 3:16). This tells us much about the heart of God and the quality of that perfect, sacrificial love.

We need to examine our passions, priorities and lifestyles. If the world is to be reached for Christ we need to share God's heart desire. God is the first and greatest missionary and all of Scripture bears testimony to that. The Bible is the revelation of his unfolding endeavours to reach and redeem the lost. We must begin to realize that mission is not just based on a few proof texts of Scripture rather it is rooted in the compassionate heart of God and evident in all his activity with humanity. Robert Speer comments on the great commission:

> The last command of Christ is not the deep and final ground of the church's missionary duty. That duty is authoritatively stated in the words of the great commission, and it is of infinite consequence to have had it so stated by our Lord Himself. But if these particular words had never been spoken by Him, or if, having been spoken, they had not been preserved, the missionary duty of the church would not be in the least affected. The supreme arguments for missions are not found in any specific words. It is in the very being and character of God that the deepest ground of the missionary enterprise is to be found.[2]

It is good to read books about mission; to have an interest in mission; to be excited about mission; to be stimulated by mission stories; but we need to be aroused from our inertia and motivated to engage in mission.

We are to be spiritually and morally distinctive from the world around us but we are to be physically involved in it. We do and must have contact with the world. The Christian cannot and should not be cloistered away from outsiders in holy huddles and lives of seclusion. Such spiritual enclaves would be a kind of neo-monastic existence. But we must not withdraw from the world for fear of contamination.

Our involvement in the world comes about in a variety of natural and intentional ways. As we interact with the world we have opportunity to bear testimony to the grace of God in word and deed as we bring a Christian perspective to bear in conversations about social and spiritual issues as opportunity allows.

Our example in all things is Christ. We have already noted that he ate with tax collectors and sinners (Matthew 9:11) and how the religious leaders of the day grumbled about that (Luke 19:7). But the writer to the Hebrews informs us that Christ was, 'holy, innocent, unstained, separated from sinners' (Hebrews 7:26). In the same way as Jesus was not of the world his disciples are not of the world. So the permission and privilege of involvement in the world must be balanced with the obligation to be a distinctive community. We should not live according to the values of the world. Our priorities are to be fundamentally different and distinctive. This may bring criticism because non-Christians will resent it when Christians don't join in sinful activity. Thus we may expect a backlash. Peter commented on this:

> For the time that is past suffices for doing what the Gentiles want to do, living in sensuality, passions, drunkenness, orgies, drinking parties, and lawless idolatry. With respect to this they are surprised when you do not join them in the same flood of debauchery, and they malign you (1 Peter 4:3–4).

I wonder how many believers today are maligned for not participating in dubious social practices. We are not to be materialistic by indulging in the carnival of consumerism. We are not to be hedonistic in a heathen world. There are many practical and positive ways in which we can let our light shine. Our good deeds give credibility to the gospel message which we proclaim. The Christian is to be concerned for good works as well as good words. If we are to model the master we must realize that he was compassionate and went about doing good (Acts 10:38).

But there is a difference between the work of secular development agencies and Christian mission. It is not merely that the Christian is motivated by faith. There are Christian charities and mission societies which have a distinctively Christian ethos. The Christian does not have a monopoly on love, compassion, morality and charity. Many non-Christian organizations (either secular or religious) engage in tremendous work for the poor and marginalized of this world. But there is a difference between humanitarianism and Christian mission. We need to ensure that we engage in more than philanthropy. The essential difference is the gospel message of salvation. Christian mission ministers to the soul of humanity and its greatest need: that of a Saviour.

There are certain structures that create inequalities and make life difficult for some people. Their lives will not be radically improved unless such structures are changed and that necessitates social and even political action. It is at this point that Christian opinion diverges. Some will say that we must distinguish between the calling of the Christian citizen to engage in social and political action and the mandate of the church. Others will see the church as an agent of bringing about social reform. The issue is not so much about Christian mission organizations' or para-church agencies' involvement in social and political campaigns and development activity. Rather it is about the church's role in this regard.

The Gospel of John relates how Jesus on one occasion, moved with compassion, healed the sick and fed five thousand people. The crowds wished to make him king, undoubtedly supposing he would redress the injustices of the Roman occupation. But Jesus withdrew from them and later told them to seek food that endures to eternal life (John 6:14–15; 25–27). Certain sections of evangelicalism identify this as a text which teaches that the church's mission is *essentially* spiritual and *incidentally* material. In other words the Church's duty is to communicate the gospel message of salvation and lead people to faith in Christ and anything else is *relatively* unimportant. According to this view social action is not essential to the church's role and is, therefore supplementary. These people will argue that Christ's priority was spiritual, not physical. They will point out that Jesus could have gained enormous popularity if he had been willing to respond to the people's political agenda but he resisted. They will deduce from this that we must do likewise by resisting such temptations and being alert to the danger of being used to further the world's agenda, even when aspects of that agenda are good causes. They will tell us that history abounds with sad examples of the church allowing herself to be hijacked in this way.

Though Christian mission may have (indeed should have) a humanitarian dimension it is not humanitarianism. Mission is not essentially about development in the sense that it is not about bringing the benefits of the developed world to the underdeveloped or developing world, though that may be a consequence or outcome of mission activity it is not the motivating factor. Neither is it the benchmark for determining the success of missionary endeavour. Mission is not a process of civilizing or westernizing other cultures. It is not a means of socialization. Mission must be a Christ-centred intentional process of communicating the gospel in word and deed. The missionary mandate is about living out the Great Commission with the passion of the Great Commandment. Let us, therefore remind ourselves of the words of Scripture. The Great Commission is:

> 'All authority in heaven and on earth has been given to me. Go therefore and make disciples of all nations, baptizing them in the name of the Father and of the Son and of the Holy Spirit, teaching them to observe all that I have commanded you. And behold, I am with you always, to the end of the age.' (Matthew 28:18–20).

We must bear in mind that this has not been rescinded and the task will only be completed when all have heard. The Great Commandment is:

> 'You shall love the Lord your God with all your heart and with all your soul and with all your mind. This is the great and

> first commandment. And a second is like it: You shall love your neighbour as yourself. On these two commandments depend all the Law and the Prophets.' (Matthew 22:37–40).

This is to be the regulating principle of all mission activity. There is a danger that mission may be perceived as the spiritual colonization of non-Christian cultures. This politicizes and polarizes communities and gives impetus to polemical rhetoric and nationalistic resistance.

Nevertheless, in certain contexts, the gospel has unavoidable political implications. Sometimes those who cross geographical and cultural boundaries to preach the gospel where Christ is not known (or where little is known of Christ) are insensitive or indifferent to the new environment. Often it is not the message of the gospel that offends but the method of disseminating it. The missionary frontier is the line which separates belief from unbelief, but it is also the line between false and true religion.

All missionary activity should remain rooted in Scripture. This will involve remaining faithful to the biblical witness as a whole. The church's mission is about presenting the unique and universal claims of Jesus. The church's mission is about calling people to repentance, faith and community relationship.

The truth is that most Christians are not living for Christ but for themselves. Paul challenges the Corinthian believers with these words, 'and he died for all, that those who live might no longer live for themselves but for him who for their sake died and was raised' (2 Corinthians 5:15). Just as Christ was completely obedient to his Father's will and just as Paul lived solely for God's purposes and glory (Philippians 1:21) so we too must live for God. Is this too high a calling? Is this fanaticism? Is this just for Jesus and Paul and an elite group of devotees? Or is this the attitude that God wants from all of us? I think we know the answer to these questions. We need to forsake self-centred living for the sake of the kingdom of God.

Christ's mandate to us is a missionary mandate: 'As the Father has sent me, even so I am sending you' (John 20:21). If we are to keep mission central to church life we must keep it central to our preaching and programs. We must not allow mission to be perceived as something peripheral. We must dispel the notion that mission is an optional extra for Christians. It is not an elective element of the spiritual life rather it is (or ought to be) the core constituent of faithful living.

Mission did not begin with the incarnation. Christ's first coming was not plan 'B' to redress the fall of man. The missionary heart of God and his missionary purpose is revealed from Genesis, right throughout the Old and New Testaments up to the book of Revelation.

To some the Great Commission is the only known reference to the subject of mission in Scripture. Certainly it marks a turning point in redemptive history where the Messiah's kingdom had dawned in new power. But it is not the beginning of mission. There is an interesting connection between the opening and closing of Matthew's gospel. Matthew opens his gospel account with the genealogy of Christ in the line of Abraham and David: 'The book of the genealogy of Jesus Christ, the son of David, the son of Abraham' (Matthew 1:1–2). This reference to Abraham at the beginning of Mathew's gospel reminds us of the promise that through Abraham's offspring, 'all the nations of the earth shall be blessed' (Genesis 26:4). When we look at this promise it is clear that God was/is interested in the rest of the world also. In the closing words of Matthew's gospel we find Jesus sending his disciples to all nations: 'Go therefore and make disciples of all nations' (Mathew 28:18).

In order to trace mission in the Old Testament it might be helpful to think of a piece of orchestral music. Often the composer will weave a motif through the whole work which is recognizable from time to time. This is the essence of the piece. It might be introduced by the violins, picked up later by the oboes and again included in the brass section. Each time we hear it we say, 'There it is again!' In a similar way the mission motif is woven into Scripture. Abraham was the father of the Jews, God's chosen people. They were chosen to be a light to all nations. Initially God chose a man and extended the blessing to his family, his clan, his tribe, all twelve tribes and now, through Christ the blessing is extended to all nations. The blessings of salvation were never intended only for Jews. God's ultimate plan includes all nations, every tribe and tongue.

So right from the first book of the Bible the desire of God's heart (that all nations of the earth will be blessed with salvation) is clearly expressed. Here we see the first note in that motif being struck. This is the keynote. This motif was to be heard again and again at the most critical times in redemptive history. The blessing promised not only *to* but *through* Abraham was for all nations. This blessing was to be received through Christ. It is received through faith:

> Just as Abraham 'believed God, and it was counted to him as righteousness' Know then that it is those of faith who are the sons of Abraham. And the Scripture, foreseeing that God would justify the Gentiles by faith, preached the gospel beforehand to Abraham, saying, 'In you shall all the nations be blessed.' So then,

> those who are of faith are blessed along with Abraham, the man of faith. (Galatians 3:6–9).

Look at how Solomon prays for non-Jews who visit the temple:

> Likewise, when a foreigner, who is not of your people Israel, comes from a far country for your name's sake (for they shall hear of your great name and your mighty hand, and of your outstretched arm), when he comes and prays toward this house, hear in heaven your dwelling place and do according to all for which the foreigner calls to you, in order that all the peoples of the earth may know your name and fear you, as do your people Israel, and that they may know that this house that I have built is called by your name (1 Kings 8:41–43).

See how this is similar to a declaration in Isaiah:

> And the foreigners who join themselves to the LORD, to minister to him, to love the name of the LORD, and to be his servants, everyone who keeps the Sabbath and does not profane it, and holds fast my covenant—these I will bring to my holy mountain, and make them joyful in my house of prayer; their burnt offerings and their sacrifices will be accepted on my altar; for my house shall be called a house of prayer for all peoples.' (Isaiah 56:6–7).

Mission is what the Bible is all about. Mission is the church in motion to the rhythm of God's heartbeat. God's heart is a missionary heart and the hearts of Christians need to be like his. In the light of all of this there can be no doubt that God wanted (and still wants) the message of salvation spread to all nations through his chosen people. The Old Testament sets forth the missionary purpose of God. The church needs to be converted to mission!

Dvorak's *New World Symphony* is my favourite piece of classical music. I have listened to it so many times that I sometimes find myself humming it. We need to listen to the mission motif in God's Word so that it becomes a familiar tune that touches our hearts. We cannot allow mission to be marginalized in our churches. It must be kept central. Mission must be returned to its rightful place at the heart of the church. Martin Goldsmith speaks of the situation like this:

> … mission appears to be an optional extra to be indulged in by those who are spiritually keen and who happen to be interested in it. Furthermore, those who try to stimulate a belief that world mission is an integral part of the life of the church find that such exhortations fail to make much impact.[3]

Trevor Harris has put his finger on the problem: '… part of the problem is that our churches are failing to teach worldwide mission as a basic theme of the whole Bible.'[4] A church should not become inward looking. But in reality the self-centred ethos which pervades society is becoming increasingly prevalent in the church. Harris points out that a genuine concern for mission is based on a deep sense of personal indebtedness to Christ and an appreciation of the great cost of our redemption.[5]

All people are created in the image of God. This image is reflected clearer (or ought to be) in those who are called Christians. This image is not only reflected in who we are but also in what we do. As such, those who are called by his name are to seek to accomplish his purpose and to serve his mission. Christopher Wright says that it is 'not just that the Bible contains a number of texts which happen to provide a rationale for missionary endeavours but that the whole Bible is itself a missional phenomenon.'[6] He points out that, from the opening accounts in Genesis, God is revealed as one who seeks relationship with his creation.[7] Thus, after the fall of man into sin, the stage is set for the rest of the Bible to describe and recount God's single-minded purpose to reconcile his creation to himself. This is a crucial spiritual perspective.[8]

As already stated the mission of God is clearly expressed in the call of Abraham recorded in Genesis chapter twelve. While God's words of promise certainly include rich blessings for him and his family, the key to understanding their missional significance lies in the purpose clauses. God's promise was given, 'so that' (Genesis 12:2) all the people of the earth would be blessed.[9] Israel was to be God's missionary people to the rest of the world and that plan is still being rolled out: 'Now we are Abraham's seed by faith, and the earth's families will be blessed only if we go to them with the gospel. This is God's plain purpose.'[10]

So it should be clear by now that an informed biblical missional view goes beyond the frequently quoted commissioning passages to a more comprehensive perspective from Genesis to Revelation.

The incarnation literally embodies the heart of God for mankind and is the missionary model for reaching the world with the gospel. Christ's ministry was missional and focused on establishing the kingdom of God:

> It is the glory of God's kingdom being launched on earth as

> in heaven, generating a new state of affairs in which the power of evil has been decisively defeated, the new creation has been decisively launched, and Jesus' followers have been commissioned and equipped to put that victory and that inaugurated new world into practice.[11]

We are ambassadors for Christ. One author has said, 'we cannot be ambassadors for a kingdom that does not have our full allegiance'[12] Christians must have a missional perspective and be the people God intends them to be. Robert Coleman expresses it like this:

> Christian disciples are sent, men and women—sent out in the same work and world evangelism to which the Lord was sent, and for which He gave His life. Evangelism is not an optional accessory to our life. It is the heartbeat of all that we are called to be and do. It is the commission of the church which gives meaning to all else that is undertaken in the name of Christ. With this purpose clearly in focus, everything which is done and said has the glorious fulfillment in God's redemptive purpose.[13]

John Piper points out that the goal of mission is to bring people into the worship of God and sees mission as a natural outcome of worship. He says, 'Missions begins and ends in worship.'[14] The church exists to worship God, to fellowship with God's people, to disciple believers, to minister to the needs of those in the church and last (but not least) to engage in evangelism.

Ministering to the needs of its members is essential to a church's health and survival. This does not mean that all activity should be focused on caring for its own membership. We must go beyond maintenance mode and be intentionally missional. Mission is essentially a work of the Holy Spirit and he is the Spirit of truth and holiness and will not be involved in activity that is untrue or unholy.

Contemporary culture presents many opportunities for the entrance of the gospel. Today's cultural setting bears similarities with that of the early church. Christ ministered at a time when institutional religion had virtually collapsed. The legalistic rituals of the Pharisees created a dead spiritual environment but there was a surge in spiritual interest and many were searching for God.

Our time is a time when interest in spirituality is rising and, paradoxically, interest in the Christian church is in rapid decline. So each church must find ways of having meaningful interaction with those outside the church. But this must be done without capitulating to the prevailing culture. The problem with the church abstaining from involvement in social issues is that it does not help to bridge the credibility gap between the church and the world.

8

Following Carey: The Contemporary Challenge

There is a place in Co. Limerick, in Ireland called, 'Plassey'. It is an old and enchanting landed estate of magnificent beauty accessed by a riverbank walk. Once frequented by generations of locals it is now the campus of the University of Limerick. In my youth it was an angler's paradise, a lovers retreat, a place where children frolicked in the summer sun and families had picnics.

Among the young lovers who dreamed of their future lives together, as they walked hand in hand, were my sweetheart and I. We were young believers in love with Christ and with each other. Often we sat in a favourite spot in the shade beneath the canopy of mature beeches and elms with our bare feet dangling in the cool stream of the River Maigue. Around that time I read the story of Sadhu Sundar Singh, the Indian Sikh who converted to Christ and suffered rejection and persecution for his newfound faith in Jesus. I also read a biography of the Baptist missionary to India, William Carey. We talked about them and their courage and the mystical land of India. Our hearts were excited with the idea that God had plans for us that would one day allow us to follow in Carey's footsteps to minister in India.

Plassey was once the Ballykilty estate and manor house owned by Thomas McMahon, until it was acquired by Robert Clive and took on its peculiar name. The story of how it came to be called 'Plassey' is interesting. On 23rd of June, 1757 Robert Clive (an officer in the British army) led the final battle in the conquest of India, which took place in the village of Plassey, near Kolkata. The outcome of this decisive conflict determined India's place in the British Empire and secured great wealth for Clive.

On his return to England in 1760 he received a cordial welcome from King George II and shortly afterwards was conferred with an honorary degree from Oxford. Yet he was denied the honour of an English title for his loyal service to the Empire. Instead he would be granted an Irish title, which (unlike an English one) did not entitle the holder to a seat in the House of Lords. To qualify for his Irish title he first had to purchase an estate in Ireland. The reason for this lukewarm reception for the homecoming hero

Plassey House, subsequently occupied by a succession of residents, situated on the campus of the University of Limerick

appears to be that he fell out of favour with several directors of the East India Company.

The retired military officer bought properties in Limerick and Clare consisting of several thousands of acres in a disjointed estate, thus securing an appropriate holding for the new landlord to become, 'Baron Clive of Plassey, Co. Clare, Ireland'.[15]

Continuity with Carey

William Carey (1761–1834) was founder of the Baptist Missionary Society, with thirteen other men, in 1792. His conviction that the gospel should be made known throughout the world led him to set sail for India the following year, never to return to his native England. For over forty years he engaged in preaching, lecturing, translating and publishing. He had many heart-breaking disappointments which tested his faith. But through it all he proved that God is faithful to those who obey his call. The impact of his work is evident today on the sub-continent and beyond. Many Indian Christians today are spreading the gospel in neighbouring countries that are hostile to the gospel, such as Myanmar (formerly Burma).

Mission today

Today India does not welcome missionaries. So those from outside the country, who desire to spread the gospel in that land, cannot apply for a visa as a 'missionary' because it would not be granted. Carey and his contemporaries had to contend with the hostility of the East India Company. They had the right to grant or refuse permission to reside in India and they did not want missionaries.[16] On that score not much has changed in over two-hundred-and-fifty years.

What is the state of mission in this post-Carey world and how can we best imitate Carey's example in mission? Today's world (as distinct from Carey's) cannot be as easily or neatly divided into Christian and non-Christian regions. The contemporary missionary frontier is not framed by longitude or latitude. Rather it is the line that separates belief from unbelief. Most communities in Western culture now have many Asians (including Indians) living among them.

An inspiring experience

In a visit to Serampore University (where Carey was the first principal, 1818–1832) I saw the desk on which he translated the Scriptures into many Indian languages. People often quote Carey: 'Expect great things from God, attempt great things for God', but he was certainly a man who practiced that in his life and it is a challenge to all of us. I felt ashamed of how little I had achieved and my lack of vision. Is there reluctance on the part of God's people today to take the gospel to distant and difficult places?

William Carey's desk at Serampore University

Previous generations have made heroic sacrifices to enter the mission field. When a missionary left his native homeland it was with a certain knowledge that he would be overseas for many years and might not ever return. Such journeys took several months. Correspondence between mission field and home for Carey took eighteen months to complete the circle. These were the days before flights, cheap air-fares, email, internet, mobile phones, smart phones, laptop computers, air-conditioning, effective medications against tropical diseases and CNN and Sky News on television. It is a sad fact that many Christian people today have no interest in what is happening beyond the boundaries of their narrow horizons.

The greatest obstacle to be overcome in fulfilling the missionary mandate is not opposition from those outside the church but rather the selfish indifference of God's people. A church devoid of missionary vision is a flickering light in danger of being snuffed out.

How can we best follow Carey today?

The apostle Paul urged the Corinthians, 'Be imitators of me, as I am of Christ' (1 Corinthians 11:1). The word 'imitators' here literally means 'followers'. Following Carey means imitating him. We can do this confidently because he imitated Christ. Christ was a missionary who left heaven and came to earth. Jesus left the realms of glory to be born in lowly circumstances. He left the mansion of heaven to be born in a manger and live much of his life as a homeless person. Jesus became poor so that those who believe in him might become rich. When we think of what Jesus set aside in order that we might become rich it is quite astonishing. He set aside his privileged place and position in heaven. In the light of this, Christian complacency about mission is an offence to God. Everything in the humiliation of Christ is for our sakes. He left heaven so that we could go to heaven. He was rejected so that we might be accepted. He was born in flesh so that we might be born of the Spirit. He became a servant so that we might become sons. He died so that we might have eternal life. These truths demand our attention and call for a response.

If we are called to follow the example of Carey what attitudes must we cultivate and what actions must we emulate? It was Carey's vision to reach the lost in India that put mission back on the spiritual agenda in a church that had lost this vision. Following Carey will mean keeping the idea of mission central to church life.

Carey was focused, determined and consciously dependant on God. His commitment to the gospel was sacrificial. The world was opening up at the time of Carey; new lands were being discovered. This new geographical frontier presented new opportunities and new challenges for the spread of the gospel. Today we are in a new frontier situation with mission in a postmodern world and a new pioneering attitude is needed to engage with and evangelize this world. Thus the gospel needs to be translated afresh in this generation with the vision and values that inspired and motivated Carey.

Ironically, Carey faced more opposition from within the church than the world. But he sought to develop understanding as a basis for supporting the work. He did not blaze a trail on his own, though he might have been tempted to do so. We might tend to see Carey as a trailblazer but he saw himself as a plodder, 'If anyone should think it worth his while to write my life, if he give me credit for being a plodder, he will describe me justly. I can plod … to this I owe everything.'[17]

The situation in India today is that 3%-6% of the population is deemed to be Christian, depending on how one counts heads.[18] The threats to the health of the church in India are similar to those things which threaten the health of the church in the West: nominalism, syncretism, pluralism and ecumenism. As India aspires to a Western economic model of development we can expect materialism to be added to this list.

The missionary enterprise undertaken by Carey involved great personal sacrifice. How many today are willing to put mission before their own interests, careers and comforts? Carey had an unshakeable conviction that the gospel needed to be preached throughout the world. He let no discouragement stand in his way. In seeking how we might best follow Carey we must look to the God in whom Carey believed. His disappointments and heartbreaks served to refine his faith by fire. His was a life invested in God and his legacy to mission is very significant because there are now large numbers of Indian missionaries in other parts of Asia and beyond.

Following Carey must mean a willingness to bear the reproach of the cross. A verse of Scripture that inspired and motivated Carey was, 'Therefore let us go to him outside the camp and bear the reproach he endured' (Hebrews 13:13). This sacrificial attitude was evident in every aspect of Carey's life. His desire to identify with Christ and to proclaim Christ was paramount.

When Carey was a schoolteacher he was often in tears when teaching geography because he was aware that many people in the world were lost souls. Today there is paganism all around us. Not, necessarily the crude variety of idol worship evident in primitive societies but certainly an idolization of things that displace God. But how do we respond? Do we see them as Carey saw them? Sadly, many do not. The world map he made for his classroom wall had statistics added regularly (population, religion etc.) and this map became his prayer chart. He began to see the world as God sees it and he began to love the world as God loves it and he decided to follow Jesus, who was the greatest missionary! Part of the problem is that eternal judgment and hell are not given proportionate emphasis in preaching today. As a consequence the church does not properly understand the seriousness of the situation.

Following Carey will involve obedience to God. He read a pamphlet written by Andrew Fuller: 'It is the duty of those who are entrusted with the Gospel to endeavour to make it known among the nations' and was persuaded to fulfil that duty. He understood that those who are called and converted to Christ are also commissioned. For Jesus commanded (not advised), 'Go therefore and make disciples of all nations, baptizing them in the name of the Father and of the Son and of the Holy Spirit, teaching them to observe all that I have commanded you' (Matthew 28:20). That commission has not been rescinded.

Carey responded to the call of the Lord in spite of the fact that there would be killer tropical diseases like malaria as well as cholera and dysentery to contend with. These diseases killed many of his contemporaries and colleagues. There would be financial difficulties, language barriers, translation problems. He published: '*An enquiry into the obligations of Christians to use means for the conversion of the heathens*' (known simply as *Enquiry*). Obedience and obligation were central themes in *Enquiry*; themes that need to be stressed again today. Carey was resilient and courageous in the face of adversity and in this he is an example to all believers today. In faith he left family, friends and fatherland like the patriarch, Abraham. In doing this he was following the Lord, whom he loved. He once said, 'Few people know what may be done, till they try and persevere in what they have undertaken.'[19]

The Dalits

The work that Carey commenced is continuing but by no means complete in the land of India (or, indeed in any land).

But in the Indian context the fields are white unto harvest. The caste system causes complications for those involved in evangelism in that land. But it is only the power of the gospel that can deliver people from the spiritual darkness which is so evident in Hinduism and its caste system.

There are approximately 200 million Dalits (outcasts) in India. They have been outcasts for centuries. They live in appalling conditions and are deemed by the *dharma* (Hindu moral law) to be defiled from birth. If they work at all it is for the higher castes that view them with disdain and treat them contemptuously. They engage in menial labour such as sweeping the streets, removing the carcasses of dead animals and cleaning toilets. The Dalits have no occupational choice and are not adequately compensated for their work. They are relegated to life outside the boundaries of civilized human society. They are the untouchable, social lepers of India. Their culture is despised and they are deprived of housing and education.

The rising tide of economic prosperity in India will not lift the Dalits boats. No matter how prosperous India becomes a Dalit will always be a Dalit. It will take the transforming power of the gospel to change this. These people are susceptible to disease, suffer from malnutrition and sometimes starve to death. They are an oppressed and powerless people characterized by hopelessness. They believe that they are under such conditions because of their faults in a previous life. They believe the more severe the conditions into which they are born the greater the possibility of being elevated to a higher form of existence in a future life. Because of this they tend to be fatalistically resigned to their circumstances. Therefore they accept servile work under humiliating, degrading and exploitative conditions. The standard of living has not improved for Dalits in India's post-independence era. It is wonderful when Dalits are converted to Christ but in Indian culture they remain Dalits.

The spread of the gospel and the creation of Christian communities will inevitably assist in the subversion of political and religious structures and dominant cultural customs as it facilitates the liberation and transformation of people's lives. The gospel is subversive and radical but we have allowed it to become conservative. The gospel must enable Dalits to find their identity, dignity and freedom as members of the family of God. Christians in such a context must work toward a more egalitarian social order. Casteism must be rejected in the creation of alternative Christian communities (churches). To the world this kind of interference is deemed to be postcolonial anathema because the world professes that all cultures must be respected.

Christians who resist the saffronisation of society (i.e. the move toward a traditional Hindu society) in India are resented as colonialists and sometimes suffer severe consequences but they have not only the right to resist and oppose such moves but the moral duty to do so.

The magnitude of the poverty (illiteracy, unemployment etc.) faced by Dalits is difficult for people in the West to comprehend. The Dalits have been conditioned within the context of an oppressive religious framework to think of themselves as sub-human. The gospel can address their psychological condition and reconstruct their psyches, thereby liberating them from feelings of inferiority and shame. The gospel proclaims in this context that their condition is neither natural nor willed by God. It is rather the yoke of religious, cultural and political oppression.

To the shame of Christianity it has to be acknowledged that

Dalits suffered discrimination at the hands of Christians. A policy of apartheid was applied whereby they were obliged to sit separately from other Christians in church buildings. They could receive communion only after higher caste Christians and they had to have separate grounds for burial.

Proclaiming the gospel in such a context will necessarily involve rejecting as false the world-view of *karmasamsara* (successive rebirths based on karma). It will also involve a rejection of the notion of a hierarchical society based on the caste system which claims divine origin. Will this offend? Yes! Is this dangerous? Yes! Is this radical? Yes! Is this subversive? Yes! Is it the gospel? Yes! This is not a 'social gospel' but in certain contexts the gospel will have unavoidable social implications.

Postmodernists say that Christianity is an oppressive metanarrative ('meta' = great; 'narrative' = story) but Christianity in such a context is not exploitative but potentially liberating and profoundly relevant. Imagine what the grace of the gospel can do in such circumstances. Christians must re-imagine the gospel in all its potency as a force for individual and societal transformation. The gospel in such a context must offer emancipation and alleviation of poverty. It is our responsibility in the West to assist as best we can to that end. Surely the gospel demands our solidarity with such people.

The oppressors of the Dalit people also need to be set free from the ideation that binds them to their place in this oppressive system. Only the gospel can do this. Until the caste system is abolished there can be no freedom for Dalits. Until then a (*bhangi*) sweeper must scavenge because he is not allowed find alternative employment. But the caste system has its vested interests.

The Dalit people need to be respected and positively affirmed in counter-cultural Christian communities. The gospel can be both liberating and empowering for the Dalits only when others in society are also transformed by the gospel. Dalits need to be set free from their superstitious view that their suffering is atonement. Mission directed towards Dalits is not just about social and economic improvement, it is also about the emancipation of minds that have been enslaved to the cultural norms and the healing of hearts that have been wounded.

The church must preach salvation: by grace alone, through faith alone in Christ alone. It must proclaim how Christ's death secures the salvation of those who believe. It must proclaim biblical doctrine and hold forth the eschatological hope of all believers. But the church must not over-spiritualize (allegorize) the Nazareth Manifesto and eviscerate it of its potency.[20]

The caste system remains a challenge in the Indian Christian context. The Christian church has, in the past, capitulated to a form of syncretism which discriminated against the Dalits. All this was a serious departure from the scriptural values of Carey. It is clear that the egalitarian principles of the gospel (that we are all one in Christ) is attractive to Dalits because it is liberating but it is equally clear that it is perceived as a threat to the higher castes, who have a vested interest in preserving the status quo.

But the story of Krishna Pal shows what the gospel can do. Krishna Pal, the first convert in Carey's mission was a carpenter. His daughter (a Christian) married the first Brahmin (highest caste) convert. One of the missionaries wrote in a letter home that this 'was a glorious triumph over caste.' The Christian funerals in Carey's day were a great testimony to unity and equality among Christians. One such burial, of a Bengali Christian, was public evidence of the power of the gospel.

Officiating at that funeral were Marshman (fellow missionary), Felix (Carey's son), a former Hindu (Brahmin) and a Muslim. The local Hindus would have nothing to do with it but they witnessed the unifying love of Christ. Christian unity was also evident at public baptisms.

The torch that Carey carried to the Indian sub-continent is still burning brightly. Many have lit their torches from that flame and spread the fire throughout the land. But we are still facing an unfinished task in India and other lands. Who will heed the call to go with the gospel in all its potent force as a redeeming and transformative power?

9

China: Changing Contours

The church in China is beginning to cast off its chains and it is emerging as a powerful force for change. Is this phenomenon likely to ultimately transform the communist culture of a repressive regime into a more open and tolerant society?

Article 13 of the Constitution of the Republic of China provides that the people shall have freedom of religious belief. Whereas the constitution provides for freedom of religious belief the government restricts religious practice to government-sanctioned organizations and registered places of worship and controls the growth and scope of the activity of religious groups.

Despite formal recognition of religious liberty, religious freedom is accorded little respect in China. Every year since 1999 the U.S. State Department has designated China as a country of particular concern with regard to religious freedom. Anecdotal accounts through clandestine mission agencies report widespread abuse of human rights with regard to religious freedom, including 'disappearances', imprisonment and torture.

Many Chinese people today still regard the militantly atheist Mao Zedong as a national hero. Mao detested religion almost as much as capitalism and was responsible for the execution of clergy, the expulsion of foreign missionaries and the destruction of churches.

But China is now undergoing a new kind of revolution not just in terms of phenomenal economic growth and rapid development but also in the growth of religion, particularly Christianity. One could be cynical and say that the pace of change is driving people to seek the consolations of religion in new communities. But whatever the reason it is a new reality that cannot be denied.

Official Chinese government statistics indicate that the number of Christians rose from fourteen million in 1997 to twenty-one million in 2006, with an estimated fifty-thousand Protestant churches and forty-six hundred Catholic Churches.[1]

The government incorporated religious freedom into its constitution in 1982, although it restricted worship to five official religions: Buddhism, Taoism, Islam, Protestantism and Catholicism—each overseen by a 'Patriotic Association'.

These statistics do not include house churches or the underground Catholic Church, believed to be larger than the official one. One source suggests, 'A conservative guess is that there are at least sixty-five million Protestants in China and twelve-million Catholics—more believers than there are members of the Communist Party. Some local Christians think that the flock is well over one hundred million.'[2]

Official figures indicate that there are about twenty-five million Muslims in China. This is likely to be an underestimate.

But even if that number is taken to be the real figure, China has almost as many Muslims as Saudi Arabia and almost twice the number of the European Union's twenty-seven countries. In the Xinjaing Province the mosques have so much control that the state government is worried about Muslim separatism. In a few decades from now China could well be the world's largest Muslim nation as well as the biggest Christian one!

With regard to first place as a Christian nation (speaking strictly of numbers of adherents rather than the institutions of state reflecting this) China could well have competition from India. In the sub-continent the number of Christians is estimated variously at between three per cent and six per cent. This means that there are between thirty-million and sixty-million Christians in India, depending on how the head-count is conducted. But the numbers of Christians is growing rapidly. One state in India (Nagaland) is close to one-hundred per cent Christian, which is all the more remarkable when one considers the fact that a couple of generations ago they were a tribal people who practiced head-hunting! There are elderly people still living in Nagaland who engaged in this activity. But they have gone from head-hunting to church-planting.

There is a Protestant university in China, close to the North Korean border. The Fengcheng Fellowship of house churches (based in the Henan Province) is an association of small autonomous churches which claims to have ten million members.[3]

But the leader of the Fengcheng Fellowship, Zhang Rongliang, has been in and out of prison since the 1970s. China is nervous about independent thought and organization. This is also evident in the way China has relentlessly persecuted the Falun Gong cult.

Christianity is viewed with suspicion by the Chinese authorities because it seems to be a force for change and there is hard-line resistance to it. Many of the protesters at Tiananmen Square in 1989 have become Christians. The authorities think that Pope John Paul II played a significant role in the disintegration of the Soviet Union. Mistrust thrives in such an environment.

The house-church movement in China is spreading rapidly. This is partly due to the fact that the Chinese government has set an informal limit of twenty-five people for an unauthorized religious gathering. Thus it is forced to replicate itself in cell-like structures in an ever increasing web. These churches are autonomous and self-governing but they are associated under the Fengcheng Fellowship umbrella and are almost a quasi-political organization akin to an indigenous Non Governmental Organization (NGO). They have pastors, schools, libraries and even some unofficial seminaries.

There is no doubt that much of the opposition to the house church movement is politically or religiously motivated. But that is not always the case. Rather it can sometimes be the outcome of more pragmatic considerations. For example, when twenty-five people (or more) gather at a person's apartment for prayer and Bible study they take the parking spaces of residents who become frustrated and report the matter to the police. The police arrive, disperse the group, take the names of those in attendance and perhaps make some arrests. The same thing sometimes happens when these groups of Christians sing hymns in an apartment and the occupants of neighbouring apartments complain about the disturbance.

On moral issues such as abortion (which is routine in China) these churches are united in their understanding of the sanctity of life and disseminate this in their teaching. The regime seems to be increasingly accepting of the idea that a moral code can act as a cohesive force in constructing a harmonious society. But some hardliners in the regime are wary that such a force could undermine the communist ideology and destabilize society.

In October 2007 the Communist Party amended its constitution which urged members to 'rally religious believers in making contributions to economic and social development.'[4] Thus the Chinese government seems to be edging towards acceptance of Christianity as part of its progress toward modernization. Whereas the conventional, mainstream denominational church with its stained glass windows and pews is in decline in Europe the church in China is new and vibrant and is seen as part of a new order rather than an institution of the old regime.

The world is aware of the astonishing and rapid transformation of socio-economic development in China. The world is aware (and somewhat concerned) that such a political regime is emerging as an economic superpower. But there is less awareness of the profound changes taking place in the contours of the religious landscape within this Asian nation. The process of transformation is well under way as Christianity continues to win hearts and minds. But as the balance of power shifts it remains to be seen if this process will radically alter the political reality in China or meet with resistance and repression.

10

A Call for Holistic Mission

Mission needs to be understood within its biblical and historical context. It is not necessarily limited to distant lands and foreign peoples. Mission can take place in any local community. What does Scripture say about holistic mission? What light can history shed on holistic mission? How can we conduct holistic mission within our local community? Is international mission still feasible? All Christians agree that the church has a missionary purpose but what constitutes mission is debatable. One side of the debate claims that the church's mission is essentially evangelism; that is leading people to faith in Christ. But the other side emphasizes the need to care for the poor and social action which addresses the causes of poverty and the suffering it produces. Which of these positions is valid? The answer is that they are both valid. They ought not to be mutually exclusive positions.

Effective mission is naturally holistic as it addresses people's spiritual and temporal needs. John Stott has said:

> A Christianity which has lost its vertical dimension has lost its salt and is not only insipid in itself, but useless to the world. But a Christianity which would use the vertical preoccupation as a means to escape from its responsibility for and in the common life of man is a denial of the incarnation.[1]

Evangelism is the announcement of the good news of Jesus Christ. Mission is that and more. It is about social justice and responsible Christian participation in society. It is wrong to focus on either one or the other. They belong together. In the past the church has erred by focusing too much on either one or the other. We cannot separate evangelism and social action. Together they constitute mission and wherever it is conducted with these dual strands working in harmony the results are evident in many conversions. If we focus on the proclamation of the gospel alone we are failing to conduct mission. If we focus on the practical demonstration of the gospel alone then we are failing to conduct mission. It is not even that 'proclamation' and 'demonstration' work alongside each other. Rather they are both an integral part of mission.

If we are to understand mission there are some important biblical terms which need to be clarified. They are 'gospel', 'kingdom', 'mission' and 'salvation'. The gospel is, of course, the good news about Jesus Christ coming as Saviour and Lord. It contains a message of salvation and an invitation to submit to the lordship of Christ. So it is not surprising that our understanding of the kingdom of God and salvation is central to the nature of the gospel. The kingdom of God has, through the centuries, been interpreted in many different ways, influencing how the gospel and ultimately mission are perceived. To appreciate the holistic nature of mission it is necessary to understand the comprehensiveness of the terms, gospel, kingdom and salvation.

The kingdom is often perceived as an inner spiritual experience. Here the gospel is understood as an invitation to personal salvation, and mission is exclusively about the saving of individual souls. The kingdom is often perceived as a future heavenly state. Here the gospel is seen as an invitation to eternal life and mission is primarily about preparing the church to meet Christ and serve him in his kingdom. Other interpretations include the kingdom as the Church (a widely held view from the time of Augustine to the Reformers) and the kingdom as a manifestation of power.[2] The kingdom is sometimes understood as a new social order with justice and righteousness as characteristics of the new kingdom. Here the gospel is understood as participating in the struggle for social justice and the exclusive aim of mission is to remove causes of human suffering.

The kingdom of God is a complex concept that was inaugurated in the coming of Jesus, evident in his casting out of demons, his healing acts and the breaking of Satan's power. However, the full realization of the kingdom is a future event and only the person who has acknowledged Jesus as Lord and King will enter into it. This view, which reflects the *'already—not yet'* character of the kingdom, is a widely held view that does not allow us to forget our evangelistic responsibility in mission, nor to ignore the world around us.

Like the kingdom of God, salvation can be interpreted in a number of different ways. We might describe salvation simply as salvation from sin whereby individuals are saved from their personal sin into a new relationship with Jesus Christ. But there is more to sin than this. It can be thought of as structural as well as personal. Many would argue that there is such a thing as structural sin, which not only affects individuals but also the society in which they live. Sin within society includes political, social and economic injustices from which we must also be saved. Salvation, then, can be thought of as liberation from this type of oppression and injustice.

The Greek verb *sozo*, meaning 'to save', also incorporates the idea of deliverance from personal danger (Acts 27:20, 31, 34), and healing (Matthew 14:36; Luke 7:3; John 4:22). Interestingly, in the Old Testament the word 'salvation' speaks of *shalom*, that is wholeness or completeness in every aspect of life.

It is not surprising that an exclusive focus on the future aspect of the kingdom leads to an understanding of salvation as nothing more than preparation for what is to come, (important though that is), and results in mission strategies which see concern for the world as secondary.

To focus exclusively on the present reality of the kingdom leads to an equal but opposite extreme in salvation theology and mission strategy, with so much attention being paid to the injustices and suffering in the world that spiritual wellbeing is neglected.

Holistic mission attempts to hold together the importance of 'gospel', 'salvation' and 'kingdom', whilst appreciating that, 'The alternative between evangelization and humanization, between interior conversion and improvement of conditions, or between the vertical dimension of faith and the horizontal dimension of love is untenable.'[3]

Some important biblical themes

The Bible reveals that mission originates from the very nature of God and so it is not surprising that the biblical story is one of mission from start to finish. A survey of some themes from the biblical story reveals that God's concerns are all-encompassing and that mission is all that God sends his people into the world to do. In other words, God's mission is holistic.

Creation and the Fall

When God made the world and human beings he pronounced that everything was 'good': 'And God saw everything that he had made, and behold, it was very good.' (Genesis 1:31). Human beings were created with an identity (created in the image of God) and with purpose (to tend the earth and make it productive) as well as being created to exist within four perfect relationships—with God, with self, with community and with the environment. However, man's disobedience not only resulted in flawed human identity and purpose but also in a distortion of all relationships.

The rest of the biblical story tells of how God purposed to restore these broken relationships and so great was his concern that he ultimately sent his son to earth to make this possible.

Paul writes, 'For in him all the fullness of God was pleased to dwell, and through him to reconcile to himself all things, whether on earth or in heaven, making peace by the blood of his cross' (Colossians 1:19–20). The creation story invites us to have a similar holistic approach to mission. As God is concerned with all things and all aspects of human life, we too must have a broad concern for the world and human beings. If we are to help a human being fully, for instance, we must recognize all types of human need. To place all the emphasis on an individual's eternal salvation while paying no attention to his/her material or social needs does not show concern for his/her total welfare. James is aware of this when he writes, 'What good is it, my brothers, if someone says he has faith but does not have works? Can that faith save him? If a brother or sister is poorly clothed and lacking in daily food, and one of you says to them, "Go in peace, be warmed and filled", without giving them the things needed for the body, what good is that? So also faith by itself, if it does not have works, is dead' (James 2:14–17). Holistic mission seeks to satisfy basic human needs—the need for God as well as the need for food, education, healthcare, and housing.

The Exodus: God's full liberation

The Exodus story tells of how God liberated the people of Israel from the oppression of Egypt, portraying a God who cares about sin and suffering in the world. Israel's liberation was not simply spiritual, but the people were delivered from every dimension of human and spiritual oppression. Chris Wright summarizes the totality of their liberation:

> The Exodus was real redemption. It was a real act of the living God, for real people, who were in slavery and it really liberated them. They were liberated from political oppression as an immigrant community into independent nation status. They were liberated from economic exploitation as a slave labour force into the freedom and sufficiency of a land of their own. They were liberated from social violation of basic human rights as a victimised ethnic minority into an unprecedented opportunity to create a new kind of community based on equality and social justice. They were liberated from spiritual bondage to Pharaoh

> and the other gods of Egypt into undeniable knowledge of and covenant relationship with the living God.[4]

It is important to interpret the Exodus not merely as a promise of liberation for politically oppressed peoples in the way liberation theologians do. When seen through New Testament eyes, the exodus becomes a picture of our redemption from sin. The Exodus event reinforces the fact that God is concerned for the well being of the whole person—his/her physical, spiritual and social needs.

God's concern for justice

Throughout the Old Testament, God's concern for the poor and oppressed is a recurring theme. The exodus story reveals how God responded to the anguished call of the people in their misery and oppression. After their liberation from slavery in Egypt, God's abhorrence of injustice and oppression continued. He commanded his people, 'You shall not wrong a sojourner or oppress him, for you were sojourners in the land of Egypt. You shall not mistreat any widow or fatherless child. If you do mistreat them, and they cry out to me, I will surely hear their cry' (Exodus 22:21–23). When the people were about to enter the Promised Land God reiterated his concern for justice, 'Justice, and only justice, you shall follow, that you may live and inherit the land that the Lord your God is giving you' (Deuteronomy 16:20). The biblical emphasis on justice reflects the very nature of God. The psalmist says that the Lord 'loves righteousness and justice' (Psalm 33:5).

Furthermore, he is the one who protects the oppressed, feeds the hungry and sets captives free. The psalmist says the Lord is the one who executes justice for the oppressed, who gives food to the hungry. 'The LORD sets the prisoners free; the LORD opens the eyes of the blind. The LORD lifts up those who are bowed down; the LORD loves the righteous. The LORD watches over the sojourners; he upholds the widow and the fatherless' (Psalm 146:7–9). God desires a world where justice reigns and so called his people to wash and make themselves clean: 'Wash yourselves; make yourselves clean; remove the evil of your deeds from before my eyes; cease to do evil, learn to do good; seek justice, correct oppression; bring justice to the fatherless, plead the widow's cause' (Isaiah 1:16–17).

It is clear from these passages that God hates oppression and injustice and longs to encourage justice among his own people and the surrounding nations also. Amos plainly rebuked Judah and Israel for their acts of injustice while admonishing the surrounding nations' oppressive, cruel behaviour. God declares, 'But let justice roll down like waters, and righteousness like an ever-flowing stream' (Amos 5:24).

The strong emphasis on social justice in these Old Testament passages highlights the fact that total biblical mission is not simply about personal salvation from sin. It is more than that. In the words of John Stott, 'His [God's] concerns are all embracing … not only justification but social justice in every community … So we must not attempt to narrow down his interests. Moreover, ours should be as broad as his.'[5]

Jesus Christ: our model for mission

The Johannine form of the Great Commission is significant—'As the Father has sent me, even so I am sending you' (John 20:21). It invites us to model the mission of Jesus. As we reflect upon the life of Jesus it becomes clear that he came not only to preach the forgiveness of sin and to offer eternal life. Jesus was also moved with compassion when he saw the hurt and suffering, the helpless and despised, the bereaved and rejected. And so he walked with the poor, he healed the sick, and he reached out to the needy. If we are to model Jesus' mission, our mission must also be similarly multi-faceted including both evangelistic and social concerns.

The church is called to continue the mission of Christ. Matthew 5:13 makes it clear that the church is to be light and salt in the world. Just as light shines into the darkness and as salt prevents decay, so too the church has a responsibility to be involved in non-Christian society. Involvement at all levels of society will naturally mean social action as well as evangelism. To help us we have the Holy Spirit, the source of power for our mission. We also have the Bible, the living Word of God, which when we use it will speak into the lives of those we seek to reach.

Scripture is a like a lens in that it invites us to see the world from God's perspective. A look through this lens reveals that God views the world with a great love that issues in action. We have been created in the image of God and through the gospel of Jesus Christ we are saved from our personal sins and are invited to live under God's kingdom rule. Although the word *holistic* may be a relatively new term, its principles and values are found on the pages of Scripture. Holistic mission issues from the very heart of God and throughout the history of the church there have always been Christians who have, in their proclamation of the gospel, also demonstrated a deep concern for social justice.

A poem to ponder

I was hungry,
and you formed a humanities group to discuss my hunger.
I was imprisoned,
and you crept off quietly to your chapel and prayed for my release.
I was naked,
and in your mind you debated the morality of my appearance.
I was sick,
and you knelt and thanked God for your health.
I was homeless,
and you preached to me of the spiritual shelter of the love of God.
I was lonely,
and you left me alone to pray for me.
You seem so holy, so close to God
but I am still very hungry—and lonely—and cold.[6]

Holistic mission in church history

The early church was influenced by the dualistic thought of Greek culture.[7] Dualistic thought distinctly separates human nature and the world into spirit and matter. As a result, from as early as the first century, this dualist thought has influenced the western church. Consequently, throughout the centuries the church has struggled against heresies springing from the dualistic Greek worldview, which for example, 'made Christ either man or God, but not both.'[8]

Contrary to the dualistic thought of the day, the gospel of the early church, in the main, saw no conflict between the spiritual and material, as it concerned itself instead with heaven and earth, and the things of this life and the next. The Christians of the early church were concerned with the social evils of their day, ranging from cruelty in the amphitheatre to labour relations. They recognized that their faith was not isolated from their everyday situations and that, as Michael Green comments,

> There was no dichotomy between a social and a spiritual gospel to those who held a unitive concept of truth. So far from being so heavenly minded that they were no earthly good, they demonstrated that those who are genuinely heavenly minded are the very people who are deeply committed to doing God's will on earth.[9]

The early church fathers encouraged the early Christians to be concerned about the sick and the poor. As Christian communities worked on behalf of others, the gospel's political implications were increasingly being expressed in the writings of the early church fathers such as Tertullian.[10]

There is no doubt that holistic ministry, the striving for personal and corporate transformation, was crucial to the early church believers. This was evident in the way they acted as salt and light wherever they lived and worshipped.

In the Middle Ages the Christian Church grew in material power and prosperity and in many ways it alienated itself from the ordinary lives of people.[11] The church, as it was then, was often unable or unwilling to help those who faced economic and political hardships. However, there were exceptions such as Francis of Assisi who, being true to the biblical mandate of helping the less fortunate and marginalized, sought to be a 'church among the poor'. Although a great amount of good was done for the needy, especially by the Dominican and Franciscan orders, it was a time when serious distortions of the doctrine of faith and works were being promulgated.

Due to the church's hierarchal structures, the church became progressively more dualistic, both in practice and theology. The gulf between heaven and earth also widened as a result of the church's concentration on the afterlife and the trials and terrors awaiting those who did not obey its teachings. However, a contradiction between this teaching and the actual practice of the church emerged as it seemed more intent on building its treasures here on earth, rather than in heaven. A growing unease developed with certain questions being asked that needed to be addressed.

Reformation

It is beyond dispute that during the Reformation period justification by faith was the central tenet of faith and all theology, including mission, orbited around this doctrine. Thus the emphasis of the Reformers was not what people could do to earn salvation but what had already been accomplished by Jesus. The renewed understanding that people could be saved by grace alone, through faith alone, in Christ alone, led away from the sacramental role of the Roman Catholic Church to the Protestant rediscovery of the priesthood of all believers. Inevitably (but not immediately) this resulted in a greater subjectivity, especially in relation to the Christian response to the Great Commission, particularly among the Anabaptists.

It is often thought that the Reformers were uninterested in mission. Gustav Warneck the father of missiology as a theological discipline, promoted this view. According to Warneck they did not engage in missionary activity because the concept of mission (as we understand it today) was not in their framework of thinking. He claimed that 'fundamental theological views hindered them from giving their activity, and even their thoughts, a missionary direction.'[12] But more recently other scholars have pointed out that evaluating the thinking of the sixteenth-century Reformers by a nineteenth-century standard in relation to mission is both unfair and absurd.[13] Scherer says that Luther was 'a creative and original missionary thinker.'[14] Luther's understanding of the relationship between faith and works was solidly biblical. He clearly understood that, although one could not be saved by works, one ought to engage in good works. He said 'But if there be no works, there must be something amiss with faith'[15]

Calvin took the believer's responsibility in this world very seriously. Bosch's summary of this issue is: 'On the whole, then, there can be little doubt that at least Luther and Calvin as well as some of their younger colleagues (such as Bucer) propounded an essentially missionary theology.'[16] Undoubtedly there was very little missionary activity during the first two centuries of the Reformation. This was due primarily to the fact that they understood their primary task as reformers of the church. That was the mission to which they dedicated themselves. Another factor was that Protestant nations (unlike Catholic nations such as Spain and Portugal) did not have colonial territories.[17] Also the churches of the Reformation were struggling to survive. Protestants were being drawn into the vortex of dissentions and disputes among themselves. In such circumstances, mission, although important, was not an urgent priority for many. Nevertheless the Anabaptists did engage in missionary outreach.

Although it seems peculiar to Christians today it must be stated that the Reformers, generally, did not consider the 'Great Commission' as binding.[18] Anabaptists however put great stress on the texts (Matthew and Mark) of the Great Commission. Bosch points out that 'They were among the first to make the commission mandatory for all believers.'[19] Nevertheless there was at least one theologian of the Reformation era who advocated the binding nature and relevance of the Great Commission, the Dutchman Adrian Saravia (1531–1613), a younger contemporary of Calvin.[20] Savaria published a tract in 1590 arguing in favour of the abiding validity of the Great Commission. But this opinion was vehemently opposed by Theodore Beza, Calvin's successor in Geneva and also by the Lutheran Johann Gerhard.

For the Reformers (generally) the Great Commission had been fulfilled in the apostolic era and therefore the church had no business getting involved in reaching the heathen. This is similar to the kind of objection William Carey encountered in the eighteenth-century.

With regard to their attitudes to mission one noticeable difference between the Reformers and the Anabaptists was their diverging view on the relationship between the church and state. Whereas Anabaptists believed in the separation between church and state, the Reformers did not. If the Reformers could conceive of mission at all it would be in cooperation with or under the auspices of the state.

Another reason for the lack of missionary endeavour by the Reformers was their eschatological views. They had a fervent expectation that the second coming of Christ was imminent. Luther, for example, believed that this would occur in 1558. It is interesting however that Luther's eschatology did not inhibit him from wholeheartedly advancing the idea of reformation. As Bosch points out: 'Apocalyptic expectations do not necessarily paralyze missionary efforts (as later Protestant missions history also demonstrated)'[21] After all, the Anabaptists held similar eschatological views but it acted as a stimulus to mission (evangelism). Is it not true that the missionary endeavours of the apostle Paul were conducted in the belief that the Lord's second coming was imminent? Both Anabaptists and Reformers had different understandings of their times. The Reformers were primarily concerned for the reformation of the church. They believed that the Catholic Church was salvageable. They accepted the baptism of its priests. The Anabaptists, by contrast rejected all manifestations of Christianity to date. For them both Catholics and Protestants were pagans and so the need for mission was both important and urgent. If all Christianity was apostate then Europe was a mission field. For the Anabaptists there was no essential difference between mission in a Europe that was nominally 'Christian' and mission in other parts of the world. But it was Lutheran orthodoxy that prevailed in Europe.

The doctrine of predestination was a double-edged sword which meant that people were either predestined to salvation or predestined to perdition. This too had a paralyzing effect on the development of mission. This coupled with the notion that people were incorrigibly corrupt by nature meant that any effort to address social issues (unemployment, poverty, sickness ...) was deemed futile.[22] This kind of pessimism stifled any attempt at improving conditions or reforming the structures that perpetuated them, especially by means of missionary activity. So pessimism produced passivity.

Justinian von Welz (1621–1666) believed that the Great Commission was still valid for the seventeenth century and he published a number of tracts advocating involvement in the missionary enterprise, in which he criticized the position of the Lutheran Church. But he was ahead of his time. The Lutheran

Church believed there were insurmountable obstacles to engaging in missions to the pagan world. Thus, for them it was impossible. They perceived that pagan peoples were incapable of receptivity to the gospel. They believed that the peoples of the non-Christian world (i.e. anywhere outside Europe) were savages (a subhuman species, incapable of conversion). They did not see these peoples as possessing souls.[23] Welz's ideas did not find fertile soil and essentially died with him. Consistent with his conviction he went to Surinam in South America in 1666 where he died, probably very shortly afterwards and no remnant remains of his missionary endeavour.

The Reformation during the sixteenth century and also the rise of Puritan theology during the seventeenth century occurred against the backdrop of the new opportunities provided by the printing press for private reading and personal interpretation of the Holy Scriptures. With Scripture in the hands of the masses, the church's declarations of faith and practice were no longer accepted without question. Fortified with biblical truth, communities began to object to the policies of both church and state. We see this in Luther's 'Ninety-five Theses', which proved to be the catalyst for great religious and political reform.

Pietism

The pessimism and passivity of orthodoxy would be replaced by fervour for the missionary enterprise. This breakthrough emerged with the Pietist movement of the eighteenth-century. This was characterized by a passionate zeal to engage in mission throughout the world. Its most famous son is Nikolaus Zinzendorf (1700–1760), the founder of Moravianism. When he was fifteen years old he naively thought it possible that all pagans would be converted before he had grown up but if there were any left unconverted he would bring them to Christ! The Pietists were opposed to orthodoxy and breathed new life into the mission enterprise. Their understanding of mission could not have been conceived outside the idea of the priesthood of all believers and the subjective element of faith it introduced. Both were products of the Reformation. The Pietists were marked by faith, courage, energy, passion and endurance.

The Pietists had a more holistic approach to mission. It was a renewal movement that desired the tangible improvement of every aspect of life, in Germany, Europe and all parts of the world. Bosch points out that in Germany Pietists were extensively involved in domestic mission 'ministering to the destitute and deprived people of Halle'. He points out that they founded 'a school for the poor, an orphanage, a hospital, a widows home and other institutions'. He goes on to say of Pietism:

> It was this dynamic and comprehensive understanding of the reign of God—in which salvation and well-being, soul and body, conversion and development were not to be divorced one from the other—which Ziegenbalg and Plutsschau took with them to India. To give one example, before their arrival schools were the prerogative only of Brahmins, and even then only for boys; the missionaries founded schools for members of the other castes and for girls as well.[1]

A few decades later (in the 1730s) the theology of Pietism began to mutate into something else. Distinctions between the secular and the sacred emerged and they began to concern themselves primarily with the spiritual dimension of mission.

Herein were the seeds of a dualism between the sacred and the profane, undoubtedly influenced by Enlightenment thinking which was beginning to permeate all forms of thought, including theology. Pietism had not penetrated to the core of the German church. Even though Pietism remained a peripheral movement it had a significant and enduring influence on the concept of mission. As a result of its theology and activity, mission could no longer be regarded as the sole prerogative of colonial governments. Neither could it be confined to an ecclesiastical hierarchy. Mission became an enterprise in which ordinary Christians could participate. Pietism heralded the advent of an ecumenical approach to mission, because it envisioned a Christian fellowship that transcended the boundaries of nations and confessions of faith.[2] Thus ordinary Christians engaged in cross-cultural mission living sacrificially amongst the people whom they served in word and deed. During the first thirty years of the Moravian movement, missionaries went to twenty-eight territories. The criteria for selecting a place to go reflected a commitment to holistic mission as they chose to go to the most deprived areas with the gospel.

The influence of the Pietism of the late seventeenth century and into the eighteenth century is much debated. It is often characterized as an escapist, world-negating style of Christianity focusing on an individualistic interpretation of salvation which led to a world of personal piety. However, the social commitment of the Pietists is commendable. For instance, the missionary work carried out by the Moravians (e.g. Zinzendorf and Ziegenbalg) in the eighteenth century is an excellent example of holistic mission. Their social commitment to help the marginalized and deprived sectors of society was further enhanced by their desire to live among those they were serving, often under very difficult circumstances.

Puritanism

The frustrated attempts of the Puritans to live out their understanding of faith and practice within the constraints imposed by English government led them to the new land of America. Although it is generally true that orthodoxy shaped both Lutheranism and Calvinism on the European continent it is nevertheless true that both English and Dutch Calvinism developed a healthier missionary spirit.

Socio-political factors contributed to puritan missionary activity. England and Holland, both strongholds of Calvinism were maritime powers with extensive colonies. This factor combined with the 'Second Reformation' in Holland and Puritanism in England, Scotland and the American colonies was decisive in determining the future of mission. For Calvin the Holy Spirit was the agent by whom the inner life was renewed and by whose power the face of the earth could also be transformed.

For Calvin the idea of the exalted Christ, active in the church and in the world, played a key role in extending the reign of God on earth. Thus mission activity involved spreading the message of the gospel as a means of extending the reign of Christ. Gisbertus Voetius (1588–1676) was the first Protestant to develop a systematic theology of mission. According to Voetius mission had three broad aims. First, there was the conversion of the heathen. Second, there was the planting of the church. But the third and ultimate goal was to manifest the glory of God's grace. He regarded mission as deriving its warrant from Scripture and conceived in the very heart of God. As such he is one of the first proponents of what subsequently became known as the *missio Dei*. He regarded the church as the only valid agent of mission.

The Puritan understanding of mission was similar to that of Voetius who played a prominent role in the Synod of Dort (1618–1619) where he would have interacted with delegates from churches in England and Scotland. Thus it is likely that some degree of mutual influencing took place.

John Eliot (1604–1690) served in mission for almost half a century (from the 1640's until the end of his life) among the Native Americans of Massachusetts. Dutch overseas mission work began on Formosa (Taiwan) in 1627. The New England Company was founded in England in 1649. Its *raison d'être* was to guarantee the missionary venture in the overseas colonies. It was the first Protestant society dedicated solely to missionary aims. Classical Puritanism endured until the beginning of the Great Awakening (c.1735). Along with Eliot the theologians who shaped the development of the missionary idea at this time were Richard Sibbes, Richard Baxter, Cotton Mather and Jonathan Edwards.

What are the essential characteristics of Puritan mission theology? The doctrine of 'double predestination' whereby some are predestined to salvation and others are predestined to damnation is a central tenet of faith amongst the Puritans. Belief in predestination has the potential to paralyze the will for mission. But it was not always held in such a rigid sense.

It is true that some Puritans thought of themselves as God's elect sent to cultivate a garden in the wilderness of North America, where they could populate God's kingdom by displacing the native population. Thus a Puritan pastor could thank God for sending 'a mortal sickness among the Indians

... which destroyed multitudes of them and made room for our Fathers.'[3] But in the mission activity of John Eliot there was a noticeable change. He was supported by the colonists who learned to accept that God's reign was to be spread by the conversion rather than the annihilation of the native people.

For the Puritans the ultimate goal of mission was the glory of God which was made manifest through his mercy and grace. Eliot established fourteen settlements known as 'praying towns' in Massachusetts. Indian converts were gathered in these and regulated in accordance with Scriptural principles. The colonies of North America were envisioned as a manifestation of the kingdom of God on earth. Meanwhile back in the mother country (England) Oliver Cromwell (in the 1640s and 1650s) was seeking to establish a theocracy. So the Puritans were trying to establish Christ's rule on earth. But the Enlightenment would destroy the theocratic model before it was fully formed by banishing religion to the private sphere. This put an insurmountable obstacle in the way of developing mission as an instrument and sign of Christ's rule on earth. Although the hope would survive and it would continue to manifest itself in various ways, the theocratic ideal was moribund.

The notion of cultural uplift was part of Puritan thinking. They believed that the gradual improvement of human conditions through benevolent and educational programs would be best accomplished when God's rule was established in society. There is undoubtedly an idea of cultural superiority underpinning this. The Puritans did, after all, believe that England was divinely mandated to guide history to its destiny. There was, in their mission, therefore, a process of Anglicizing, civilizing and Westernizing the recipient culture.

Today the Great Commission is understood as a mandate

text for mission but this emphasis is conspicuously absent with the Puritans. Bosch suggests: 'Perhaps the main reason for the absence of this motif is that the validity of the commission was not disputed and that the Puritans did not have to appeal to a command to justify what they were doing.'[4]

One might tend to assume that the Reformers and Puritans had little time for holistic mission. This mistaken assumption is reinforced by the legacy of spiritual material we inherit from them. Much of this material is excellent but it primarily relates to a person's salvation and subsequent walk with God. However, the Reformers generally promoted a holistic approach to ministry with John Calvin, for instance, taking a keen interest in the social and political questions of Christian belief and practice. We see a similar concern amongst the Puritans as evidenced by the example of the Puritan minister Thomas Case, who in 1641 declared, 'reformation must be universal' and 'all places, all persons and callings' should be reformed.[5]

Social conscience

The social conscience of evangelicals continued to grow as a result of the Great Awakening in the American colonies and the Methodist revivals of Great Britain and Ireland. Social activism and the awareness of the need to minister to soul, body and community/society energized evangelicals to witness in word and deed initially at home, but also overseas, through the emerging missionary movement.

The efforts of John Wesley, in the context of the new and developing denomination of Methodism, showed how the preaching of the Word and the task of improving society were not mutually exclusive but complementary to each other.[6] The generation of evangelicals spanning the eighteenth and nineteenth centuries understood the relationship between the spiritual and the social or the heavenly kingdom and the earthly kingdom. That they understood it in the context of the present rather than the hereafter was evident in the way they practiced their faith.

A rich heritage of holistic ministry, which is still remembered today, was instigated by many great evangelicals of this era. People like Granville Sharp, Thomas Clarkson, James Stephen, Zachary Macaulay, Henry Thornton, and most famously, William Wilberforce, had enormous impact on all levels of British society and the furtherance of the gospel. Many of these men lived in Clapham and so they became known as the 'Clapham Sect.' It was largely due to this group that slavery was abolished. But they were also involved in penal and parliamentary reform and factory legislation. Political activism was seen especially in the life of Anthony Ashley Cooper (better known perhaps as the Earl of Shaftesbury) who was most famous for his concern for child workers in factories and mines and children living in slums with no schooling.

Others such as Elizabeth Fry, Josephine Butler, George Müller and Doctor Barnardo are remembered for their contribution to social work. Edward Miall was deeply involved in political activism at a grass roots level and Thomas Chalmers and Thomas Guthrie were proactive in socioeconomic ministry in Scotland.

The rise of co-operative societies at this time, many with evangelical roots, showed how communities could work together for their own betterment. However, economists such as Adam Smith and David Ricardo began to have an influence on society. This resulted in the growth of the middle classes who espoused Victorian values and 'a gospel-of-work' philosophy. By the end of the nineteenth century, a different form of evangelicalism was beginning to emerge, with many conservative evangelical Protestants embracing the message of 'free enterprise economics, success orientated competitive individualism, extreme fear of socialism, flag-waving patriotism and imperialism.'[7] This attitude continued for most of the twentieth century. However, evangelical preachers such as C. H. Spurgeon understood the need to recognize injustices that had been carried out. For instance, he encouraged a fast day for the Indian mutiny in 1857.

Shifting paradigms

There is no doubt that during the nineteenth century there was a great desire among the evangelical community in Britain and also in America to lessen human misery. However, during the first thirty years of the twentieth century, a major shift occurred as evangelicals began to renounce their social responsibility. This shift became known as 'The Great Reversal.'[8]

There are a number of reasons for the Great Reversal. World War One showed the depth of human evil and led to pessimism about the possibility of reforming sinful human beings. The rise in pre-millennial eschatology, which viewed the world as beyond improvement, promulgated the idea that the only thing worth saving was a person's soul.[9] Evangelism in word, therefore, was greatly encouraged as an attempt to usher in the return of Christ.

The growth of liberal theology forced the evangelical church to expend all its time defending the biblical gospel. There was little time to be concerned about social justice. In the opinion of evangelicals the content of the 'social gospel' being widely preached misrepresented the true biblical nature of the gospel, and consequently they naturally distanced themselves from this deviation and, in turn, their involvement in social reform declined.[10]

While the social gospel had wide influence in America, the effects of the Industrial Revolution and the rapid increase in urbanization were creating problems of acute poverty, human rights, inequalities and exploitation among the working classes in Great Britain.

The rise of interest in the social sciences and the realization that the Christian Church was becoming progressively more irrelevant to the working classes, led to greater discussion of social problems. The earlier brief analysis of the eighteenth century indicates that this was nothing new. John Wesley stated, 'The gospel of Christ knows of no religion but social, no holiness but social holiness.'[11] It is not necessarily a view that can be ascribed to his Arminianism so let us not throw the baby out with the bathwater!

In the first half of the twentieth century there was a growing misunderstanding between evangelicals, who defended what they called 'the fundamentals of the faith' and other evangelicals who, although agreeing with 'the fundamentals of the faith', also had a growing unease about the lack of concern for loving one's neighbour holistically. According to Jacob Thomas 'the authentic gospel had to be rediscovered to rectify costly mistakes and to reverse the Great Reversal.'[12]

One of the most vocal theologians, in the USA, to articulate the message of regaining an evangelical social conscience was Carl F. H. Henry. He challenged evangelicalism to rethink its 'withdrawing mentality', which was characterized by an attitude of escapism, spiritual individualism and an indifference to social and political activism. This misunderstanding showed how evangelicalism in certain respects had seriously undermined the whole gospel of the kingdom of God, something John Wesley warned about nearly two hundred years before. He said, 'Christianity is essentially a social religion. To turn it into a solitary religion is indeed to destroy it.'[13] Those who oppose a holistic approach to mission might tend to suppose the opposite to be true: 'Christianity is essentially a solitary religion. To turn it into a social religion is indeed to destroy it.'

It may seem peculiar to Christians today but many classic works of systematic theology which date from the early part of the twentieth-century either omit missiology altogether or pay it scant attention.[14] Even today missiology is not universally part of the curricula of Bible colleges and theological seminaries. Many Bible schools include it on their syllabi but many do not.

By the end of the 1960s and the beginning of the 1970s, Christians in the United Kingdom and the USA had to take stock of their contribution to a fast-changing world. As society was gradually becoming post-modern serious questions about the need for public religion were being asked and traditional Christian values were being eroded, due in some measure, to the strong grip of materialism and secularism upon western culture.

In the developing world, the unjust systems of colonialism, and the growth of large commercial institutions alienated those caught in the cycle of poverty as a result of both lack of education and lack of opportunity. Nonetheless, by the 1960s and 1970s, the growth of the evangelical church was far more visible in the developing nations of Africa, the Far East and Latin America than in the historical Protestant countries of northern Europe. The growing 'voice' of these new centres of evangelicalism could no longer be ignored, and so in the mid-1960s the thinking and intellectual insights of theologians from developing nations began to influence a number of conferences and consultations.

At gatherings such as Wheaton (1966) and Lausanne (1974), Christian leaders from growing churches in the developing world challenged evangelicals to include social activity as a vital part of mission. Manila (1989) is well known for its call for 'the whole church to take the whole gospel to the whole world' and the *Consultation on the Relationship between Evangelicalism and Social Responsibility* (CRESR) in Grand Rapids (1982) showed how the imbalance between social action and evangelism was changing.

In Great Britain, events such as the 'Salt and Light' consultation in 1988, (sponsored by the Evangelical Alliance, Tear Fund and the Evangelical Missionary Alliance), and the National Assembly of Evangelicals in Bournemouth in 1996, promoted the social agenda to a new place of prominence. Stott comments on how Tearfund and Evangelical Alliance's 'UK Action' program enabled 'an increasing number of local British churches to develop holistic ministries among the urban poor.'[15]

This type of approach builds on the principles of Christian community development, often experienced in an overseas context, and is one way forward for Christian churches wanting to reach their local community with the gospel of Jesus Christ. By the beginning of the twenty-first century many other initiatives, such as the *Micah Declaration* in 2001, were set up to give both theologians and practitioners the opportunity to express their views on a large number of holistic issues being faced daily by both Christians and non-Christians.[16]

Many people today have embraced the importance of holistic mission as the outworking of the Great Commission and also the Great Commandment to love others. Waldron Scott says of this approach, 'It seems a true reflection of Jesus' way of ministering to people.'[17]

From this very brief historical overview of holistic mission within the Christian church it is clear that, through the ebb and flow of thought and practice, evangelicalism has rediscovered a belief and application of holistic mission similar to that of the early church believers. In the early church there was no dichotomy between a social and a spiritual gospel. Similarly in our present time:

> It is now commonplace to affirm in International gatherings of evangelical leaders that there is no dichotomy between evangelicalism and social responsibility; that both proclamation and social action must go together in the gospel ministry. There is a strong conviction about the social implications of the gospel; that salvation is for the individual and for the benefit of society; that the Christian message is for life beyond the grave and life this side of the grave.[18]

Holistic mission in the local community

If the mission of the church is to reflect the mission of Jesus Christ it must include both social and evangelistic activities. However, church history has revealed that the balance between the two has not always been easy with the church tending to emphasize either one or the other. Sadly, confusion over the roles of evangelism and social concern still exists within the local church today. Should evangelism be the primary focus of the church's ministry? Should Christians be bothered with social justice? If the local church desires to have an effective ministry within its community then a balanced understanding of the relationship between the two activities of social action and evangelism is necessary. A number of attempts have been made to define this relationship:

Social action as a means to evangelism

Here evangelism is the primary focus of mission but social action is undertaken as a preparation for the gospel. In this approach social action is in danger of becoming little more than 'bait on a hook' and there is a very real risk of creating what has been called 'rice Christians'.

Social action as a manifestation of evangelism

This is similar to the previous view with social action being seen as a legitimate part of mission. This view says that what we do in terms of social justice reinforces the message we preach through evangelism. Social action, then, is seen as a type of visual aid or in Stott's words, 'social action becomes the "sacrament" of evangelism, for it makes the message significantly visible.'[19]

Social action as a consequence of evangelism

This view believes that society will be transformed through transformed lives. Therefore, the priority is to evangelize people and see them converted so that they can begin to change their own society. Conversion, then, is the necessary starting point for any form of social action.

Social action and evangelism as equal but distinct aspects of mission

Bosch is critical of what he terms the 'cause-effect' approach to the relationship between evangelism and social action that sees evangelism as primary.[20] In a desire for a more holistic approach, he suggests that social action and evangelism are equal but distinct aspects of mission. Such an approach refuses to prioritize between the two aspects maintaining that each aspect needs the other because people need to be set free from both personal and structural sin.

Social action as a partner of evangelism

Evangelism and social work belong together but remain independent of each other and so they need not always go together. Although each is considered equal, this approach allows us to choose what the greater need is for a particular situation at a particular time.

A holistic approach to mission invites local churches to recognize their responsibility to evangelize and show social concern. Bosch, a strong advocate of holistic mission, rejects the view of mission as evangelism plus social action (evident in a number of the approaches outlined above) because this suggests that evangelism is the essential part of mission while social action is an optional extra. The danger with Bosch's approach is that mission becomes literally everything the church does—a very broad and therefore, unhelpful definition. To see social action and evangelism as partners, however, is a useful way to understand holistic mission. John Stott is an advocate of this approach but he cautions:

> This does not mean that words and works, evangelism and social action, are such inseparable partners that all of us must engage in both all the time. Situations vary, and so do Christian callings. As for situations, there will be times when a person's eternal destiny is the most urgent consideration, for we must not forget that men without Christ are perishing. But there

> will certainly be other times when a person's material need is so pressing that he would not be able to hear the gospel if we shared it with him. The man who fell among robbers needed above all else at that moment oil and bandages for his wounds, not evangelistic tracts in his pockets! Similarly, in the words of a missionary in Nairobi quoted by Bishop John Taylor, 'a hungry man has no ears'. If our enemy is hungry, our biblical mandate is not to evangelize him but to feed him (Romans 12:20)! Then too there is a diversity of Christian callings, and every Christian should be faithful to his own calling.[21]

How is your church involved in the local community? Jesus commanded all of his followers: 'You shall love the Lord your God with all your heart and with all your soul and with all your mind. This is the great and first commandment. And a second is like it: You shall love your neighbour as yourself.' (Matthew 22:337–39). Our relationship with God, then, must impact all areas of our lives: our attitudes and words; how we relate to others; the way in which we spend our time and money; our behaviour at work and among our friends and neighbours. Further, if as Christians we claim to love God then our church should endeavour to meet the needs of people in the community.

This command calls for a holistic approach, which will involve leading people to Christ and working for social transformation within the community. To know how the church can do this in its local community, it is necessary to know the community and the kind of people who live there.

Financial pressure

At a pastor's fraternal some time ago I presented a paper

entitled 'The Church Community in Contemporary Culture: Evangelism and Engagement.' In this paper I presented a critique of the 'Missional Church', affirming its positive aspects and cautioning about its more radical influence. In the course of my presentation I advocated a holistic approach to mission and cited India and Romania (two countries where I have been involved in leadership training) as excellent examples of a successful holistic approach. In the question time one pastor suggested that it was a pity we, in Ireland, did not have such opportunity for social action. This was in March 2011 during the worst economic crisis the country has ever experienced and after the nation had lost its fiscal sovereignty and was under the auspices of the International Monetary Fund governors and the governors of the European Central Bank. Thousands of people had lost their jobs. Many more were unable to meet mortgage repayments and were losing their homes. Marriages were under pressure and domestic violence was on the increase. My own son (who has an excellent degree and professional qualification as a secondary school teacher) had to go to China to find employment! I could continue to delineate the very grim situation the country was in and the bleak prospects for the future. There was a tangible air of doom and gloom and people were without hope and despairing. Yet this pastor seemed to be unaware of how the church could connect with the community in a holistic way. How can this be? Have we come to inhabit spiritual ivory towers far removed from the reality of people's lives?

As the economic crisis deepens and wages are cut more and more families struggle to pay the weekly bills. Many people are out of work and trying to survive on meagre resources. People are losing their homes and the stress of such pressures is taking its toll on relationships. Even families in well-paid employment are experiencing the pressures of paying off high mortgages and end up working very long hours to make ends meet. It is no surprise that in the past twenty years debt has become an increasing problem, with the average household owing thousands on credit cards.

Broken families

Financial pressure is one among many factors contributing towards breakdown in husband/wife relationships and so it is not surprising that the divorce rate is escalating. This fact along with the rising number of pregnancies among young single women means that the stable family unit is no longer the norm for many people in our society today. Many children grow up in single parent families.

Immigrants

The face of society has changed considerably in the past decade and the ever-increasing number of immigrants has been another factor in this change. Being a foreigner in a strange land brings its own challenges. Often it is difficult for immigrants to adapt culturally and linguistically to their new country. They can be unwelcome by people in the host countries who feel they are either a drain on limited resources or that they are taking local jobs from local people. As such they are vulnerable to racial attacks, they are often unaware of their legal rights and they face diverse social problems.

Others

The community is made up of a wide range of people, young and old, churched and un-churched, each with differing needs and problems. Young people today no longer see the importance or relevance of church and some become involved in potentially harmful activities, including alcohol or drug abuse. The elderly within the local community are often the most vulnerable with feelings of loneliness, helplessness and fear. People of all ages suffer from worry or stress, evident in the increase of stress-related illnesses but also in the recent rise of suicides, especially among teenagers.

So what can the local church do?

The challenges and struggles faced by people in society today open up limitless opportunities for churches to be salt and light within their local communities. Once the community and its needs have been carefully researched, steps can be taken towards supporting and encouraging the people who live there. Debt counselling, parenting classes, toddlers groups, pregnancy counselling, English language classes, legal advice, addiction support groups and general mercy ministries are some ways in which the church can address the needs of the local community.

As the church sets up new groups and undertakes new ventures to address the real issues in the community there is no need to be ashamed of the reasons for doing this. The church engages in this in obedience to the Great Commandment of Jesus Christ and so as Rob Warner suggests: 'We need to find the confidence and creativity to give appropriate expression to our Christian convictions.'[22]

Nevertheless, it is often difficult to bridge the gap between evangelism and social action and between the church and the community. Realistically, many people who are willing to attend the new toddlers group or parenting class on church premises are often reluctant to return to the same building when invited to attend church services. As Christians the onus is on us to bridge this gap. One way of doing this might be to involve the whole church in the new venture, not just as leaders but also as participants. This generates real opportunities for relationships and friendships to be forged between the churched and the un-churched in the community, and these naturally formed relationships are an effective means of evangelism. This type of involvement with the community can really make a difference.

Poverty

Many people tend to think of poverty as the lack of tangible things like food, shelter, clothing, medicine and education. But Bryant Myers, in his book *Walking with the Poor,* suggests that there is more to being poor than this. After a detailed discussion on the theories of poverty put forward by Robert Chambers ('poverty as entanglement'), John Friedman ('poverty as a lack of access to social power'), Jayakumar Christian ('poverty as disempowerment') and finally Ravi Jayakaran ('poverty as a lack of freedom to grow), Myers concludes that poverty must be understood in a holistic way as 'a complicated social issue involving all areas of life – physical, personal, social, cultural and spiritual.'[23]

The Bible also portrays poverty as being much more than a lack of material means. In the Old Testament 'poor' is translated by several main terms incorporating a much broader meaning than material poverty. The 'poor' are depicted as weak, miserable, helpless and destitute, oppressed and crying out for justice, downtrodden and humiliated. In the New Testament the 'poor' are described as those who are economically destitute as well as those who are spiritually humble. Throughout the Bible the most vulnerable to poverty are the marginalized groups of society such as widows, orphans and strangers, but at no time does the Bible suggest that poverty is an acceptable condition; rather it is one that must be challenged.

What does it mean to be needy?

It is necessary to define what it means to be poor. It is estimated that more than a billion people (that is, one in every five of the world's population) live in extreme poverty, surviving on less that a dollar per day. On average 10 million children die each year before their fifth birthday, mostly from preventable diseases, and more than 115 million children do not attend school.[24] Recognizing the complexity of poverty, we need to consider the reasons for poverty. Myers suggests the following reasons.[25]

Physical causes such as lack of food, shelter, water or clean air can be attributed in part to the inhospitable geography or isolation in which many poor people live. Other factors like lack of land or livestock or employment also contribute towards poverty.

Then there are social causes. Every person lives within a social context but sadly the poor often find themselves trapped in social structures that perpetuate injustice and misery.

There are also mental causes such lack of education, knowledge and technical information can result in poverty. Often the poor blame themselves for their poverty and are overcome with feelings of hopelessness.

But there are also spiritual causes. In many societies the spirit world, witchcraft, gods and ancestors have power over the people and contribute towards their poverty. For instance, fear of how the gods might react can prevent poor people from accepting technical improvement. However, one other important factor needs to be taken into account: poverty occurs within the context of relationships that are not functioning in the way God intended. Human beings exist within four relationships—with self, environment, community and God. Sin distorts each of these relationships and also contributes to the causes of poverty.

The needy often do not understand who they are, why they were created and the reason they exist, thus their relationship with self is distorted. Their relationship with the environment is also distorted due to, for example, lack of land or possession of infertile or overused land. Furthermore, they live within oppressive societies with no access to social power and the non-poor playing god in the lives of the poor, creating brokenness in the relationship with community. Their relationship with God is also distorted, as often they place their trust in spirits and other gods.

How can we help the needy?

From the discussion so far it is clear that being needy is a complex issue impinging on every area of life. Therefore, our approach to the needy must be holistic in nature. Recognizing that sin and sinful relationships are the root cause of their poverty, it will not be enough to simply supply the tangible things that so many people lack. No doubt such a short-term solution will address the immediate needs of the people but it is not a sustainable or whole solution. Holistic solutions often require a commitment of time as well as financial resources. The real needs of the people in the community can only be seen and understood when time is spent living in the community building relationships.

These relationships then facilitate the inclusion of the

community in the process of reaching a long-term solution. Of course, it is also important to look beyond the immediate community (regional, national and international) since many poor people suffer the consequences of unjust relationships imposed by the social and political structures within the country and beyond its borders.

Myers suggests that any effective work carried out among the socially, materially, physically and spiritually poor must involve working towards a 'better future' for the poor.[26] He goes on to suggest that, 'The kingdom vision for the better human future is summarized by the idea of shalom: just, peaceful, harmonious, and enjoyable relationships with each other, with ourselves, our environment, and God.'[27]

Clearly such an approach will involve tending the sick, educating the uneducated, providing water, reconciliation and kingdom building. All are legitimate ways of moving towards a better future. This better future will also be seen in changed people who realize that they are created in God's image with identity and purpose, and in restored relationships which are just and peaceful.

Christian development agencies are mission agencies striving to reach the neediest peoples of the world. Such agencies seek to partner with believers in the developed world to use their professional skills to address urgent and important needs. Thus doctors, dentists, teachers, community developers, pastors, theologians, businessmen and women, and many more have given of their time, energy and expertise (usually on a voluntary basis, though there are paid professionals also in the field) to serve within needy communities.

People who cannot go can give financial and prayer support to those who can. Thus each contributes in ways that will bring a better future to the people of the community. At a national level Christian agencies strive to challenge those in government and other bodies whose decisions and actions affect the poor. Thus, advocacy and reconciliation ministries are becoming increasingly more important.

The ultimate goal of mission is to make manifest the glory of God by establishing worshipping communities of redeemed people who testify to his mercy and grace. It is also a goal of mission to share God's love and compassion. Spiritual transformation and economic and social change go together as mission is shared in word and deed. Believers need to proclaim and demonstrate the whole gospel to those who are spiritually, materially, physically and socially deprived. It is not so much about the tasks undertaken but rather our very identity as God's people. This will be reflected in Christian lifestyle (behaviour and attitudes) as well as professional activities. How believers relate to others is as important (perhaps even more important) than the expertise they offer. This is a holistic approach to ministry.

Mission is about bearing witness (*martyria*) to the character of God and his mighty acts of redemption. This includes proclamation (*kerygma*). Thus the church must announce the good news of repentance and faith in Christ. The church must engage in serving the needy (*diakonia*) and countering evil and injustice. The church must bring others to share in fellowship (*koinonia)* in the body of Christ In this way the church fulfils the mandate to make disciples, to reconcile and restore broken relationships in a sin-spoiled world, and so reflect the unity of the Triune God.

Part 2

Preface to Part Two

The chapters that follow are reports from the mission field which were written and published in 2004 and 2005, with the exception of 'A Taste of India' (2009) and 'A Student's Story' (2011).[1] As such they are snapshots which capture the context of the times in which they were written. I have updated this material wherever possible. They are stories which give insight to fascinating people and circumstances and the challenges they face with courage and commitment to the gospel. Their faith in God is inspirational. These portraits of diverse cultures reveal what God can do and indeed has done in these lands. As such they serve as a virtual tour of the mission field. I trust they will help readers to gain a better understanding of mission. The first part of this book contains chapters which are theoretical but this second section is about where the rubber hits the road. These chapters talk about real people in real places who trust in the real and living God. The former communist regimes of Eastern Europe are now open to the gospel. But in some countries (like

Serbia) there is opposition and resistance, especially from the Orthodox churches. However, the countries of Eastern Europe are not only open to the gospel but they are also open to other influences, many of which have a negative impact on society. The Arab world has seen the dawn of a new era but it is still a crime in such lands to seek to lead people to faith in Jesus. India has had centuries of missionary activity and has between thirty and sixty million believers (depending on how one counts heads). Yet it has its own challenges, particularly syncretism and nominalism. One thing is clear from the chapters that follow: God is active in this world in building his church and in spite of all that Satan has thrown at it the church is alive and growing. Nations rise and fall but God's plans are not thwarted. His kingdom is growing and his love is being made known.

11

Adopted by God

On a teaching trip to Serbia I made an unscheduled visit (for lunch) to the home of a lady named Zivana, in Belgrade.[1] Her story is truly remarkable. Her father was killed in the Second World War. This would have been tragic enough but things were to get worse. One day German soldiers arrived in the village where she lived with her mother and older sister. Zivana was about nine years old and her sister was about eleven. The able-bodied young men of the village were away, fighting with the Partisan Army against Hitler's troops. Women, children and old men were taken from their homes into the streets and shot. Zivana's mother threw herself on her youngest daughter in an effort to save her.

What a terrible choice that woman had to make! Obviously that effort was successful but in that last act of heroic love Zivana's hips were broken. She lay on the ground in pain with her dead mother on top of her and her dead sister beside her. She was now alone in the world and was sent to an orphanage.

Slavice, Zivana and Jasmina

Eventually she grew up and married and gave birth to a baby boy (Goran) but her husband left her for another woman. In 1989 she learned of Christ's heroic sacrifice for her soul. She was converted and adopted into the family of God. In 1996 she was baptized in the River Jordan.

A much-loved Bible in Serbian hands

She found work with a Christian group (in Belgrade) called *Bread of Life*. This was during the war in Serbia. In this job she was able to minister in a practical way to those who were displaced, hungry, lonely and traumatized by war. It is truly wonderful how God uses all our experiences in ministry.

Studying the Scriptures

Bread of Life ministry was set up during the Bosnian-Croatian-Serbian conflict (1991 to 1995) to provide food for hungry people but subsequently developed into more diverse areas of ministry.

God grows beautiful things even in wastelands and I am so glad to have met these people. It is often the unscheduled stops in our lives that are God's appointments for us.

I have been very impressed with students in Serbia who were willing to spend about six hours each day listening to teaching from the Scriptures on the intensive courses I taught. They are all people with stories of how God reached into their lives.

Teaching about heaven

It was a privilege teaching these people (Zivana was one of my students) who were newly adopted into God's family. The subject we were studying was 'Heaven'. I was explaining what Scripture had to say about it. I started off by saying that according to Scripture heaven is part of God's creation. It is God's sanctuary and the place where God's throne is positioned. Heaven is the place to where Jesus ascended and from where he will return. In redemptive history God has not been a detached observer from some distant location. This is a false concept of God.

God is active from heaven

God has been active, from heaven, in the affairs of humanity and particularly in the lives of his people. He is not an aloof occupant of some remote and lofty elevation. God communicates with his people from heaven; he speaks to them and listens to them speak to him in prayer. He has always been receptive and responsive to his people. God sent bread from heaven to nourish his people. He sent fire of judgment and fire to guide the wandering remnant in the wilderness. God is continually active from heaven. He reigns so that his sovereign will is never thwarted. He observes human actions.

The Bible tells us how we can enter heaven by making it clear that we must be chosen and called by God; we must be born again; we must trust in God and in Jesus; we must have our names recorded there. Heaven is the place where we should store treasure. It is the final destination of the believer; the place prepared by Christ. Jesus dwells there at God's right hand. Christ intercedes for the saints from there. Satan has been cast out of it; angels inhabit it and Gods will is unobstructed in that place.

As I spoke about the joy and comfort in that place I could see the tears roll down the cheeks of people who had suffered much in recent years. We rejoiced in the fact that heaven is free from death, pain and sorrow and crying. It is a place of eternal light, peace, harmony and unity. It is the place of eternal praise to God; a place of exquisite beauty and purity.

During the coffee break we had been discussing how people tend to imagine their own heaven. We were talking about the common idea that what is heaven for one person might not necessarily be heaven for another person. I explained that according to Scripture heaven is not just a state of mind but is in fact an actual place. I spoke about how Christ ascended into heaven and that this can only mean that he went from one place to another. When we resumed the lecture I referred to the verse where Jesus described heaven as the house of the Father with many mansions (John 14:1).

Golden harps

I went on to say that in spite of the teaching of Scripture concerning heaven, including limited physical descriptions of the place, it is hard to imagine because it is difficult for mortal minds to conceptualize eternity.

I scornfully referred to the notion that believers will one day become disembodied spirits and spend eternity flitting about from cloud to cloud, playing golden harps on an endless day off. This is an impression reinforced by numerous poems throughout the centuries and some hymns, such as William Cowper's, 'There is a Fountain Filled with Blood'. The last verse of this hymn says:

> Lord, I believe Thou hast prepared,
> Unworthy though I be,
> For me a blood bought free reward,
> A golden harp for me!
> 'Tis strung and tuned for endless years,
> And formed by power divine,
> To sound in God the Father's ears
> No other name but Thine.

I was explaining that this view of heaven was merely a fabrication of people's imaginations. I told my students how nothing could appeal to me less because I get bored easily and need occupation. I speculated that perhaps God would assign work to us and that we would be fulfilled in these specific and challenging roles and responsibilities.

There was a murmur of discontent among a few of the women who told me that they quite liked the notion of eternal leisure! We laughed; a token of the joy that awaits those adopted by God.

12

Religious Freedom in Serbia

Evangelical Churches have existed in Serbia from the second part of the nineteenth century. Baptists, for example, received legal recognition in 1905 in some parts of the country, and after the formation of The Kingdom of Serbs, Croats and Slovenians in 1918 they enjoyed recognition in the legislation of the newly formed state.

After the Second World War the communist government did not differentiate between religious communities. They were all considered second-class citizens. In the nineties, with the beginning of democracy other developments took place in relation to religious minorities. Evangelicals found themselves subjected to intense media hostility. Their properties became targets of regular attacks by nationalistic organizations. Evangelicals were frequently subjected to threatening behaviour in their communities. Many evangelical churches had windows smashed and walls daubed with offensive graffiti. In some instances church services, concerts, and other gatherings were interrupted. On one occasion a bomb was thrown into a crowd gathered for an evangelical youth concert. The police rarely find the culprits.

In Serbia today evangelicals are deemed to be a sect and associated in the public mind with cults. In the last twenty years many books have been published against 'sects'. Many of these books have contributed to the formation of public opinion, which is anti-evangelical. Four of these titles have been published (or at least sponsored) by the Orthodox Church. Two by the national army! Two by the police! Two by secular publishers ... Some of these works are textbooks of the Orthodox theological schools. The titles alone are provocative and contribute to the incitement of hateful acts of vandalism and violence. One of these books is called *Sects, Satanism, and False Prophets*. Another is called *Soul Hunters*. The material for this latter work was initially published in the *Yugoslav Army Journal*.

Many books include reference in their titles to *Orthodoxy and Religious Sects*, clearly indicating the official and popular Serbian mindset. One police officer still working in the Ministry of the Interior wrote a work called *A Manual for Self-Defense*. It is about how to defend Serbia against sects (meaning evangelicals and other religious minorities). This has been reprinted many times in large quantity print-runs. The Army publishing house also produced *A Lexicon of Religions, Mythology and Religious Sects*. This is what is being produced in post-communist Serbia!

There have been numerous (hundreds/thousands) of anti-evangelical articles published in secular and Orthodox Church magazines. Similar numbers of radio and T.V. programs adopt the same position. There are several nationalistic organizations whose statements of purpose are the fight against sects. In some instances they co-work with some extreme individuals in the Orthodox Church. The Serbian government has not taken appropriate measures against them.

Legislation

Serbia did not have religious laws. So in 2001 the first democratic government brought out a draft proposal for new religious laws. This proposed legislation was based on the law of the Kingdom of Yugoslavia, which existed in 1918. At that time most of the evangelical churches did not exist. Some evangelical communities which did exist at the time were not legally recognized. There was in the new draft legislation an omission which can only fuel an already volatile situation. Baptists, who had been recognized in the 1918 legislation, were not included in a positive way in the proposed legislation.

That draft introduced the terms 'traditional' and 'historical' referring to particular churches and religious communities. Thus seven churches were assigned special rights. All other religious minorities were labelled 'legal entities with religious purposes'.

Evangelical churches were not included in discussion concerning this bill. When they learned what was going on they eventually managed to make a contribution to the debate which resulted in the draft failing to pass into law.

Although the bill failed, some of its ideas survived and have become part of other laws. For instance, the selection of seven recognized religious communities indicates a pro-orthodox and anti-evangelical bias. Each of these seven privileged groups now has the right to its own religious education in public schools. The children of evangelicals were not granted the right to learn the religion of their parents, but have to choose one of the seven.

The later draft of a religious law was similar to the former one. It too neglected post-1918 legislation in which most of the evangelical churches gained their legal status. It not only assigns special rights to the seven selected national religious churches but it also introduces a hierarchical division of religious communities at four levels.

Level one is reserved for the Orthodox Church. At the top of this pyramid she holds the title *primus inter pares* (first among equals). Level two belongs to other 'national' religious communities. Level three is for 'religious associations' (this level is shared by existing evangelical churches and religious minorities). New religious communities are assigned to Level four.

From that draft it was obvious that the bias still greatly favoured the Orthodox Church. As we descend to the lower levels, rights diminish further, and controls over certain 'religious communities' become greater. Articles 4 and 62 most explicitly show how this draft removed earlier achieved legal status from the evangelical churches and religious minorities, and reduces them from the status of 'church' to the status of 'religious association'.

Such a law could result in widespread discrimination, not only with regard to religious education in public schools, but also in relation to other institutions such as hospitals (consider ethical issues) and the use of state resources. This legislation would present difficulties in establishing/developing theological education. Concerning confiscated property, article 45 anticipates that another law will regulate the return of property confiscated from 'churches' but will not apply to 'religious associations'.

This draft restricts the religious rights of evangelical churches. Some evangelicals in Serbia are seeking to lobby the Ministry for Religious Affairs. Their hope is that this draft will be replaced with a law which will give much better assurances for their religious liberty.

Relationship to the government

The democratic government of Serbia is making some effort towards religious liberty. However, it seems that it has deficient knowledge about evangelical churches. It is influenced by many prejudices accumulated from a negative media campaign against evangelicals over the last twenty years. Reforms are superficial and slow. Both the former and the existing Ministry for Religious affairs personnel have rejected direct, official contacts with evangelical representatives.

Evangelicals don't expect more rights than others but they have come to hope that the new democracy will guarantee equal rights for all religious communities in Serbia including evangelicals.

Today the constitution of Serbia and other laws and policies restrict religious freedom, and, in practice, the government generally does not respect religious freedom for evangelicals. There is ongoing discrimination based on religious affiliation, belief, or practice. Evangelical representatives continue to advocate for changes in the laws on religion and restitution that would rectify the discriminatory aspects of some current legislation.

In 2011 there were 16 'nontraditional' religious communities registered: Seventh-day Adventist Church, Evangelical

Methodist Church, The Church of Jesus Christ of Latter-day Saints (Mormons), Evangelical Church in Serbia, Church of Christ's Love, Spiritual Church of Christ, Union of Christian Baptist Churches in Serbia, Nazarene Christian Religious Community, Church of God in Serbia, Protestant Christian Community in Serbia, Church of Christ Brethren in Serbia, Free Belgrade Church, Jehovah's Witnesses-Christian Religious Community, Zion Sacrament Church, Union Reform Movement Seventh-day Adventist, and the Protestant Evangelical Church Spiritual Center.

The Law on Religion recognizes seven 'traditional' religious communities: the Serbian Orthodox Church, Roman Catholic Church, Slovak Evangelical Church, Reformed Christian Church, Evangelical Christian Church, Islamic Community, and Jewish community. The religion ministry's web site contains links only to these 'traditional' communities. Although there is, officially, no state religion the Serbian Orthodox Church receives preferential treatment.[1]

Although registration is not mandatory for religious communities, those who do not register encounter considerable difficulties when seeking to open a bank account, purchase or sell property, or publish their literature. The property and tax laws grant property and value-added tax (VAT) exemptions only to registered religious communities; implementation of these laws allows registered communities to claim VAT refunds.

Registration requirements include submission of members' names, identity numbers, and signatures; proof that the religious group has at least 100 members; the group's statute and summary of its religious teachings, ceremonies, religious goals, and basic activities; and information on sources of funding. The law also provides that no religious community may register if its name includes part of the name of an existing registered group. However, the religion ministry has registered several 'nontraditional' churches and religious communities bearing the words 'Protestant' and 'evangelical' in their names. Religion ministry officials explained that this was the result of efforts to 'creatively interpret' the law to permit registration of non-controversial groups as long as similarities between the names would not cause public confusion or provoke legal challenges.

Students in primary and secondary schools are required to attend classes on one of the seven 'traditional' religions or on civic education. Representatives from the Ministry of Religion stated that the law also permits registered, nontraditional religious groups to offer classes, but none has attempted to do so.

The Ministry of Religion continues to deny registration to the League of Baptists, Hare Krishna Movement, Pentecostal Church, and Protestant Evangelical Church of Subotica. In January 2012 the Union of Baptist Churches hearing before the Supreme Court appealing the ministry's decision to deny them registration was rejected. They have submitted a new legal action (Request for Reviewing the Court Decision). This review has not yet taken place.[2] They continue to claim restitution of the Belgrade church and after six years they have not even received a response. The reason for this is that under the 2006 Law on Restitution to Churches and Religious Communities, unregistered religious communities cannot seek restitution of property. The law still does not allow for the restitution of properties that previously belonged to unregistered religious communities.

Societal abuses and discrimination based on religious affiliation, belief, or practice continues to be a reality for evangelical Christians in Serbia today. There are physical attacks, vandalism (of church buildings and cemeteries), hate speech, and negative media reporting. The police response to vandalism and other societal acts against them rarely result in arrests, indictments, or other resolution of these incidents. Some right-wing youth groups openly denounce 'sects', including evangelicals such as Pentecostals and Baptists). In addition, the press (mostly tabloid media) continues to publish 'anti-sect' propaganda that labels smaller Christian churches (including Baptists) as 'sects' and claims they are dangerous. Right-wing youth groups and Internet forums continue to use hate speech against evangelicals. Evangelical Christians continue to advocate for changes in the religion and restitution laws that would eliminate discriminatory elements.

13

Religious Revolution in Romania

The Romanian religious landscape is not what we Westerners might expect to find in Eastern Europe. The country has a population of twenty-three million people with a very small percentage of believers. Nevertheless God has done something extraordinary in that land. We will trace God's hand at work in just one church in Romania. Emanuel Baptist Church is situated in Western Romania, near the Hungarian border in the city of Oradea. This Baroque style city has a population of 230,000 people. It is 250 kilometres from the Hungarian capital, Budapest and further away from its own capital Bucharest which is in the south of the country near the Bulgarian border. Oradea is located in the region known as Transylvania, a very picturesque area with beautiful mountain scenery and spectacular caves.

Soviet occupation following World War II led to the

formation of a Communist People's Republic in 1947 and the abdication of the king. The decades-long rule of Nicolae Ceaușescu became increasingly draconian through the 1980s. He was overthrown and summarily executed in late 1989. Former communists dominated the government until 1986 when they were swept from power. Much economic restructuring remained to be carried out before Romania could achieve its goal of gaining accession to the E.U. in 2007.[1]

Romania has various ethnic groups with 90% Romanian; 7% Hungarian; 2% Roma; 0.5% German; 0.3% Ukrainian; others 0.8%. Regarding religious affiliations 70% are Roman Orthodox; 6% Roman Catholic (of which 3% are Uniate); 6% Protestant; 18% unaffiliated. The languages spoken in the country are Romanian, Hungarian and German.

Since the fall of the anti-Christian Ceaușescu dictatorship in December 1989 Christians have been very keen to use their freedom to reach Romania with the gospel. With tremendous sacrificial giving from inside Romania and generous help from outside the country Emanuel Baptist Church in Oradea, began to play a crucial role in evangelism, training pastors and church planting. It has several institutions in the areas of health-care, vocational training schemes, social programs and education which have established vital links with the community. Emanuel has known phenomenal growth and has planted many churches throughout Romania.

Courage and commitment

Behind all this there is an amazing story of courage and commitment to Christ by some spiritual leaders. In 1989 Baptist Pastors were granted permission to meet to discuss budgetary matters. This permission was necessary for such a group and was allowed only on the basis that nothing else should take place on that occasion. Secret police kept a close eye on all such gatherings, including church meetings/services. There are heartbreaking stories of pastors being betrayed by their closest friends who had worked for decades as informers or even agents of the secret police. These people were themselves victims of an oppressive system and were threatened or bribed.

Pastors had to report every Monday morning to a local official whose responsibility it was to oversee denominations. The report required specific information such as numbers in the church, new converts, religious background of the convert(s), details of the sermon, foreign visitors' details and so on. These atheistic and anti-Christian bureaucrats could decide who could be baptized and become members of the churches and who could not. Although the churches knew it was better to obey God rather than men.

Signing their death warrants

When almost fifty pastors met in December 1989 to consider their financial affairs there was another item on the agenda, to write a letter to Ceaușescu. The letter reminded the dictator that he was not God and that he was subject to God. They demanded the right to meet as believers without the scrutiny of the state and accountability to the state as it existed. They requested permission to import Bibles (Bibles had been recycled as toilet paper in Ceaușescu's time). They made many appeals for religious freedom, including permission to translate and print Bibles in the Romanian language and freedom to conduct evangelism. The signatories (43 of the 47 men at that meeting) were very afraid of the likely consequences. It was like signing their death warrants. One pastor told me he returned home and told his wife and they both cried, realizing that this action could lead to a long term of imprisonment. Within a few days Ceaușescu had been overthrown and killed.

Using the time wisely

The country was exhilarated with a new sense of freedom and Christians were concerned to use this freedom wisely, to God's glory. When the microphone was snatched from T.V. news reporter (in studio) the first words proclaimed in the new situation were: 'Romania, God is with us!' If Ceaușescu had survived the rebellion he might well have tried to falsify a link between the political uprising and the signatories of that letter. There was no political connection but there was a spiritual plan unfolding and the timing of this letter cannot be a coincidence. It may very well be that this correspondence from the spiritual leaders was the last thing he ever read. The writing was on the wall. God had spoken and Ceaușescu's evil regime was at an end.

It is an astonishing and inspiring story. God began to bless the leaders who were prepared to put their lives on the line. Men like Paul Negruț and the youngest signatory on that day Doru Hnatiuc (married with two children at that time).

The story that follows is a brief sketch of what God has been doing over the past 15 years in Romania through Emanuel Baptist Church. Where the pastoral team consists of Paul Negruț, Doru Hnatiuc, Peter Vidu and the mission's pastor Cosmin Marc.

Growing in maturity, unity and numbers

The first missionaries arrived in Oradea (from Hungary) in 1902. Since then Emanuel Church has known continuous growth. In 1912 there were 12 members. In 1924 there were 45 members. In 1934 there were 70 members. In 1961 there were 404 members. The church was known during those times as the 'Second Baptist Church of Oradea'.

1974 was the year of a great spiritual revival. 399 people got baptized that year which doubled the membership! The church had 1,800 members in 1977. In 1993 there were 3,020 members and by the end of 2003 the number grew to 4,029 members. Counting the men in the second row, beginning with the man who is standing we can identify the pastor who saw revival under his ministry. He is third from the left.

Since 2003 approximately 175 members have been added to the church. The church met in the same building until February 1995, although it underwent several changes

Emanuel Baptist Church, Oradea, Romania

Candidates for Baptism

Packed church (view of balcony)

Packed church (ground floor view)

along the years. The hall in this picture is the last extension to the old church.

Building for God

The old church building had about 700 seats but many people (up to 1,500)—were standing regularly during the services of the church. Because of that, in the spring of 1991 the construction of a new church building started.

Church in construction

It took 4 years to build the new church. With God's help, financial support from churches around the world, and with the hard work of its members the project was completed in February 1995. The official opening of the new church building took place on the 26th of February, 1995.

Choir at official opening

The church has 2,300 seats in the main hall. Some additional seats are available in the auxiliary rooms with closed–circuit video transmission everywhere. Today it is the largest Baptist Church in Europe. There is a wedding hall with a canteen, a room for mothers and toddlers, several Sunday-School classrooms and additional meeting rooms in the basement. There are also guest rooms (where I stayed). There are 1,000 children involved in Sunday-School, aged between 1 and 14 years. In 2003 the church had

Empty sanctuary

Full sanctuary

Overflow into hallway

Overflow into basement

4,029 members. Since then it has had hundreds more added to membership.

Even though they built a large church building to have enough seats for everyone, it often happens that people still have to stand in the hallways because of the lack of space.

In these pictures you can see people watching the closed-circuit video transmission in the hallway and basement during special services in the month of January 2004. The space problem is not only found inside but also outside where parking is a problem with so many cars everywhere, even on the footpaths.

Parking problems

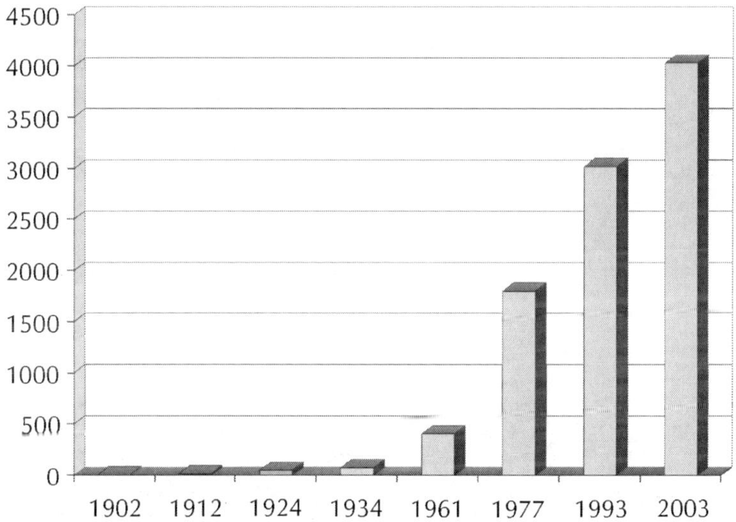

Bar chart showing growth rates

Emanuel University

An accredited University was founded in Oradea, 1990. It has 428 students (384 full-time, 44 part-time) and 78 lecturers.[2]

It has a *Faculty of Theology* with 4 majors: Pastoral Theology; Literature; Social Science and Music. There is also a *Faculty of Management.* There are excellent facilities for students and staff. There are 260 students resident in the dorms on campus. There are two chapels, one cafeteria, five music rooms, two computer labs (60 computers) and a very large library over 60,000 books—mostly in English. 936 students have graduated since 1990.

Emanuel University

The High-School was founded in 1990. Today it functions in a building close

University Lecturer

Students in Library

Students in robes

Junior school

to the church. Facilities include 3 gyms; several labs (Physics, Biology, Chemistry, Romanian literature, History, Foreign Languages, Computer-Science) and a sports field.

The junior (primary) school commenced in 1997. Since 2002, the school has a new building with 4 floors, 18 classrooms with all the necessary facilities. At the moment, the school has 35 teachers and 540 students. In 2002 the elementary school commenced as well.

Junior School (new building)

A kindergarten was founded in 1996 and it now has 6 employees. There are 70 children in the three age

Junior students

Campus

groups (3 years, 5 years and 5–6 years).

Bethesda Medical Clinic

Bethesda Medical Centre was founded in 1992. There is a team of employees consisting of 7 full-time and 11 part-time staff. There are 12 doctors, 2 nurses, 1 lab technician and 3 other staff. There are surgeries such as family and general medicine, ultrasound, obstetrics-

Pharmacy

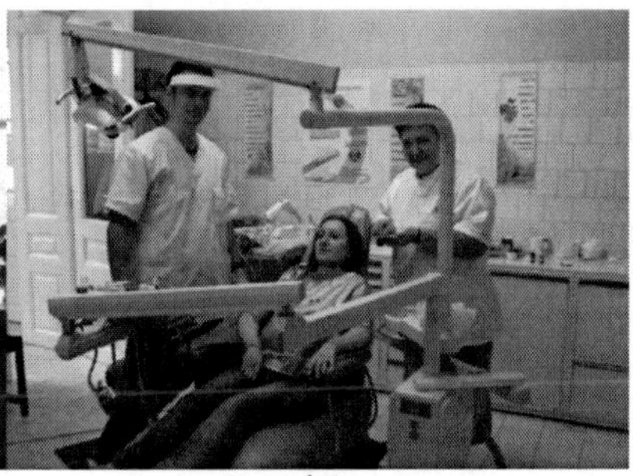
Dental Surgery

gynaecology, dentistry, ophthalmology, endocrinology, paediatrics, and surgery. 12,592 people received free medical treatment at Bethesda Medical Clinic and Pharmacy in 2003.

A Charity Centre called 'Casa' (home) was founded in 1996.

Vocational Centre

Tailoring/dressmaking class

Projects include 'Briana' Maternal Centre (focused on the prevention of abortion and child abandonment after birth). There are 1 million abortions in Romania every year. This means that since the Revolution in 1990, 15 million abortions have taken place.[3] It also caters for Families in Difficulties (150 families have been helped). Furthermore it provides Foster Care. As if that was not enough to keep them busy they also have a Vocational Centre providing training courses in tailoring/dressmaking and computers. They also have a project called Kingdom Kids which gives occupational therapy at the orphanage in Oradea—more than 500 children are involved.

A Hospice Centre was founded in 2003. Seven people are currently employed there. The Centre's mission is to help people suffering from terminal illness. Many in the hospice have found the hope of heaven in Christ.

The School of Prophets was founded in 1987. This activity was stopped (1991–1995) but restarted in 1996. Its mission is to train ministers from evangelical churches through

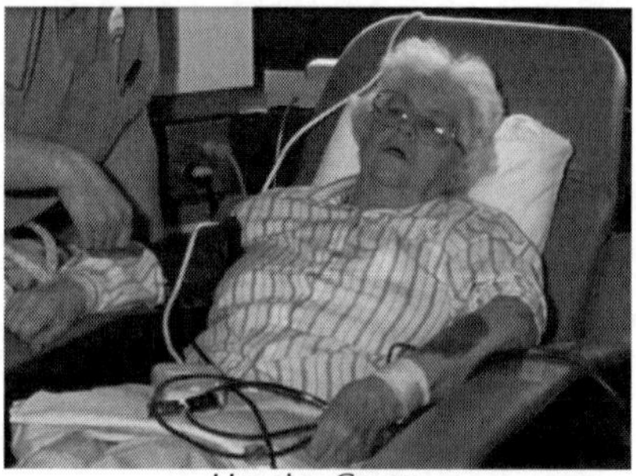

Hospice Centre

Bible study courses. This is an investment that promotes and preserves the truth of the gospel.

Evening courses are mostly taught by Slavic Gospel Association, U.K. (SGA) Lecturers. 1998 was the year with most graduates (42). During 2003–2004, 18 people graduated. Other S.G.A. projects involve helping pastors, helping widows and printing Christian literature.

School of the prophets

The priority of mission over maintenance is evident in Emanuel Baptist Church. Many members from Emanuel are involved in missionary activity in churches around Oradea, especially in churches planted by Emanuel. This Church has planted other churches in many locations in Romania.[4]

Living in liberty

Freedom is a precious thing for Romanian Christians and they are making the most of every opportunity for the gospel. The word 'holistic' has been stolen from our vocabulary by New Age Philosophy but we can see a holistic approach to people's needs (spiritual, material, mental, health, welfare and sense of belonging) being rewarded by God in Romania. This is a model church that God has blessed because they valued their new freedom and seized every precious moment for God. The story of Emanuel is one that is saturated in prayer.

Preaching and the power of God

I asked Doru Hnatiuc (a pastor in Emanuel): 'What one thing

is central to the growth and health of Emanuel Church?' His reply came without hesitation or doubt: 'Preaching, the Word of God!' Everything else emerged from a Christ-like compassion for the poor, sick, abused and abandoned in their community.

Romania has much to teach us about the love of Jesus, a love expressed in word and deed. In Romania the church cares for people not just from the cradle to the grave but from conception to resurrection. It is amazing what God has done in such a short space of time. Let us pray that the gospel will continue to prosper there and here in our generation and let us work toward that end.

14

Rejoicing in Service

I had been to Moldova in April 2003 as member of a pastors' team invited by the Slavic Gospel Association (UK).[1] On that occasion I was engaged in preaching, usually twice a day, for the duration of the ten-day visit, in churches in rural, northern Moldova. I also spoke in a hospital to medical staff and to the senior students in a second level school. I did not know at that time that I would return to Moldova a year later as a member of the Slavic Gospel Association staff to teach in the Mission School in Balti. Through a series of providential circumstances God brought me into the work of the mission.

Eastern Orthodox Church in Moldova

It was a privilege and a

Pastors and church-planters studying Scripture

joy to teach the twenty-five well motivated students. To be involved in the training of men who are active in church planting is a thrill. My responsibility was to deliver twenty-five lectures; sixteen on 'Apologetics' and nine on 'The Cults' and I thank God for his enabling power in the classroom. We had breakfast, lunch and dinner together each day and I got to know and love these men. By the time I had learned who was who and how to pronounce their names it was time to say goodbye, in Russian, of course!

They need much prayer for the many difficult situations they face such as opposition from the Orthodox Church and the corruption of some civic leaders who expect to be bribed before they will grant planning permission for 'Houses of Prayer'.

House of Prayer in Moldova

I listened to many requests for prayer from these people who are materially poor but spiritually rich. None touched me more than a request brought by a student named Victor Kutsky who asked for prayer for a lady in his church whose husband is an atheist. He is making it very difficult for her to attend church as he sends her to the market on Sunday morning with the milk from their cow and she may only go to church if/when all the milk is sold. As a result she does not get to church often and is spiritually weak but still has the desire to attend. May God watch over Moldova.

15

On a Hill Far Away

When I was in Hungary a few years ago (to teach theology in Bicske) I visited Tatabánya, a city located 30 miles from Budapest on the way to Vienna. On a hill overlooking this city there is a statue of a large bird that looks like the griffon of mythology (a large vulture), wearing a golden crown that sparkles in the sunshine. This is known as 'The Turul Monument'. According to local superstition this inanimate object is meant to safeguard the city.

But at the very feet of this fierce-looking image of a flesh-eating monster with its outspread wings there is a steep precipice which is a popular suicide location. It is heart-breaking to think of the emptiness and sorrow that has led so many people to hurl themselves from this cliff. It is ironic that this pagan symbol of defence has become a monument to despair.

Monument overlooking Tatabánya has a wing span of 15 meters

The name Tatabánya is made up of two words, *Tata* means 'grandfather' and *Banya* 'mining'. That tells us something about the industrial history of the place as an old mining centre. But today it is a dark city with occult practices and all its attendant evil. It is in this place that I met a student who has started a prayer and Bible-study group. I attended this meeting to share fellowship and encourage this fledgling group (about 10 souls). Their vision is to see a church planted that will shine forth the light of the gospel, bringing hope to the hopeless and salvation to the lost.

Prayer/Bible-study group in Tatabánya

We may be sure that they will experience opposition and discouragement but they will have the abiding presence of Christ who promised that he would be with those whom he commissioned with the task of making disciples (Matthew 28:18–20).

When I visited the Turul monument I looked out over the panoramic view of Tatabánya from the feet of this sinister creature and a verse came to mind: 'For we do not wrestle against flesh and blood, but against the rulers, against the authorities, against the cosmic powers over this present darkness, against the spiritual forces of evil in the heavenly places' (Ephesians 6:12). Here in this city is a group of people

Head of Turul Monument

who, in their desire to serve God in church planting, have stepped into the arena of a great spiritual battle against the hosts of darkness.

Satan brought Christ to a great height where he tempted him to cast himself down. Jesus was taken to a very high mountain by Satan who showed him the kingdoms of the world and offered all their splendour if he would abandon his mission.

These events may be seen as rather crude attempts to destroy Christ but the enemy is also subtle and chooses the timing of temptation to coincide with occasions when those who belong to Christ are most vulnerable. The lure of the world's luxuries may be a temptation to those who have very little by way of material possessions. What we learn from the temptation of Christ is that if Satan fails to destroy us he will attempt to distract us.

We can enter the battle with this group in prayer, asking God to keep them focused on the work of the kingdom. Pray that God will restrain the powers of darkness in Tatabánya and prosper the work of the gospel. The master is our model and he anguished on a hill overlooking Jerusalem for its inhabitants. He longed to gather them as a hen gathers her chicks under her wings. Oh that many would come to love the one who suffered and died on a hill outside the city gates.

Pray that Jesus, the one who is worthy to wear the golden crown will be lifted up and become the focus of the inhabitants of Tatabánya so that many will come to live in the shadow of his wings.

16

A Student's Story

There were eleven postgraduate students in my 'Advanced Hermeneutics' class at the Theological College in the Middle-East.[1] They came from several countries in the region and from Africa. They were excellent students (judging by the quality of the challenging questions and the nature of the interaction in class). It is deeply rewarding and very humbling to serve these fearless and fervent saints. May God richly bless them! They were being equipped for work in the Arab world. A glance at a map revealed just how strategically placed this school was to reach the Arab/Muslim world in Syria, Saudi Arabia, Egypt, Iraq, Iran and Lebanon. Many of its citizens are Palestinians.

One morning one of my student's, Ezzat, was late for class. He apologized and explained that he had to go to an embassy in relation to his visa application for residency in a foreign country. Later that day he told me why he was planning to move. His work involved sharing the love of God in word and deed in North Africa for seven years up until September 2009. In April 2009 something was published in a local newspaper about his work. The article also contained personal threats against him and his dear friend and fellow Christian, Chris. It was the start of a chain of events which culminated on June 23, 2009.

Ezzat had been with Chris from 7:30pm to 10:30pm the previous evening. They were with a new contact talking about the Lord. The next morning (23 June, 2009), because it was his turn in the carpool, Chris dropped Ezzat's son and his own daughter off at school. From there Chris headed to the office to begin another day of work. Upon arriving at the office, however, he was accosted by two men, who jumped out of a nearby car and tried to abduct him. Chris fought off their efforts until a third man got out of the car, he was holding a gun. He pointed the gun at Chris and shot him three times in the head at point-blank range. Chris fell down dead in front of the office where he had shared God's love through his project of relief and development. This dear man, who had been a light of truth to so many in the neighbourhood, gave his life serving the Light of the World. Needless to say Ezzat was shocked and terribly upset. His eyes were filled with tears as he spoke of this painful incident in his recent past.

Some weeks earlier masked men arrived at the office of Chris where both Ezzat and Chris spent time sharing God's love with others. They asked questions about their work. Ezzat noticed that he was being watched and followed. He received anonymous (threatening) phone calls. His home (where he lived with his wife, Jacklin (an Iraqi) and two children, Matthew (8 years old at the time) and Judy (18 months old at the time) was being watched by these 'anonymous' people. It later came to light that they were *Al-Qaeda*. When the police apprehended those who killed Chris they had in their possession a list of twelve people who were to be killed. Ezzat's name and Chris' name were on the list.

Working in the Arab World

Ezzat, Jacklin & family *Chris, Jackie & family*

Chris was an NGO director with an excellent reputation for helping the citizens of the region climb out of poverty. That legitimate work gave Chris and Jackie the opportunity to share God's love and truth.

Prayerfully considering what he should do next Ezzat went to the theological college and is currently completing a Master's degree in Theology. But his heart remains in the Muslim countries of North Africa and he plans to work in North Africa and focus on reaching people with the love of God.

He is interested in settling in a strategic location where diverse cultures and religions converge as this will provide a perfect platform for his work. He hopes it will be possible to visit and continue following-up those with whom he had worked during his seven years in that place. In order to obtain residency the government has to give official approval to Ezzat and his family.

A condition of the visas will be that they have raised sufficient financial support. He hopes to raise his support in the Middle-East (he is Egyptian) where he is based. Of course he will be pleased to receive prayerful and practical support from other countries! Please pray that the Lord will provide what is needed so that Ezzat can continue to focus on continuing this valuable work. Also pray that God would raise up those who can join with Ezzat in this new project. He is actively seeking partners. Ezzat is committed to working in the Muslim world. He is a challenge to many of us who would be afraid to do this. But we can uphold him in prayer.

I would like to give Chris's wife the last word here. In response to correspondence from me Jackie said: 'I agree with you that the story of my late husband's sacrifice can and will be used by the Lord to challenge and inspire others'. She added 'and most importantly bring God the glory He alone deserves'.

17

A Taste of India

My first visit to India was a six week missionary trip in 2009 where I taught at the Calcutta Bible Seminary.[1] I subsequently returned in 2010 to speak at conferences in Delhi and Kolkata (Calcutta) and in 2011 I visited Nagaland to speak to a Theological Association.[2]

Calcutta Bible Seminary Campus

Great Expectations

On that first occasion as I was flying over the Himalayas I was anticipating encounters with tribal groups, trips to scenic locations (especially breathtaking Himalayan panoramas), quaint and serene hill stations, fabulous wildlife-spotting opportunities, mystical Buddhist temples and colourful Hindu festivals. What I experienced was quite different. I was located on campus one hour's drive north of Kolkata in a densely populated area that was spiritually dark, dirty and dangerous. There are, of course, very beautiful places in India. Darjeeling and Nagaland in the north and Kerala in the south are just two examples of landscapes which are exceedingly picturesque.

Violence on the streets

While I was in West Bengal a man was slaughtered with a machete just ten kilometres from the campus where I lived. It was a politically motivated crime. His body was hacked to pieces. A man was decapitated in Kolkata in a road rage incident. In a separate occurrence an angry mob burnt a bus which had been involved in an accident where a little boy, who was being carried on his father's bicycle, was knocked down and killed.

Orissa

I have not been to Orissa but students and staff told me of the situation there. The neighbouring state of Orissa continues to be in the grip of sporadic gory anti-Christian riots. Many Christians have been burnt alive. Countless churches, houses and shops have been gutted. Even Christian orphanages have not been spared. In the village of Barakhama extremist Hindus attacked Christian dwellings with guns and bombs. Hindu extremists are involved in torturing church members, especially leaders. They have tortured Christians into falsely confessing to crimes, or tortured them to make false accusations against other believers. Christians are being tortured in an attempt to have them renounce their faith. Buildings used for worship or prayer meetings have been destroyed. Bibles and other religious materials have been confiscated and Christians have been beaten up by police and government officials.

A country of contrasts

India is a country of magnificent beauty and terrible ugliness. In Kolkata there are the splendid architectural reminders of its colonial past (such as the Victoria Memorial) juxtaposed alongside the shocking slum dwellings. Environmental pollution is evident everywhere. There are extremes of wealth and poverty. Men are beasts of burden and women toil endlessly to make as good a life as possible for their families. It is however, a very colourful place with women dressed in Saris and Salwar of every hue, which reflects something of the amazing variety of ethnicities. The geography and history of India are fascinating but it is more than the sum of its parts. The peoples of India are very beautiful (every other woman could be cast as a *femme fatale* in a Bollywood movie). The

Victoria Memorial Kolkata

Slum dwellings

Salwar Girls

people of West Bengal are not just physically attractive but more than that I found them to be gentle and generous.

Ministry in the slums

Ministry teams of staff and students from the college visit slums every Saturday evening. I was in one of these dwellings where I had opportunity to pray for the family who lived there. The lady of the house provided the team with a meal. She insisted. Their hospitality is amazing.

Street scene

Assault on the senses

Being driven from the airport to the college campus was an amazing experience. The roads were congested so the driver decided to drive at high speed on the wrong side of the road. With oncoming traffic flashing their lights and blowing their horns my '*chauffeur*' adroitly weaved his way merrily onward at an astonishing velocity. The principal of the college, who had met me at the airport, and was sitting in the front seat, turned around and said with a twinkle in his eye and a smile on his face, 'welcome to India'. I later learned that this was 'normal' driving.

Aromas

With the windows open in the car I managed to regain enough

composure to notice the foul smells of stagnant water, sewage and rotting vegetation which are so common. These odours contrasted with the delectable aromas of spicy food (cooked on the streets) and burning incense from Hindu shrines which were all mixed with carbon monoxide and sweat in the intensely hot and humid air of the monsoon season.

Sounds

Then there were the sounds. Beeping the horn seems to be a national pastime which is as popular as cricket and about as ineffective as a neon sign in Tokyo. My apartment was about 200 metres from a runway of the international airport. There were open-air political rallies conducted through public address systems with the communist party and the national party vying for power. When these speeches abated the Hindu horn blowing, bell-ringing and chanting began and continued well into the hours of darkness. At 5.30 a.m. the first Muslim call to prayer was heard from the nearby mosque. After a night of broken sleep and drenched in sweat I awoke to curried goat and rice for breakfast, and trudged wearily to my classroom. But it was here that I came into contact with what God is doing in India.

Naga warriors in ceremonial dress

The students and staff

The students and staff were Baptists or members of the Evangelical Church of India and were mostly from the North-East part of the country (Orissa, where there is serious persecution from Hindu extremists, West Bengal, or one of the sixteen tribes of Nagaland, a state which was predominantly animistic and whose near ancestors were head-hunters!).

All classes are conducted in English (the language of theological education in India) and students have varying ability in spoken and written English. It is hard to comprehend the amount of languages spoken in India. For example each of the sixteen tribes of Nagaland has their own language but they also speak English, which is taught in school and Hindi, which is the national language. The local community spoke Bengali, Hindi and a little English. Some of the students from Chennai (formerly Madras) in the state of Tamil-Nadu spoke Tamil (their mother-tongue) and English and Hindi. The curse of Babel with a confusion of languages is evident on this amazing subcontinent.

The lecturers are very dedicated and godly people who earn a salary of $120 per month. The students spend most of their free time (after lectures) in the library and when the library is closed it is a moving sight to see dozens of pairs of sandals outside the prayer rooms where the students spend hours on their knees talking to God. The college did everything possible to make my stay as comfortable as possible. The principal, Rev. A. Jayakumar, is a capable and kind man whose gentle ways strike the right keynote on campus and contributes to an environment where the goodwill of the staff is harnessed so that learning can be effectively accomplished.

The needs are very great. For example many students cannot afford fees and the college supports them. Other students are supported by their local churches. The Annual fee for a B.Th. student is Rs.28000 ($550), which includes tuition, mess, accommodation etc. For a M.Div student, the fee is Rs.30000 ($600). But the college is currently providing free education to the students from West Bengal and Jharkhand (20 in number out of a total of 80 students). This is unsustainable without regular support. While I was there students were asked to each contribute 100 Rupee ($2) for dining hall plates but they could not afford to pay so the college had to purchase them from its limited resources.

My students (M.Div.)

I made new friends in India and fell in love with the people there. One of my third year M. Div. students has now taken on ministry in Orissa.

C.B.S. Projects

C.B.S. is also involved in community development programs like tailoring, handicrafts, spoken English, a girls' education program and a crèche. At present 30 women learn tailoring and handicrafts. These women come from very poor backgrounds and support their families through the income they generate.

Around 25 students attend spoken English class. Even though some of them are graduates, their inability to communicate in English is a handicap which prevents them from getting good jobs. But through the Spoken English classes they not only learn how to speak English but they also build their confidence.

Through the Girls education program, C.B.S. supports female children to pursue their education and C.B.S. takes care of all their expenses. It is not uncommon for girls at the age of 12 to get married in West Bengal. At present C.B.S. has 13 girls in this program.

C.B.S. also runs a crèche especially for the poor children. At present they have 15 children in this project where Bible verses and Christian songs are taught. This year 3 children (3 & 4 years of age) have been included in the crèche. These children were literally on the streets begging with their grandmother. C.B.S. brought them to the crèche and is taking care of them. The other children also come from homes where the families have nothing.

The Evangelical Church of India

The Evangelical Church of India (ECI) is composed of more than 3,300 local congregations that are spread over at least 15 Indian states and represent some 30 languages. Every Community for Christ (ECC) teams have been responsible for planting more than 600 of the ECI churches. There are three university accredited seminaries which meet the needs of formal theological education for clergy level evangelists, district and area pastors and other Christian workers for the various ECI ministries in India. These are Allahabad Bible Seminary in Allahabad, Calcutta Bible Seminary in Kolkata and Madras Theological Seminary and College in Chennai.[3] ECI also has numerous regional Bible schools to serve the needs of the church. These regional Bible schools meet the needs of informal theological education for lay level evangelists, pioneer church planters and local lay leadership currently expanding the church throughout India and beyond.

Partnerships

The ECI partners with missionary organizations (such as OMS International) and these alliances assist work in evangelism, church planting, church growth and development, theological education and leadership training. These partnerships help the ECI address more holistic ministry needs, such as literacy, primary education and health care (including HIV/AIDS ministries).

The scale and pace of growth

The scale and pace of spiritual growth in India is phenomenal. For example the ECI estimates that there were 52,115 conversions in 2008. This does not include statistics from other very large denominations, like Baptists or Pentecostals).[4] They have calculated that 415,137 unbelievers have attended evangelistic events/services. There have been 5,548 baptisms; 7,199 people were in discipleship or lay-leadership training and 117 new churches were established.

Former Hindu family converted to Christ

Their home on Sunderban Island

Plinth of destroyed Hindu Shrine

Site for church building (school in background)

A humbling experience

One of my more memorable experiences was shortly after I arrived in India. I was taken on a relief mission to the Sunderban Islands. Many people in the region have dug large ponds beside their homes (mud huts with straw roofs). In these artificial lakes they keep fish and bathe. The water is quite stagnant and many people have skin diseases. But this is how they live. A typhoon flood brought salt water to these ponds and the surrounding land which killed the fish and destroyed crops. Until heavy rain washes the salt down these problems will persist. The team distributed parcels of food and clothing.

5 A.M. loading aid parcels

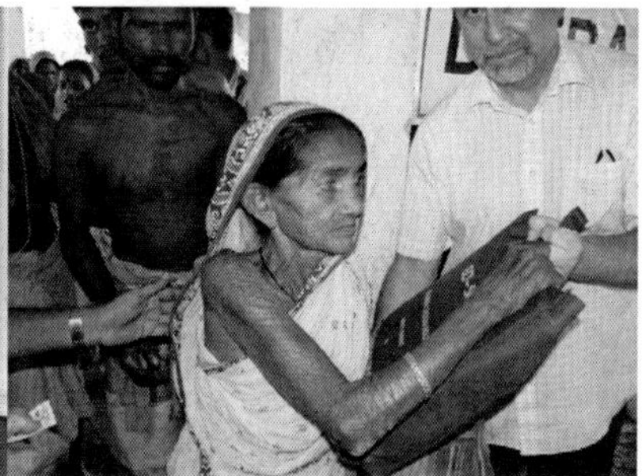

Distributing aid at Sunderban

As the road had been washed away I had walked some distance barefoot and my feet were covered in mud. We were expected and so a lady in the village had prepared something for us to eat. I hesitated to enter her home for fear of getting food-poisoning (I confess this to my shame). The lady noticed my brief pause and thought I was reluctant to enter her home with such dirty feet. Instantly she knelt at my feet and using the bucket of water (a scarce commodity) outside her house, she began to wash my feet. I protested and asked others to tell this woman to stop (while Jayakumar, the principal of

The lady who washed my feet

C.B.S, photographed it). But she continued and completed the job. I felt so ashamed. I accepted hospitality from this dear lady and it was delicious and I was not poisoned! It was a humbling experience. I later learned that this woman and her entire extended family had been converted to Christ. They had a Hindu shrine on their land beside their house but knocked it down

One in Christ

and all that remains is the plinth. On the other side of their house is the site for the construction of a church building on land donated by this family. I feel honoured to have met these people and to be a witness and participant in what God is doing in that land.

God is moving throughout this world redeeming the lost and raising up communities of believers who worship the Lord Jesus Christ. It is a privilege to be partners in mission, not only with the Lord's people but also with the Lord himself. May kingdoms of darkness be conquered by the power of God through the love of Christ to the praise and glory and honour of his precious name!

Endnotes

Chapter 1

1. The word 'atheist' is derived from Greek, '*a*' means '*not*' and '*theos*' means '*god*'. Thus its very name expresses its negativity.
2. Similar to what is happening in North Korea today.
3. *The System of Nature or, the Laws of the Moral and Physical World* (*Système de la Nature ou Des Loix du Monde Physique et du Monde Moral)* is a work of philosophy by Paul Henri Thiry, Baron d'Holbach (1723–1789). It was originally published under the name of Jean-Baptiste de Mirabaud, a deceased member of the French Academy of Science. D'Holbach wrote and published this book anonymously in 1770, describing the universe in terms of the principles of philosophical materialism: The mind is identified with brain, there is no 'soul' without a living body, the world is governed by strict deterministic laws, free will is an illusion, there are no final causes, and whatever happens takes place because it inexorably must. Most notoriously, the work explicitly denies the existence of God, arguing that belief in a higher being is the product of fear, lack of understanding, and anthropomorphism. The book was considered extremely radical in its day and there were many refutations written in response. The version I am citing is from Vol.1, The Echo Library, Middlesex, England, 2007, p.57.
4. c.f. Burleigh, Michael. *Sacred Causes* (HarperCollins, 2006), 41–43.

5. Elsie, R. *A Dictionary of Albanian Religion, Mythology, and Folk Culture* (New York: NYU Press, 2000) 18.
6. This 11.9% 'Nonreligious' refers to persons professing no religion, nonbelievers, agnostics, freethinkers, uninterested, or the lapsed religious secularists who are indifferent to all religion but not militantly so. The 2.3% 'Atheist' refers to persons professing atheism, skepticism, disbelief, or irreligion, including the militantly antireligious who are opposed to all religion. Although there are millions of Christians and millions of people of other faiths in China the vast majority of people are irreligious. Including them in the statistics would change the percentages significantly. However, is irreligion not an imposed order? As religion is licensed and monitored to ensure compliance with strict regulations much of the Christian church in China is, of necessity, underground and therefore under the radar of accurate/reliable statistical analysis.
7. *Social values, Science and Technology*, 7–11. This survey was requested by Directorate General Research and coordinated by Directorate General Press and Communication. The fieldwork was conducted January–February 2005 and Published in June 2005. It is available on the internet in PDF at the following link: http://ec.europa.eu/public_opinion/archives/ebs/ebs_225_report_en.pdf (Retrieved 1/3/2012).
8. Zuckerman, Phil and Michael T. Martin, (eds.), *The Cambridge Companion to Atheism* (Cambridge, England: Cambridge University Press) 51.
9. 'Characteristics of the Population', Australian Bureau of Statistics, 2006.
10. 'Worldwide Adherents of All Religions by Six Continental Areas' (*Encyclopedia Britannica*, 2005).
11. 'Worldwide Adherents of All Religions by Six Continental Areas' (*Encyclopedia Britannica*, 2005)
12. Baggini, Julian, *Atheism: A Very Short Introduction*, Preface (no page number), (Oxford University Press, 2003).
13. Op. cit., 10.
14. Op. cit., 21 and 17 respectively

15. Howard-Snyder, Daniel and Paul K. Moser, cited in the introduction to *Divine Hiddenness: New Essays* (New York: Cambridge University Press, 2001).
16. John L. Schellenberg, (2005). 'The Hiddenness Argument Revisited (I)', *Religious Studies*, Cambridge University Press, 41 (2), 201–215.
17. Helm, Paul. 'John Calvin, the *Sensus Divinitas*, and the Noetic Effects of Sin', *International Journal for Philosophy of Religion* 43 (2), 1998, 87–107.
18. Moser, Paul. 'Cognitive Idolatry and Divine Hiding', *Divine Hiddenness: New Essays* (New York: Cambridge University Press, 2001).
19. Ibid
20. Novak, Michael. 'Lonely Atheists of the Global Village', *National Review*, March 19, 2007.
21. Gould, Stephen Jay. 'Darwinian Fundamentalism', *The New York Review of Books*, June 12, 1997.
22. Eskow, R. J. 'Blind Faith: Sam Harris Attacks Islam', *The Huffington Post*. 11 October 2005; 'Reject Arguments for Intolerance – Even from Atheists', January, 2006, *The Huffington Post*.
23. Bunting, Madeleine. 'The New Atheists Loathe Religion Far Too Much To Plausibly Challenge It', *The Guardian*, 17 May, 2007.
24. Keller, Catherine *On the Mystery: Discerning Divinity in Process* (Fortress Press, 2008) 5.
25. Feinberg, John S. and Paul D. Feinberg, *Ethics for a Brave New World*, (1993), 2nd edition, updated and expanded (Wheaton: Crossway, 2010) 697.
26. Boyd, Richard 'How to Be a Moral Realist', *Essays on Moral Realism*, edited by G. Sayre-McCord (1988) 181–228.
27. McGrath, Alister. *Why God Won't Go Away: Engaging with New Atheism* (SPCK, 2011); Timothy Keller, *The Reason for God: Belief in an Age of Scepticism* (Penguin, 2008); Francis Collins, *The Language of God: A Scientist Presents Evidence for Belief* (Pocket Books, 2007); Anthony Flew, *There is a God* (HarperOne, 2007).
28. Micklethwait, John and Adrian Woolridge, *God is Back: How the Global Rise of Faith is Changing the World* (London: Penguin, 2009). This work succeeds

in triumphantly debunking the myth of an emerging secular civilization. See also Alister McGrath, *Engaging with New Atheism: Why God won't Go Away* (London: SPCK, 2011), also Harvey G. Cox and Jan Swyngedouw 'The Myth of the Twentieth Century: The Rise and Fall of Secularization', *Japanese Journal of Religious Studies*, Vol. 27, No. 1/2 (Spring, 2000) 1–13, published by Nanzan University.

Chapter 2

1. 13th February, 2012.
2. 15th February, 2012.
3. The decision to re-establish diplomatic ties was taken by the former Prime Minister Margaret Thatcher in 1982. The diplomatic relationship between the UK and the Holy See is the oldest as it was first established in 1479.
4. Micklethwait, John and Adrian Wooldridge. *God is Back: How the Global Rise of Faith is Changing the World* (Penguin, 2009 USA, 2010 UK).

Chapter 3

1. See Walter Truett Anderson, *Reality Isn't What It Used To Be: Theatrical Politics, Ready-to-Wear Religion, Global Myths, Primitive Chic, and Other Wonders of the Postmodern World* (San Francisco: Harper & Row, 1990).
2. Thomas Guarino, 'Postmodernity and Five Fundamental Theological Issues' (*Theological Studies*, 57, no. 4, December 1996) 654.
3. Daniel J. Adams, 'Toward a Theological Understanding of Postmodernism' (*Cross Currents*, 47, no. 4, Winter '97–'98) 518.
4. Lawrence Cahoone, ed. *From Modernism to Postmodernism: An Anthology* (Malden: Blackwell Publishers, 1997) 1. Postmodernism is characteristically anti Western civilization and opposes what it views as abuses of the West.
5. Ibid.
6. Charles Colson and Nancy Pearcey, *How Now Shall We Live?* (Nashville: Lifeway Press, 1999) 48.

7. Alister E. McGrath, *Christian Theology* (2d ed. Malden: Blackwell Publishers, 1998) 114.
8. Cahoone, *From Modernism to Postmodernism*, 1.
9. David S. Dockery, 'The Challenge of Postmodernism,' in *The Challenge of Postmodernism: An Evangelical Engagement,* ed. David S. Dockery (Wheaton: Victor Books, 1995) 16.
10. David Ray Griffin, William A. Beardslee, and Joe Holland. *Varieties of Postmodern Theology* (Albany: State University of New York Press, 1989). Some include liberation, feminist, and contemporary Catholic theologies.
11. Richard Tarnas. *The Passion of the Western Mind: Understanding the Ideas That Have Shaped Our World Views* (New York: Ballantine Books, 1991) 395.
12. Adams, 'Toward a Theological Understanding of Postmodernism', 520; Diogenes Allen, 'The End of the Modern World,' (*Christian Scholar's Review*, 22, no. 4, 993) 340.
13. Adams, 'Toward a Theological Understanding of Postmodernism', 520.
14. Cahoone, *From Modernism to Postmodernism*, 14.
15. 'The term 'postmodern' primarily refers to time rather than to a distinct ideology.' Dockery, 'The Challenges of Postmodernism', 13.
16. Ward views postmodernism more as a 'condition' than as a period. See Graham Ward, 'Postmodern Theology,' *The Modern Theologians*, ed. David F. Ford (Malden: Blackwell Publishers, 1997) 585.
17. Martyn Oliver, *History of Philosophy: Great Thinkers from 600 B.C. to the Present Day* (New York: Barnes and Noble Books, 1999) 171.
18. Oliver, *History of Philosophy*, 189.
19. Griffin, *Varieties of Postmodern Theology*, xii.
20. Cahoone, *From Modernism to Postmodernism*, 14.
21. According to Henry, much that characterized modern theology 'carries over into postmodernism's postulations.' Carl F. H. Henry, 'Postmodernism: The New Spectre?' in *The Challenge of Postmodernism: An Evangelical Engagement*, ed. David S. Dockery (Wheaton: Victor Books, 1995) 38. See also, David F.

Wells, *No Place for Truth, Or Whatever Happened to Evangelical Theology* (Grand Rapids: William B. Eerdmans Publishing Company, 1993) 61.

22. Cahoone, *From Modernism to Postmodernism,* 3. According to Grenz, Nietzsche (1844–1900) was the first to attack modernism, 'but the full-scale frontal assault did not begin until the 1970s.' Stanley J. Grenz, *A Primer on Postmodernism* (Grand Rapids: William B. Eerdmans Publishing Company, 1996) 5. See also, Tarnas, *The Passion of the Western Mind*, 395.
23. Henry, 'Postmodernism: The New Spectre?' 35.
24. Cahoone, *From Modernism to Postmodernism*, 2.
25. McGrath, *Christian Theology*, 575.
26. Allen, 'The End of the Modern World,' 340; Thomas C. Oden, 'The Death of Modernity and Postmodern Evangelical Spirituality,' in *The Challenge of Postmodernism: An Evangelical Engagement*, ed. David S. Dockery (Wheaton: Victor Books, 1995) 24.
27. McGrath, *Christian Theology*, 113.
28. Adams, 'Toward a Theological Understanding of Postmodernism,' 519. Fairlamb is correct postmodern scepticism reaches 'not only to modernism, but to Western philosophy as a whole.' Horace L. Fairlamb, *Critical Conditions: Postmodernity and the Questions of Foundations* (Cambridge: Cambridge University Press, 1994) 1.
29. McGrath, *Christian Theology*, 575. According to Christopher Norris, postmodernism 'is a 'family resemblance' term deployed in a variety of contexts (architecture, painting, music, poetry, fiction, etc.) for things which seem to be related—if at all—by a laid back pluralism of styles and a vague desire to have done with the pretensions of high modernist culture.' Christopher Norris, 'Postmodernism,' *The Oxford Companion to Philosophy*, ed. Ted Honderich (Oxford: Oxford University Press, 1995) 708.
30. Veith says, 'If the *modern* era is over, we are all postmodern, even though we reject the tenets of postmodernism.' Gene Edward Veith, *Postmodern Times: A Christian Guide to Contemporary Thought and Culture* (Wheaton: Crossway Books, 1994) 42.

31. Dockery, 'The Challenge of Postmodernism,' 14.
32. Dockery, 'The Challenge of Postmodernism,' 14.
33. Millard J. Erickson, *Christian Theology* (Grand Rapids: Baker Books, 1998) 160. Adams writes, 'One cannot speak of the postmodern without first speaking of modernity and modernism.' Adams, 518.
34. Millard J. Erickson, *Postmodernizing the Faith,* 2d ed. (Grand Rapids: Baker Books, 1998) 15.
35. Ibid.
36. Stanley J. Grenz, *A Primer on Postmodernism*, 61.
37. Erickson, *Christian Theology*, 160.
38. Henry, 'Postmodernism: The New Spectre?' 36. See Erickson, *Christian Theology*, 160.
39. Erickson, *Christian Theology*, 161.
40. There is no consensus on the exact beginning of the Enlightenment and the modern era. Oden specifically says the modern period lasted from 1789 to 1989. This offers a simplified and rather neat period of time which at least offers a handle on the subject at an elementary level. Oden, 'The Death of Modernity and Postmodern Evangelical Spirituality,' 23.
41. Henry, 'Postmodernism: The New Spectre?' 37.
42. See Grenz, *A Primer on Postmodernism*, 2–3.
43. Tarnas, *The Passion of the Western Mind*, 279.
44. D. A. Carson, *The Gagging of God: Christianity Confronts Pluralism* (Grand Rapids: Zondervan Publishing House, 1996) 61.
45. As Henry notes, 'The intellectual order of the world was relocated in human reasoning. This control over nature and history would free humankind from … a predetermined universe.' Henry, 'Postmodernism: The New Spectre?' 36.
46. John Locke, *An Essay Concerning Human Understanding*, ed. Peter H. Nidditch (Oxford: Oxford University Press, 1975) 704.
47. Thomas C. Oden, 'The Death of Modernity and Postmodern Evangelical Spirituality', 24.

48. O. R. Jones, 'Foundationalism,' *The Oxford Companion to Philosophy*, ed. Ted Honderich (New York: Oxford University Press, 1995) 289.
49. Carson, *The Gagging of God*, 61.
50. Ibid, 59–60. Carson points out that 'this quest for certainty was supported by seminal thinkers like Locke, Kant, and Hegel; it reached out to embrace almost every discipline.' 60.
51. Ibid., 63.
52. Cahoone, *From Modernism to Postmodernism*, 482, fn. 1. See Patricia Waugh, *Postmodernism: A Reader* (London: Edward Arnold Publishers, 1992) 1.
53. Jean-Francois Lyotard, 'The Postmodern Condition: A Report on Knowledge,' in *From Modernism to Postmodernism*, 482.
54. Anderson, *Reality Isn't What It Used To Be*, 5. Henry points out that many thinkers are convinced that postmodernism has 'the status of a major irreversible movement.' Henry, 'Postmodernism: The New Spectre?' 35.
55. Alister E. McGrath, *Christian Theology*, 113.
56. Anderson, *Reality Isn't What It Used To Be*, 5.
57. Ibid
58. Thomas C. Oden, 'So What Happens after Modernity? A Postmodern Agenda for Evangelical Theology,' in *The Challenge of Postmodernism*, 395. See Henry, 'Postmodernism: The New Spectre?' 40.
59. Oden, 'So What Happens after Modernity? 395.
60. McGrath, *Christian Theology*, 114.
61. Carson, *The Gagging of God*, 100.
62. James B. Miller, 'The Emerging Postmodern World,' in *Postmodern Theology: Christian Faith in a Pluralist World*, ed. Frederic B. Burnham (San Francisco: Harper & Row Publishers, 1989) 11.
63. Tarnas, *The Passion of the Western Mind*, 399.
64. Anderson, *Reality Isn't What It Used To Be*, 75.
65. Richard Rorty, 'Solidarity or Objectivity?' in *From Modernism to Postmodernism*, 574.
66. Ibid.

67. Anderson, *Reality Isn't What It Used To Be*, xii.
68. Often the 'powerful' are identified as Christian, white, European males.
69. Christopher Norris, *The Truth About Postmodernism* (Cambridge: Blackwell Publishers, 1993), 301.
70. Anderson, *Reality Isn't What It Used To Be*, 183.
71. Henry, 'Postmodernism: The New Spectre?' 41.
72. Oden, 'The Death of Modernity,' 24.
73. Henry, 'Postmodernism: The New Spectre?' 37.
74. Ibid.
75. Henry, 'Postmodernism: The New Spectre?' 37.
76. Grenz, *A Primer on Postmodernism*, 7
77. Oliver, *History of Philosophy*, 173.
78. Oliver, *History of Philosophy*, 172.
79. Henry, 'Postmodernism: The New Spectre?' 42.
80. Cahoone, *From Modernism to Postmodernism*, 271.
81. Ibid.
82. See Adams, 'Toward a Theological Understanding of Postmodernism,' 526.
83. Adams, 'Toward a Theological Understanding of Postmodernism,' 526.
84. Lyotard, 'The Postmodern Condition: A Report on Knowledge,' 482. In agreement, Kevin J. Vanhoozer says that Lyotard's definition is, 'The best definition of 'postmodern' of which I am aware.' Kevin J. Vanhoozer, 'Exploring the World; Following the Word: The Credibility of Evangelical Theology in an Incredulous Age,' *Trinity Journal*, 16, no. 1 (Spring 1995) 3.
85. Tarnas, *The Passion of the Western Mind*, 402.
86. Timothy R. Phillips and Dennis L. Ockholm, *Christian Apologetics in the Postmodern World* (Downers Grove: InterVarsity Press, 1995) 13.
87. Kevin J. Vanhoozer, *Is There a Meaning in This Text?* (Grand Rapids: Zondervan Publishing House, 1998) 19.
88. Fairlamb, *Critical Conditions*, 5.
89. According to Cahoone, Derrida and Foucault are the 'two most famous

instigators of what is called postmodernism.' *From Modernism to Postmodernism*, 336.

90. Allen, 'The End of the Modern World,' 339.
91. McGrath, *Christian Theology*, 114.
92. See Grenz, *A Primer on Postmodernism*, 5–7
93. Vanhoozer, *Is There a Meaning in this Text?* 20.
94. Anderson, *Reality Isn't What It Used To Be*, 90.
95. Vanhoozer, *Is There a Meaning in this Text?* 53.
96. Ibid.
97. McGrath, *Christian Theology*, 114.
98. Henry, 'Postmodernism: The New Spectre?' 36.
99. Phillips and Ockholm, *Christian Apologetics in the Postmodern World*, 13.
100. Tarnas, *The Passion of the Western Mind*, 397.
101. Henry, 'Postmodernism: The New Spectre?' 41.
102. Carson distinguishes empirical or cultural pluralism from philosophical pluralism. Empirical pluralism refers to the growing cultural diversity in our society. Empirical pluralism is a reality and not a philosophical viewpoint. Philosophical pluralism is the belief that all religions are more or less true; no one religion is inherently superior to others. Carson, *The Gagging of God*, 19.
103. Oliver, *History of Philosophy*, 173.
104. David Hall, 'Modern China and the Postmodern West,' in *From Modernism to Postmodernism*, 699.
105. Anderson, *Reality Isn't What It Used To Be*, xi.

Chapter 4

1. Bonhoeffer, Deitrich. *Life Together: A Discussion of Christian* Fellowship (San Francisco, California, HarperOne, 1954) 27.
2. Benfold, Gary. 'So that I can rebuild it', *Evangelical Magazine of Wales*, May/June, 2004.
3. Van Rheenen, Gailyn, 'Modern and Postmodern Syncretism in Theology and

Missions', *The Holy Spirit and Mission Dynamics*, ed. C. Douglas McConnell (Pasadena: Wm. Carey, 1997) 173.

4. Van Rheenen, Gailyn, 'Modern and Postmodern Syncretism in Theology and Missions', 173.
5. Groothuis, Douglas, 'Facing the Challenge of Postmodernism', *To Everyone and Answer: A Case for the Christian Worldview*, Francis Beckwith, William Lane Craig and J. P. Moreland (eds.) (Downers Grove, Illinois: IVP, 2004) 253.
6. I have witnessed holistic models of mission working well in India and Eastern Europe but I acknowledge the dangers inherent in this model whereby the gospel message of salvation can become subordinate to material concerns.
7. Halter, Hugh and Matt Smay, *The Tangible Kingdom*, (San Francisco: CA, Jossey-Bass, 2008) xxii
8. Halter, Hugh and Matt Smay, *The Tangible Kingdom* 11.
9. Luke 4:18–19
10. Frost, Michael and Alan Hirsch, *The Shaping of Things to Come,* (Massachusetts: USA, Hendrickson, 2003 and Australia: Strand Publishing) 16.
11. Halter, Hugh and Matt Smay, *The Tangible Kingdom* (Massachusetts: USA, Hendrickson, 2003 and Australia: Strand Publishing) 74.
12. David F. Wells, *God in the Wasteland: The Reality of Truth in a World of Fading Dreams* (Wm. B. Eerdmans, Grand Rapids: Michigan, and Inter-Varsity Press, Leicester: England, 1994) 41.
13. 'A True Work of the Spirit', © John MacArthur, Jr, 'Grace to You'. See also: http://www.biblebb.com/files/edwards/je-marksofhs.htm
14. As far as I am aware they believe in the sinless life, substitutionary death/ atonement, resurrection, ascension, intercessory role, divinity, trinity and second coming of Christ.
15. Ward, Graham, 'Introduction: 'Where We Stand',' in *The Blackwell Companion to Postmodern Theology*, ed. Graham Ward (Oxford and Malden, Mass.: Blackwell Publishers, 2001) xv.
16. Frost, Michael, *Encounter with God*: Scripture Union Bible Reading Notes, July-Sept., 2010, p.45.

17. Guinness, Os, *Dining with the Devil*, Grand Rapids: Baker, 1993. I have been informed that Google References attributes this remark to W. R. Inge, the famed Dean of St Paul's Cathedral.
18. Migliore, Daniel L., *Faith Seeking Understanding: An Introduction to Christian Theology* (Grand Rapids, Michigan: Eerdmans, 1996) xxi.
19. Eric E. Wright, *A Practical Theology of Missions: Dispelling the Mystery; Recovering the Passion* (DayOne, UK, 2010) 10.
20. A. W. Tozer, *The Root of the Righteous* (Harrisburgh, PA: Christian Publications, 1955) 8.
21. Eric E. Wright, Op. cit. p.10.
22. Houghton, Frank (1894–1972), *Christian Hymns*, Ed. Paul E. G. Cook and Graham Harrison (Evangelical Movement of Wales, 1977).

Chapter 5

1. The issue of famine is another question not under discussion here. But it should be noted that many famines are caused by war and ecological abuse.
2. When I say 'evolved' here I mean it was gradually revealed by God.
3. See Genesis 22:1–18 and Hebrews 11:17–19).
4. Some believe the magi were kings.
5. That is, apart from the fact that the gospel was prophetically announced in the Old Testament.
6. This in no way undermines the cessationist view that the miraculous gifts of the Holy Spirit such as tongues, prophecy and healing ceased being practiced early on in Church history.
7. Though it is precious to the saints and rich in meaning it is not like a magical password to heaven.
8. Dr Umar Al-Ashqar, dean of the Faculty of Islamic Law at Zarqa Private University in Zarqa, Jordan, has written: 'Paradise is something of immense value; a person cannot earn it by virtue of his deeds alone, but by the Grace and Mercy of Allah.'

   Answering Common Questions on Salvation That Christians Pose to

Muslims, http://www.call-to monotheism.com/answering_common_questions_on_salvation_that_christians_pose_to_muslims Retrieved 1/3/2013. So it would be wrong to suppose that Islam has nothing to say about grace. We should not intentionally or unintentionally out of ignorance or malice slander other religions, even if they are false religions like Islam. Nevertheless it is not a religion based on the concept of grace. There is no assurance of salvation taught in Islam. Dr Umar Al-Ashqar's stance is supported by *hadith*. A *ḥadīth* is a saying or an act or tacit approval or disapproval ascribed either validly or invalidly to Muhammad. *Hadīth* are regarded by traditional Islamic schools of jurisprudence as important tools for understanding the *Quran*. Hadith were gathered and collated into large collections during the 8th and 9th centuries. These works are referred to in matters of Islamic law and history to this day. The largest denominations of Islam, *Sunni*, *Shi'a*, and *Ibadi*, rely upon different sets of hadith collections.

1. 'Chapter 15: None Would Attain Salvation Because of his Deeds but it is Through Lord's Mercy, Number 6764', *Sahih Muslim, Book 39*, University of Southern California center for Jewish-Muslim engagement, http://www.usc.edu/schools/college/crcc/engagement/resources/texts/muslim/hadith/muslim/039.smt.html, retrieved 2011–01–01
2. I am not saying that works such as the *Koran* are divinely inspired.
3. Even though God knows who would have responded to the gospel had they heard this does not mean they will be saved, any more than the inhabitants of Tyre and Sidon were saved (Matthew 11:21). Ultimately it is God's elect who will be redeemed.
4. Godfrey, W. D. 'Predestination', *New Dictionary of Theology* (IVP, 1998) 530
5. Arminianism is based on the theological ideas of the Dutch Reformed theologian Jacobus Arminius (1560–1609). The Calvinist-Arminian debate is best known as a dispute between Dutch Protestants in the early seventeenth century. But the theological points remain at issue. Arminianism emphasizes conditional election based on God's foreknowledge, man's free will through prevenient grace to cooperate with God in salvation.

6. Iain Murray, *Spurgeon v Hyper-Calvinism: The Battle for Gospel Preaching* (Banner of Truth, 1995) 152.
7. Op. cit.

Chapter 6

1. For a fuller explanation of *missio Dei* see L. Pachauau, '*Missio Dei*', *Dictionary of Mission Theology: Evangelical Foundations*, ed. John Corrie (Northampton: England, IVP, 2007) 232–234.
2. Eric E. Wright, *A Practical Theology of Missions: Dispelling the Mystery; Recovering the Passion*, (DayOne, Leominster: England, 2010) 18.
3. I am referring here to those who understand the church's mission as proclaiming the gospel message and inviting people to believe in Christ for salvation. It is acknowledged that evangelism can be defined in broader terms such as the Luasanne Covenant and the Manila Manifesto.
4. See J. A. Kirk, 'Missiology', *New Dictionary of Theology*, Eds. Sinclair Ferguson and David F Wright (IVP, Leicester: England, 1988, reprint, 1994) 434–436.
5. It needs to be asserted that many so called 'natural disasters' have an all-too human dimension, including floods and famines.
6. Obviously professional help is needed for such people and certain mental illnesses can cause some people to be dangerous to themselves and others and great caution is advised.
7. It is acknowledged that there is Christian involvement in environmental issues but what I am arguing here is that it should be a more pervasive element of our ethos.
8. George W. Peters, *A Biblical Theology of Missions* (Chicago: Moody, 1972) 27.
9. Eric E. Wright, Op. cit., p.46.
10. Missiology is a relatively recent subject in theological seminaries and Bible colleges and in many such places it is not on the curriculum. Many older works on systematic theology do not include sections on mission, at least as a distinct area of study.
11. See http://www.100people.org/statistics_100stats.php, accessed 13/02/14

12. Obviously reading this means you are not one of the two-billion people who can't read.

Chapter 7

1. Eric E. Wright, *A Practical Theology of Missions: Dispelling the Mystery; Recovering the Passion*, (DayOne, UK, 2010) 10.
2. Cited in George W. Peters, *A Biblical Theology of Missions* (Chicago: Moody, 1972) 55.
3. Cited in *The Great Omission* by Trevor Harris (Evangelical Press, 2005) 17.
4. Ibid
5. Ibid
6. Christopher Wright. *The Mission of God* (Downers Grove: InterVarsity Press, 2006) 32.
7. Ibid, 54.
8. Ibid, 55.
9. Kaiser, Walter. 'Israel's Missionary Call', *Perspectives on the World Christian Movement* (Wm. Carey Library, 3rd edition, 1999) 12.
10. Stott, John. *Christian Mission in the Modern World* (Downers Grove: IVP, 1975) 9.
11. Tom Wright, *Surprised by Hope* (New York: HarperCollins Publishers, 2008) 204.
12. Ed Stetzer and Philip Nation, *Compelled by Love* (Birmingham: New Hope Publishers, 2008) 26.
13. Robert Coleman, 'The Master Plan', *Perspectives on the World Christian Movement,* (Wm. Carey Library, 3rd edition, 1999) 125.
14. John Piper, 'Let the Nations Be Glad', *Perspectives on the World Christian Movement,* (Wm. Carey Library, 3rd edition, 1999) 64.
15. Plassey House is in Co. Limerick, but the greater part of his demesne was in Co. Clare.
16. That is why Carey settled in Serampore with Marshman and Ward (the

Serampore Trio) because that area was under the jurisdiction of the Danish government, not the East India Company.

17. Finney, Kellsye. *William Carey* (Carlisle: UK, OM Publishing and Didcot, UK, Baptist Missionary Society, 1986, revised edition 1992) 25.
18. This means that in a country of one billion people there are 30million–60 million Christians. That leaves 940million–970million people who are mostly Hindu (some Muslim and Sikh). That is approximately four times the population of the USA.
19. Finney, Kellsye. *William Carey*, 121
20. Luke 4:18–19.

Chapter 8

1. I want to make it clear that I believe that the Roman Catholic Church is not a Christian Church. A Christian church must, at a minimum, in my view, believe that salvation is by grace alone, through faith alone, in Christ alone and it must accept that the canon of Scripture (which consists of sixty-six books, thirty-nine in the Old Testament and twenty-seven in the New Testament) is the ultimate authority in all matters of faith and practice. Therefore I refer to the Catholic Church in this article as it is generally perceived by those outside the evangelical Christian community with the broadest use of the term, 'Christian'.
2. Micklethwait, John and Adrian Woolridge, *God is Back: How the Global Rise of Faith is Changing the World* (London: Penguin, 2009) 4–5.
3. Aikman, David. *Jesus in Beijing: How Christianity is Changing the Global Balance of Power*, New York: Regnery, 2003).
4. Dean, Jason and Loretto Chao. 'In Search of … Something', *Wall Street Journal*, April 12, 2008

Chapter 9

1. As quoted in David J. Bosch, *Transforming Mission* (New York: Orbis, 1991) 408.
2. Made popular through the ministry of John Wimber (25 February, 1934–17 November, 1997). Wimber was a charismatic pastor and one of the founding

leaders of the Vineyard Movement, a neo-charismatic evangelical Christian denomination which began in the USA and has now spread to many countries world-wide.

3. The words of J. Moltmann quoted by David J. Bosch, *Transforming Mission* (New York: Orbis, 1991) 408
4. Chris Wright, *Knowing Jesus Through the Old Testament* (London: Marshall Pickering, 1992) 31.
5. John Stott, *New Issues Facing Christians Today*—Fully Revised Edition (London: Marshall Pickering, 1999) 22
6. Stott, John, *Issues Facing Christians Today* (London: Marshall Pickering, 1984 and 1990) 19.
7. The conflict of dualistic thought and the biblical teaching of, for example, the incarnation is evident in Gnosticism, which was prevalent in the early church.
8. Hiebert, P. G. *Anthropological Insights for Missionaries* (Grand Rapids: Baker Book House, 1998) 207.
9. Green, Michael. *Evangelism in the Early Church* (Eastbourne: Kingsway, 2003) 384–385.
10. See Dowley T. et. al., *Eerdman's Handbook to the History of Christianity* (Grand Rapids: Eerdman's Publishing Co., 1977) 111.
11. Dowley T. et. al., *Eerdman's Handbook to the History of Christianity*, 279ff.
12. Warneck, Gustav. *Outline of a History of Protestant Missions* (Edinburgh and London: Oliphant, Anderson and Ferrier, 3rd English edition, translated from the 8th German edition 1906) p. 9. See also J. A. Scherer. *Gospel, Church and Kingdom: Comparative Studies in World Mission* (Minneapolis: Augusburg Publishing House, 1987).
13. Gensichen, Hans-Werner. 'Were the Reformers Indifferent to Mission?', *History's Lessons for Tomorrow's Mission* (Geneva: WSCF, 1960) 119–127.
14. Scherer, J. A. *Gospel, Church and Kingdom: Comparative Studies in World Mission* (Minneapolis: Augusburg Publishing House, 1987) 65.
15. Gensichen, Hans-Werner. 'Were the Reformers Indifferent to Mission?', *History's Lessons for Tomorrow's Mission* (Geneva: WSCF, 1960) 123.

16. Bosch. David J. *Transforming Mission: Paradigm Shifts in Mission Theology* (Maryknoll, New York: Orbis Books, 25th printing, 1991) 245
17. With the exception of Lapland which was evangelized by Swedish Lutherans in the sixteenth-century.
18. Warneck, Gustav. *Outline of a History of Protestant Missions* (Edinburgh and London: Oliphant, Anderson and Ferrier, 3rd English edition, translated from the 8th German edition 1906) 14, 17f. See also Franklin. H. Littell. *The Origins of Sectarian Protestantism* (New York: Macmilan, 3rd printing, 1972) 114–116.
19. Bosch. David J. *Transforming Mission: Paradigm Shifts in Mission Theology* (Maryknoll, New York: Orbis Books, 25th printing, 1991) 246.
20. Warneck, Gustav. *Outline of a History of Protestant Missions* (Edinburgh and London: Oliphant, Anderson and Ferrier, 3rd English edition, translated from the 8th German edition 1906) 20–22.
21. Bosch. David J. *Transforming Mission: Paradigm Shifts in Mission Theology* (Maryknoll, New York: Orbis Books, 25th printing, 1991) 246.
22. The total depravity of man is a biblical doctrine which is not in dispute here.
23. This in part explains the slave trade and its terrible cruelties. Vestiges of this thinking remained not just until the American Civil War but right into the USA of the 1960s. Manifestations of this were also evident in the apartheid regimes of South Africa until the end of the twentieth-century. In spite of William Wilberforce's success in bringing about the abolition of slavery, racist attitudes with a tenuous theological basis stubbornly remained among 'Christian' people.

Chapter 10

1. Bosch. David J. *Transforming Mission: Paradigm Shifts in Mission Theology* (Maryknoll, New York: Orbis Books, 25th printing, 1991) 254.
2. By 'ecumenical' here I mean Protestant/evangelical, non-denominational or interdenominational cooperation, not an unholy alliance with the Roman Catholic Church.
3. Bosch. David J. *Transforming Mission: Paradigm Shifts in Mission Theology* (Maryknoll, New York: Orbis Books, 25th printing, 1991) 258.

4. Bosch. David J. *Transforming Mission: Paradigm Shifts in Mission Theology* (Maryknoll, New York: Orbis Books, 25th printing, 1991) 260.
5. Smith, D.W. *Transforming its World—The Social Impact of English Evangelicalism* (Carlisle: Paternoster Press, 1998) 110.
6. Bebbington, D.W., *Evangelicalism in Modern Britain* (London/New York: Routledge, 1989) 70.
7. Quoted from George Marsden, 'The Gospel of Wealth, the Social Gospel and the Salvation of Souls in Nineteenth Century America' Fides et Historica (Fall 1972 and Spring 1973) 18, as cited by Jacob Thomas, *From Lausanne to Manila: Evangelical Social Thought* (Delhi: ISPCK, 2003) 23–24.
8. The American historian Timothy L. Smith coined the term 'Great Reversal'. See John Stott *New Issues Facing Christians Today*—Fully Revised Edition (London: Marshall Pickering, 1999) 8.
9. I am not commenting on pre-millennialism *per se* here.
10. The 'social gospel' had wide influence in America from the end of the 19th century up until the middle of the 20th century. Walter Ruschenbush (1861–1918) was one of its most well known advocates.
11. William H. Boley, *A New Dictionary of Christian Ethics*, (London: SCM Press, 1986) 659
12. William H Boley, *A New Dictionary of Christian Ethics*, 659
13. Thomas, Jacob. *From Lausanne to Manila: Evangelical Social Thought* (Delhi: ISPCK, 2003) 8
14. In spite of this many subsequent works of systematic theology glaringly omit any section on mission. One such example is Louis Berkhof's *Systematic Theology*, first published in 1939 and again in 1941 with the first British edition published in 1958 and subsequently reprinted frequently and in several languages. The edition I have (Edinburgh: Banner of Truth, 1976) contains a Preface written in 1949 which shows no awareness of such a disquieting gap. In spite of this it is an excellent work which should be included in every theological library. Even in some more modern works, such as James Montgomery Boice's

Foundations of the Christian Faith: A Comprehensive and Readable Theology, InterVarsity Press, 1986, there is scant treatment of mission.

15. Stott, John. *New Issues Facing Christians Today*—Fully Revised Edition (London: Marshall Pickering, 1999) 13.
16. For more information on the Micah declaration see http://www.micahchallenge.org/english/think/aim1/declaration/
17. Scott, Waldron. *The Quiet Revolution*, (Oxford: Lion Publishing, 1985) 110
18. Nunex, E. and W. Taylor, *The Awaking of our Evangelical Social Conscience—Crisis and Hope in Latin America* (Pasadena: William Carey Library, 1996) 432
19. John Stott, *Christian Mission in the Modern World* (Downers Grove: IVP, 1975) 26
20. David J. Bosch, *Transforming Mission* (New York: Orbis, 1991) 406
21. John Stott, *Christian Mission in the Modern World* (Downers Grove: IVP, 1975) 28
22. Warner, Rob in Fran Beckett et. al., *Rebuild* (Leicester: Crossway, 2001) 162
23. Myers Bryant L., *Walking with the Poor* (New York: Orbis, 1999) 81
24. Statistics taken from the Department For International Development (DFID), UK website at http://www.dfid.gov.uk
25. Bryant L. Myers, *Walking with the Poor* (New York: Orbis, 1999) 81ff.
26. Myers, Bryant L. *Walking with the Poor* (New York: Orbis, 1999) 113.
27. Ibid., p. 113.

Preface to Part Two

1. See 'Acknowledgement' for details.

Chapter 11

1. I have been to Serbia on a couple of occasions (teaching theology) each time in Belgrade, Vršac (a small town located 50 miles northeast of Belgrade) and Niš, the largest city of southern Serbia and the third-largest city in Serbia, after Belgrade and Novi Sad.

Chapter 12

1. The government continues to subsidize salaries of Serbian Orthodox clergy working in other countries. Other benefits, such as health care and pensions, are provided by the government to clergies of various churches on the basis of individual arrangements with the state.
2. At the time of writing (August, 2012).

Chapter 13

1. This has been achieved.
2. Accurate at the time of writing, 2004
3. That number now (at time of writing in 2013) stands at 23 million. That is more than five times the population of Ireland and it is the same as the population of Romania itself!
4. By 2004 the picture was as follows: Salard was founded in 1990 and now has 30 members and 15 adherents (regular attendees). Les was founded in 1998 and it has 15 members and 15 adherents. Săcădat was founded in 1991 and it has 20 members and 10 adherents. Margine was founded in 1998 and it has 11 members and 8 adherents. Cordau was founded in 1999 and has 14 members and 10 adherents. Bicaciu was founded in 1990 and has 7 members and 6 adherents. Gepiu Colonie was founded in 1992 and has 7 members and 6 adherents. Brusturi was founded in 2001 and it has 15 members and 3 adherents.

Chapter 14

1. This article was written in April 2005.

Chapter 16

1. May, 2011.

Chapter 17

1. I taught an intensive course to M. Div. students. This program is accredited by

the Asian Theological Association (ATA) and their B.Th. course is affiliated to Serampore University.

2. There were 1,500 delegates at that conference, which gives some insight to the scale of Christian work in India.
3. There are many other (non-ECI) seminaries and Bible colleges throughout India.
4. I am very new to the Indian scene and do not know exactly what is going on there but I know, for example, of an Assemblies of God Pentecostal Church, Park Street, Kolkata which has a regular attendance of 1,200 at each of its morning worship services (8.30a.m and 10.30a.m.) on Sundays. Here are some rough statistics that give part of the picture: the Protestant (I think Anglican) Church of South India 3,800,000; the Protestant Church of North India 1,250,000, Methodists 648,000, Baptists 2,392,694, Lutheran 1,267,78, Brethren 1,000,000, Presbyterian 823,456, Pentecostal, 600,000.